The Emerging Industrial Structure of the Wider Europe

The latest wave of European Union expansion has brought many central and eastern European countries into the fold. Unlike previous enlargements, however, the latest new members are also undergoing radical economic reform as they reintegrate into the international economy.

This book reviews the changing industrial architecture of the new wider Europe from a 'network' perspective, highlighting the importance of the linkages that develop between firms and governments in the new entrants and the EU. It does so on the basis of a series of case studies covering countries, sectors and firms, as well as providing an analysis of the underlying dynamics of production and policy integration.

The impressive group of authors go beyond traditional analyses by adopting an interdisciplinary approach drawing on the insights of economics and politics. As such, the book will appeal to students of the EU and enlargement, as well as those with an interest in foreign investment and transition economies.

Francis McGowan is Lecturer in the Department of International Relations and Politics, the University of Sussex, UK.

Slavo Radosevic is Reader in Industrial and Corporate Change, School of Slavonic and East European Studies, University College London, UK.

Nick von Tunzelmann is Professor in the Economics of Science and Technology, SPRU (Science and Technology Policy Research), the University of Sussex, UK.

Studies in Global Competition

A series of books edited by
John Cantwell
The University of Reading, UK and
David Mowery
University of California, Berkeley, USA

The Emerging Industrial Structure of the Wider Europe

Edited by Francis McGowan,
Slavo Radosevic and
Nick von Tunzelmann

Routledge
Taylor & Francis Group

LONDON AND NEW YORK

First published 2004
by Routledge
11 New Fetter Lane, London EC4P 4EE

Simultaneously published in the USA and Canada
by Routledge
29 West 35th Street, New York, NY 10001

Routledge is an imprint of the Taylor & Francis Group

© 2004 editorial matter and selection, Francis McGowan, Slavo Radosevic
and Nick von Tunzelmann; individual chapters, the contributors

Typeset in Bembo by
Newgen Imaging Systems (P) Ltd, Chennai, India
Printed and bound in Great Britain by
Antony Rowe Ltd, Chippenham, Wiltshire

British Library Cataloguing in Publication Data
A catalogue record for this book is available from the British Library

Library of Congress Cataloging in Publication Data
A catalog record for this book has been requested

ISBN 0–415–32334–7

Contents

16 Network alignment and pan-European industry networks: conclusions, contributions and policy implications

FRANCIS McGOWAN, SLAVO RADOSEVIC AND NICK von TUNZELMANN

Figures

Tables

Contributors

Stefan Dunin-Wasowicz, Center for Social and Economic Research (CASE Foundation), Warsaw, Poland and Dunin-Wasowicz Industrial Partners, Haute Savoie, France.

Michal Gorzynski, CASE-Doradcy Consulting Company, Warsaw, Poland.

Judit Hamar, KOPINT-DATORG Ltd, Budapest, Hungary.

Andreja Jaklič, Faculty of Social Sciences, University of Ljubljana, Slovenia.

Francis McGowan, University of Sussex, UK.

Cezar Mereuta, Romanian Center for Economic Modelling, Bucharest, Romania.

Jose Molero, Complutense Institute for International Studies, Complutense University, Madrid, Spain.

T. P. O'Connor, The Circa Group, Dublin, Ireland.

Slavo Radosevic, School of Slavonic and East European Studies, University College London, UK.

Matija Rojec, Faculty of Social Sciences, University of Ljubljana, Slovenia.

Geomina Turlea, Institute for World Economy and Romanian Center for Economic Modelling, Bucharest, Romania.

Nick von Tunzelmann, Science and Technology Policy Research – SPRU, University of Sussex, UK.

Richard Woodward, Center for Social and Economic Research (the CASE Foundation), Warsaw, Poland.

Deniz Eylem Yoruk, Science and Technology Policy Research – SPRU, University of Sussex, UK.

Preface

This book analyses the extent and the major determinants of pan-European or 'East–West' industrial networks in reinforcing the competitive advantages of the European Union (EU) and central and eastern Europe (CEE). It shows that the outcome of pan-European industrial integration is not automatically positive and that a variety of factors must be in place for a 'win–win' result. The volume provides new and rich empirical evidence on these processes and interprets them within a new theoretical perspective.

This approach combines economic, political and management aspects and could be in short described as the 'political economy of industry integration'. In that respect, we expect that the book will be of major interest to those investigating processes of European integration, and also industry integration, and globalization issues in general.

The volume is based on the project 'The emerging industrial structure of the wider Europe: the co-evolution of economic and political structures' (Award No. L213252037). This project was funded within the UK Economic and Social Research Council (ESRC) programme, 'One Europe Or Several?'. It was coordinated by Dr Slavo Radosevic and gathered a team of twenty-two researchers from 'old' and 'new' EU member states and candidate states. In addition to authors of the chapters in this volume the following researchers have contributed extensively to the project: Kate Bishop, David Dyker, Jen Gristock, Ulrike Hotopp, Tomasz Mickiewicz, Sangita Shah, Baroness (Margaret) Sharp and Urmas Varblane. The project outline and working papers are posted on <www.ssees.ac.uk/esrc.htm> where one can also download the policymakers' and entrepreneurs' summary of the project.

We are most grateful to the ESRC for financial assistance and to the ESRC programme directors, Professor Helen Wallace and later Professor Jim Rollo, for their support during this programme. Kate Bishop was an extremely efficient project secretary as well as a researcher on the project. We thank Cynthia Little for technical and editorial assistance in the preparation of this book.

Francis McGowan
Slavo Radosevic
Nick von Tunzelmann
September 2003

Acronyms

BEEPS	Business Environment and Enterprise Performance Survey
BERD	Business enterprise R&D
CAD	Computer aided design
CAM	Computer aided manufacturing
CDTI	Centre for Technological and Industrial Development
CEE	Central and Eastern Europe
CEEC	Central and East European countries
CEFTA	Central European Free Trade Agreement
CIM	Computer integrated manufacture
CIS	Commonwealth of Independent States (former USSR)
CM	Cut and make
CMEA	Council for Mutual Economic Assistance
CMT	Cut, make and trim
CSF	Community Support Frameworks
CSIC	(Spanish) National Council for Scientific Research
DE	Direct exporting
DE	Domestic enterprise
EBRD	European Bank for Reconstruction and Development
EC	European Community
EDI	Electronic data interchange
EDP	Electronic data processing
EEC	European Economic Community
ERO	Energy Regulation Office
ESI	Electricity supply industry
ESRI	Economic and Social Research Institute (Ireland)
EU	European Union
FDI	Foreign direct investment
FEZ	Free economic zone
FIE	Foreign investment enterprise
FSU	Former Soviet Union
FTO	Foreign trade organisation
GERD	Government expenditure in R&D
HERD	Higher education expenditure in R&D

IDA	Industrial Development Authority (Ireland)
IT	Information technology
ISDN	Integrated service digital network
ISO	International Standards Organization
M&A	Merger and acquisition
MEBO	Management employee buy-out
MNC	Multinational corporation
MNE	Multinational enterprise
MRP	Materials requirements planning
NAFTA	North Atlantic Free Trade Association
NGO	Non-governmental organization
NIF	National investment fund
NIHE	National Institute of Higher Education (Ireland)
NLP	National Linkage Programme (Ireland)
NPF	National property fund (Czech Republic)
NSAI	National Standards Authority of Ireland
NSI	National system of innovation
OBM–domestic	Original brand manufacturing (in the domestic market)
OBM–foreign	Original brand manufacturing (also in foreign markets)
ODM	Original design manufacturing
OECD	Organisation for Economic Cooperation and Development
OEM	Original equipment manufacturing
OPT	Outward processing trade/traffic
PAIZ	Polish Agency for Foreign Investment
PAT	Programmes in Advanced Technology
PC	Personal computer
R&D	Research and development
RTC	Regional Technical College
SEZ	Special enterprise zone
SIT	Slovenian tolar
SME	Small and medium sized enterprise
SOE	State-owned enterprise
TNC	Transnational corporation
VAT	Value added tax
WTO	World Trade Organization

1 Introduction

Francis McGowan, Slavo Radosevic and
Nick von Tunzelmann

This volume explores the emerging industrial architecture of the wider Europe, and, in particular, the interplay between production and policy integration in shaping the new relationships between the East and the West. Our definition of integration is a wide one, highlighting not just the roles of firms and governments, but also of networks, which we consider to be central to the development of competitive advantages for both the old and new members of the European Union (EU). However, the outcome of pan-European industrial integration is not automatically positive and a variety of factors must be in place for a 'win–win' situation.

In this volume we show, first, that the way in which central and east European countries (CEECs) integrate into the wider European economy will have important effects on the long-term growth of the EU and CEECs. Their integration through production networks, formed within intra- and extra-multinational corporation (MNC) linkages, is an essential part of wider European integration, which includes market as well as institutional or policy integration. Second, the volume analyses factors that determine different integration outcomes at micro, sectoral and country levels through a variety of empirical studies. The basic framework, which guides the empirical contributions, is that of 'alignment of networks'. By 'network alignment' we mean the effective coupling between the evolution of national (local) specific systems and the global (regional) production networks. Each system is complex and therefore the interlinking of systems is especially complex. Whether an alignment of networks will take place depends not only on such linkages, but also on the nature of each individual network and agent involved. Third, the book explores the role of state strategies and EU enlargement policy on industrial networks, as a broadening of the 'alignment' process. In this respect, we draw on experiences of Ireland and Spain as reference cases and analyse this issue in-depth in the cases of Hungary, Romania, Poland and Slovenia.

Overview of the book

The book is organized as follows: we begin with perspectives on the theoretical and conceptual issues raised in the book (Chapters 2–4); this is followed by a series of firm- and sector-level case studies (Chapters 5–9); next, a series of country case studies (Chapters 10–15); and finally a conclusion that highlights our major findings and discusses the policy implications of this project. Chapter 2 on industry integration in the pan-European economy reviews how industry integration issues have been tackled in the theoretical and empirical literature. We draw on a wide range of literatures including those dealing with economic integration, trade, foreign direct investment (FDI), international business and regionalism. We highlight the benefits and constraints of individual theories and argue for a framework that employs a broader range of variables influencing the formation of networks, including MNC strategies, CEECs' state actions, sectoral features and EU policies. This need for the inclusion of different levels of governance in the analysis arises also from the multiplicity of actors currently influencing the shaping of international production networks. In this context, we propose the alignment of network framework as the appropriate heuristic for analysing industry integration issues of the wider Europe.

Chapter 3, 'Network alignment in the catching-up economies of Europe', examines networked systems and argues that the basic failing in CEECs (and many others) is not so much 'market failures' or 'government failures', but pervasive 'network failures'. These arise either because the necessary networks have not been developed or because those that exist pursue goals inconsistent with other networks to which they are linked. With transition, global networks now dominate the domestic innovation process, and the national structures are practically all bypassed. The chapter argues that this may bring short-term benefits, but long-term sustainability of growth requires relinking with the national systems, which themselves need reorienting to demand pressures. These represent the key 'realignments of networks' needed in the CEEC systems. Policy needs to target this realignment process as its top priority.

Chapter 4, 'State strategy and regional integration: the EU and enlargement', examines the impact of European integration (and particularly the process of enlargement) upon the state strategies and production integration of the CEECs. It raises questions about the impact of accession to the EU by focusing on two areas: the orientation of policy and the capacity of states to pursue policy. In terms of orientation, regional integration of the sort carried out in the EU might be expected to narrow the range of developmental options (indeed, it may push CEECs towards a 'regulatory' rather than a 'developmental' mode of governance). In terms of capacity, incorporation into the EU may increase administrative capabilities and strengthen institutions and conduct. In both respects, however, the impact of membership is less clear-cut than might be thought, as neither existing nor prospective member states may be able or willing to adapt to the apparent logic of integration.

Chapter 5, 'Industrial networks in central and eastern Europe at the firm level: summary and overview of ten case studies' summarizes the major issues involved in industrial integration at firm level. On the basis of a number of case studies of CEECs' companies and MNCs operating in the CEECs, the major factors that either promote or hinder the deepening of industrial integration are identified. This review of case studies uses the alignment of networks perspective to analyse their common features. The essential features of each of the cases are described and compared across several network alignment elements, like market access, strategy, government policy, local policies, the EU, finance, technology, etc. This chapter provides rich new evidence on how network alignment operates at the micro level and what factors are affecting the depth and the scope of inter-company integration. These issues are then followed up in the sectoral case studies dealt with in Chapters 6–9.

Chapter 6, 'Network realignment in the CEE food-processing industry', builds on the distinction between the vertical, functional and regional networks introduced in Chapter 3 to assess overall network (mis)alignment in the CEECs food industries. FDI in the food industry has largely replaced domestic sources of technology, at the cost of orphaning much of the latter. There are indications that this has led to short-term gains, but the viability of long-term improvements is more questionable, unless the domestic sources of technology can be reactivated. However, and against their intentions, some foreign companies are being drawn into acting as drivers of upgrading in host-country supplies of materials, including primary agricultural products. Even if this happens, the host countries, nevertheless, remain vulnerable to global competition among large multinational companies, which could easily desert them in the future.

Chapter 7, 'Patterns of industrial upgrading in the clothing industry in Poland and Romania', presents in-depth evidence of processes of industry upgrading in the clothing sectors of Romania and Poland. Patterns of upgrading at the firm level include managerial, process, product and functional upgrades. Using this taxonomy, the chapter analyses the impact of industrial networks on industrial upgrading over the past decade. It explains differences in country patterns, presents a stylized process of upgrading, and depicts process-upgrading paths of different firms.

Chapter 8, 'The electronics industry in central and eastern Europe: an emerging production location in the alignment of networks perspective', analyses the emergence of CEECs as a new location for the production of electronics. The main factors that drive integration of the region's electronics firms into global production networks are analysed, as well as prospects for upgrading the industry by using network alignment perspectives. Networks that are being built in CEECs in electronics are usually confined to subsidiaries with still limited local subcontracting; but they are export-oriented and are expanding. EU demand is the main pull factor giving cohesion to the actions of MNCs as well as to the actions of local and national governments in CEECs. The layer of local firms is still very weak, with very limited capabilities in core technologies. This is the key weakness preventing further alignment of networks in CEECs' electronics. Local governments, on the other hand, play an important catalytic role in working jointly with foreign investors in establishing industrial parks and new capacities.

Chapter 9, 'Policy and production integration in the central European electricity industry', examines how the changing industrial architecture of Europe manifests itself in the electricity supply industries of central Europe, and focuses in particular on the interplay between policy and production integration. In doing so, it touches upon the issues of state strategies and regional integration with regard to the impact of integration upon the orientation and capacity of states referred to in Chapter 4. This chapter shows that the processes of policy and production have encountered difficulties over the last decade. While the formal overall alignment of national policies with the EU acquis and broader regulatory requirements has been relatively straightforward, there have been significant criticisms of the ways in which national systems operate in practice. There have been disputes over the conduct of policy, in some cases jeopardizing foreign investments. Although such friction may be an inevitable part of the transition process, it also reflects more fundamental problems in the sector. The chapter discusses whether the problems with integration are a reflection of administrative shortcomings, of rent-seeking by entrants and incumbents, or the assertion by states and their proxies in the sector of a more 'developmental' strategy in the sector.

Chapters 10–15 explore the extent of and factors that explain the uneven process of industry integration by focusing on country determinants. The chapters follow the logic of alignment of networks approach, which ensures comparability of the key issues. Chapter 10, 'Foreign direct investment and indigenous industry in Ireland: a review of the evidence', considers the development of industry and FDI in Ireland and, in particular, how linkages with MNCs in Ireland have developed. Key to the success has been consistent implementation of industrial development policy, optimization of EU membership, an enhanced education and training system and improved communications and infrastructure. The chapter shows that networks and their alignment have played an important role in Ireland's drive towards industrialization. It explains the historical roots and experiences of actors in matching different networks and explains the excellent economic outcome as the coincidence of several complementary strategies and policies. The chapter draws implications for CEECs from the Irish experience in internationalization and enlargement.

Chapter 11, 'Integration of Slovenia into EU and global industrial networks', reviews the existing evidence on the internationalization of the Slovenian economy in all the various modes. It analyses the scale and dynamics of industry integration of Slovenia into EU/global industrial networks through trade, outward and inward processing trade, subcontracting and FDI. Based on an analysis of the Slovenian car components industry in international industrial networks, it illustrates the relatively favourable strategic position of Slovenian companies. This is supported by analysis of Slovenian outward investments. However, the authors argue that Slovenia has not fully exploited its potential to grow based on FDI and discuss the policy issues involved in this strategic shift.

Chapter 12, 'FDI and industrial networks in Hungary', summarizes the micro and macro effects of FDI on the Hungarian economy, the country with the biggest presence of FDI in Europe. It discusses the issue of the increasing absolute gap between domestic and foreign firms. It also shows that there are emerging signs of improved performance in the indigenous companies sector. There is evidence that Hungarian subsidiaries seem to be closely integrated and in a highly dependent position within global networks. The chapter discusses the policy implications of this situation.

Chapter 13, 'Industrialization and internationalization in the Spanish economy', reviews the Spanish industrialization process since the 1950s, with special attention to the opening up of the country to international competition and FDI. It shows that there are two stages that can be distinguished. The first lasted until the 1980s and is clearly identified with an import-substitution strategy. The basic attracting factors during this phase were the growth of the domestic market and the low level of wages. In the more recent period, characterized by the globalizing trend of international relations, new waves of FDI and new foreign firm strategies dominate the process. Similarly, outward FDI has increased very quickly in the last ten years, dramatically modifying the relative balance between inward and outward flows. The chapter draws implications for the CEECs from the Spanish experience in internationalization and enlargement and interprets the process of industrialization and internationalization within the alignment of networks framework.

Chapter 14, 'Markets and networks in Romania: systemic unrest or life after disorganization?', characterizes the Romanian situation as 'systemic unrest' within which network alignment takes on specific shapes and dynamics. It analyses each of the nodes of network alignment (enterprises and entrepreneurs, state, regions, MNCs and FDI, enlargement) and shows how Romania's integration into the global economy is shaped through their mutual interaction. FDI operates as a major attracting factor for some network alignment. The state-owned sector and the Romanian political economy of government–business relationships on the other hand are hindering the growth process of indigenous industry. Unemployment risks and special interests seem to be behind the protraction and delays in the process of restructuring.

Chapter 15, 'The integration of Poland into EU and global industrial networks: evidence and main challenges', summarizes the extent and depth of Polish integration into EU industry networks and uses the car industry as evidence to substantiate the major hypothesis. It argues that network alignment has been shallow, with MNCs and the national government playing limited roles. In contrast, domestic firms and local governments have been disproportionately active (relative to their capacities) in the process of integrating the Polish economy with foreign firms and markets.

The concluding Chapter 16, 'Network alignment and pan-European industry networks: conclusions, contributions and policy implications', highlights the major contributions of this volume in understanding the emerging industry architecture of the wider Europe. We assess the results of the constituent chapters within the alignment of network framework. Network creation and alignment involve the conscious and sustained direction of the efforts and resources of a variety of actors. Network failures are predominant due to the poor quality of existing networks and/or problems in their alignment. The development of successful interrelationships is contingent on realigning the networks connecting several sources of governance – markets, government, MNCs, firms in the CEECs and the EU enlargement policy. This concluding chapter draws implications for policies and strategies, which aim to maximize probabilities for such alignment to take place.

2 Industry integration in the pan-European economy

A review of theoretical and empirical issues

Slavo Radosevic and Francis McGowan

Introduction

What do we know about the dynamics of industry integration and their impact on economic convergence? This chapter considers how the issue has been addressed in the theoretical and empirical literature, highlighting the insights and limitations of existing approaches and emphasizing the need for a broader framework of analysis than is usually deployed to examine this question. We draw on literature on economic integration, trade, foreign direct investment (FDI), international business, growth and regionalism with the aim of identifying the most relevant approaches and theories for understanding the relationships between industry networks and growth. Our approach employs a broader range of variables influencing the formation of networks, including multinational corporation (MNC) strategies, central and east European (CEE) state actions, sectoral features and European Union (EU) policies. Mindful of the multiplicity of actors currently influencing the shaping of international production networks, we propose an 'alignment of networks' framework as the appropriate heuristic for analysing the industry integration issues of the wider Europe.

Literature review

The subject of regional integration, whether in production or in policy, has been of concern to several interrelated streams of academic research. Literatures on economic integration, on trade and growth, on FDI and growth, on international business and on political science are all relevant for understanding the issue of international industrial networks. In the following sections we critically interpret the main issues from this body of knowledge from the perspective of our research topic.

The literature on economic integration

The literature on *economic integration* itself comprises numerous approaches. Customs union theory and common market theories are most often concerned with estimates of the static (more rarely, dynamic) effects of integration. Theories of regulation and optimal regimes are concerned with appropriate levels of regulation (subsidiarity), while public choice institutional economics considers issues like optimal club size and specific interest groups that shape the dynamics of integration. The diversity of these approaches suggests that 'there is as yet no coherent framework to explain the development of integration systems in general [. . .], nor to explain the path European integration has taken in particular' (Molle 2001: 39).

The best known approach to integration is to calculate the trade and income effects of integration. Surprisingly, static trade and income effects of integration usually turn out to be limited. For example, the static effects of the accession of the CEE countries to the EU have been estimated to be some 0.2 per cent of GDP for the EU and some 1.2 per cent increase in GDP for the CEE countries (see Baldwin *et al.* 1997; compare Baldwin 1989). Economists have difficulties in getting to grips with the dynamic effects of integration such as learning by inter-acting, specialization and network externalities. Moreover, industrial integration takes place at the micro level, which makes aggregate approaches to integration insufficient and partial.

The literature on trade and growth

The literature on *trade and growth* is relevant for understanding industrial networks since close links between trade and growth are essential in the catching-up process. Trade serves to promote specialization, increased scale of production and extended varieties of goods in which learning effects are embodied. However, our understanding of the mechanisms which drive such learning effects is very vague and the empirical and theoretical research on trade and growth tells us very little about them. Slaughter (1997) and Aghion and Howitt (1998) suggest that factors such as capital accumulation, factor price equalization, knowledge spillovers and trade-mediated technology transfer are important. However, these mechanisms are variously devoid of learning content (factor price equalization), involve unknowns (spillovers) or are insufficiently specified (capital accumulation and trade-mediated technology transfer). Instead, the empirical literature tends to focus on measures of openness (trade to GDP ratios) in order to establish links to growth. A common objection to this research is that openness may be the result of growth rather than vice versa. Data on per capita income cannot identify the mechanisms by which convergence or growth takes place. This opens the problem of endogeneity in empirical research, which has been difficult to resolve. In reality growth and trade mechanisms operate in combination, which leads to serious problems for econometric investigation. In addition, empirical research has to use proxies for its concepts, which are far from perfect.

There is thus a huge gap between theoretical models, which are by nature simplistic, and empirical research, which has developed on its own. The work on trade and growth in CEE has followed mainly the empirical route. The majority of analyses have looked at the changing patterns of CEE trade by using various factor intensity taxonomies (Guerrieri 1999; Hoekman and Djankov 1996;

Kubielas 1997; Landesmann 1997, 2000) or detailed product-level data (Kaminski and Ng 2001; Radosevic and Hotopp 1999).

The literature on FDI and growth

The literature on *FDI and growth* considers this link through analysis of the costs and benefits of FDI, or estimates of spillovers, or – at the micro level – examinations of the linkages between growth and types of FDI. Several estimates of the direct costs and benefits of FDI were undertaken during the 1970s (see Helleiner 1989 for an overview). However, such attempts faced numerous conceptual and measurement problems and were often confined to only one aspect of FDI, the costs and benefits of licences. Today cost–benefit analyses are undertaken for CEE by direct comparison of performance of domestic and foreign enterprises (Hunya 2000). The dynamic effects of FDI are taken into account by estimating spillovers or benefits to domestic firms for which no direct compensation is made. This is done either by collecting circumstantial evidence on linkages or by statistical testing of the relationship between the productivity of domestic firms and that of foreign investment enterprises.

The assumption underlying this stream of research is that spillovers are positively related to the extent of linkages. However, the actual connection between linkages and spillovers has not yet been studied. This means that the mechanisms that generate positive or negative spillovers remain basically unknown.

The main conclusions from this literature are that high growth rates and large inflows of FDI tend to go together (UNCTAD 2000). However, causation mechanisms are not clear at the macro level as they are very much context-specific: the positive effects of FDI are likely to increase with the level of local capabilities and competition, while there are inconclusive results regarding indirect effects of FDI. There is no general policy advice for maximizing spillovers as they are sector-specific and are functions of industry, market and technology factors (see Kokko 1995; De Mello 1997; Radosevic 1999; for reviews of the literature).

Empirical research on the effects of FDI in CEE (Holland *et al.* 2000; Hunya 2000a,b; Konings 2001; Meyer 1998; Resmini 2000) shows that:

- FDI is concentrated in a few countries but is dispersed across industries and geographical sources; in terms of employment FDI operates as a buffer (substitute) for large employment decreases in the CEE countries, except in Hungary where it operates as a complement;
- FDI deepens trade linkages by having disproportionately high shares in export and imports;
- the direct effects of FDI include significantly higher productivity of acquired companies/greenfields than of domestic firms. Foreign investment firms are the main profit generators in the CEE countries, with higher relative shares in investments and in R&D than domestic firms;
- in terms of industrial and market structure FDI plays a dual role as a restructuring agent by building new sectors (electronics, automotives), and as a

market seeker (food). It is involved in branches that have relatively stable and promising or growing domestic markets, and is not (at least not until recently) entering collapsing branches with shrinking domestic markets (steel, petrochemicals);

- the effects of FDI are still localized to acquired or newly erected plants. The extent of spillovers from FDI is still very limited, non-existent or even negative.

A fair conclusion is drawn by Holland *et al.* (2000) who point out that 'FDI inflows have improved the overall growth potential of the recipient economies, but primarily through productivity improvements within the foreign affiliates themselves, rather than through increased capital investment, or technology spillovers to domestic firms' (p. 211).

The international business literature

The *international business* literature is one of the major sources of theories and empirical evidence on industrial networks. The link between international business and growth is not developed in this literature; yet it seems obvious that the effects of inclusion in the global economy may vary according to the organizational types of MNCs which enter a country (hierarchy/heterarchy; closed/open; leaders/ followers). This link has been explicitly discussed in broad terms by Ozawa and Castello (2001) and has been conceptualized via the notion of development subsidiary (Birkinshaw 1996; Birkinshaw and Morrison 1995), which focuses on how MNC subsidiaries enhance their resources and capabilities, and, in so doing, add increasing levels of value *to the MNC as a whole*. A review of this literature shows that:

(a)   national subsidiary types and their positions are related to the host country and regional attributes;
(b)   the organizational type of MNC plays a role in the opportunities and modes of integration of a country at the production network level;
(c)   the organizational types of MNCs are not related to the frequency of 'developmental subsidiaries' in a straightforward manner; and
(d)   the organizational structure is secondary to the management of decision-making processes within the multinational firm.

A growing part of the international business literature is concerned with non-equity relationships or networks and marks a shift away from the internalization issues which dominated the traditional MNC literature. This reflects a fragmentation of value chains across the global economy and the changing boundaries of firms. A simple procurement or vertical integration dichotomy cannot explain the existence of network forms of organization: despite high degrees of uncertainty, frequency and asset specificity, firms in network relationships do not integrate. The source of firms' market power is far less in control of physical and other assets and much more in control of inter-firm relationships (Holmstrom and Roberts 1998). This moves the focus of analysis from individual firms to the meso level, that is, to supply chains, clusters of firms and other emerging organizational forms. For some first steps in conceptualizing the new research agenda see Casson (2000).

Unlike the literature on FDI, the empirical work on CEE from an international business perspective is much less amenable to generalizations. This literature shows that the diversity of modes of integration of CEE into the global economy runs not only across sectors but also within sectors, and is strongly shaped by the individual strategies of foreign investors. For example, Ruigrok and van Tulder (1998) showed that international production networks in the European car industry largely ran along the lines of strategic groupings, in which individual firms shaped the patterns of industrial networks. Industrial networks, in turn, had a significant impact on the nature of success of the strategies that firms pursued. Equally, individual firms are able to shape the patterns of adjustment to a large number of firms with whom they cooperate or compete.

The models of operations of foreign firms in CEE are diverse. As industry studies show, they range from operations where CEE functions as a low cost base to those where CEE operates largely as a complementary production base. However, the most widespread seems to be the position where CEE enterprises operate as extended workbenches or localizers (Lankes and Venables 1996). Based on twenty-six cases of strategic alliances in central Europe, Radosevic (2004) finds that, as a rule, firms grow either through foreign acquisition or networking (alliances), or through expansion that relies heavily on networking. Expansion as a single strategy is rare. The alliances in central Europe are being driven more by unexploited market opportunities and cost differentials than by the wish to displace competition. Alliances are more often found in vertical relationships while FDI occurs with horizontal links. The types and dynamics of alliances also reflect the political and legal situation of a country (privatization, attitude towards FDI) as well as specific sectoral features in terms of technology, finance and markets.

The political science approach

Political science approaches to integration have tended to fall into two categories: grand theories for explaining the overall dynamics of integration; and analysis of the institutions and policies surrounding specific integration experiments and their impacts on member states.

Overall theories of integration have built upon idealist traditions of international relations, which emphasized the possibilities for international cooperation. The 'neofunctionalist' school predicted a broadly positive relationship between these on the back of a steadily increasing degree of integration and pooling of sovereignty, the latter facilitated by a virtuous circle of transferred loyalties and expanding tasks (Haas 1958; Lindberg and Scheingold 1970). However, as the hopes of the most ardent Europeans were apparently dashed, a 'realist' backlash determined that power politics and national interests were still the primary forces within Europe and that these would contain the process of integration (Hoffman 1966). Events in the 1980s offered a revival of this debate (now configured as a debate between 'supranationalists' and 'intergovernmentalists', see Sandholtz and Zysman 1989; Moravcsik 1991); though more generally there has been a proliferation of approaches reflecting the more eclectic nature of the discipline of international relations as much as any specific changes within the EU. While the terms of this broader debate have ranged across many issues and motivating forces, it has bypassed the question of economic integration, even though regional integration has been predominantly focused on economic rather than political issues. To the extent that the economic dimension is included, it is usually expressed as a determinant of preferences aggregated by member state governments or as part of a virtuous circle process. An exception to this rule might be found in the concept of 'multilevel governance', but this literature tends to focus upon policy processes rather than the interplay between conditions of production and political choices.

Increasingly, however, there has been a growing interest in considering the EU as a system of governance, drawing upon approaches from political science (Hix 1999) or policy analysis (Richardson 1996). From political science, there has been a diverse range of approaches, some focusing on the institutions and their potential comparability with equivalent institutions in national settings. From policy analysis the main focus has been on organizational and administrative processes (Metcalfe 1996). Taking the mechanisms of integration as part of a system in their own right – and opening out the range of approaches which can be used to study integration – should facilitate the use of a more adequate 'political economy' approach.

Limitations of the literature: a summary

Our review of the literature reveals not only a wide range of approaches and methodologies that are of relevance for exploring the emerging industrial architecture of the wider Europe, but also filling the important conceptual and empirical gaps in understanding its determining factors and dynamics. We can rely on estimates of the static trade and income effects of economic integration, but much less on estimates of dynamic effects (Molle 2001). The empirical estimates of welfare effects of FDI are limited to the employment effects. Empirical links between trade and growth show that the relationship operates as a two-way causality (Rodrigo 2001). Theory is weak on understanding the mechanisms through which export expansion affects GDP growth, and vice versa. Empirical estimates of spillovers give an indication of the possible effects of FDI but do not specify the mechanisms by which spillovers occur. The international business literature provides evidence on the detailed mechanisms by which companies grow and integrate into global networks, but it does not normally address linkages to host countries' growth. The political science literature has traditionally over-emphasized the nation state (whether by asserting its primacy or recording its demise), though more recent approaches seem to recognize that the state is but one actor in a multi-level process of integration.

The current literature is thus:

(i)   primarily focused on macro determinants to explain trade integration, or growth via FDI (econometric proxies for determinants are often poor substitutes for real determinants);
(ii) abstracted from the broader institutional environment;
(iii) not conceptualizing micro–macro linkages, which are the key to understanding the link between international industrial networks and industry upgrading.

From the perspective of our research topic this is highly unsatisfactory. First, understanding the *process* of industry integration is equally important as understanding the determinants of integration. There is a tendency for economic integration theory to deal purely with factors of production and trade, concentrating on the *effects* of integration, while political science approaches tend to focus on the *process* of integration, concentrating on political and economic elite attitudes and preferences. What is rarely considered is the interrelationship between these two (for a slight exception see Miles *et al.* 1995). An understanding of the process variables is essential if we want to understand the potential for industry upgrading via industrial networks, which is essential in our case.

Second, understanding the broader institutional context, in particular political governance, is essential for understanding the interaction between local and foreign firms' strategies, states, the EU and regions. From a business studies perspective the problem of global production networks is predominantly seen as an issue of firms' strategies and the role of cooperative alliances (see, for example, Dussauge and Garrette 1999). Indeed, corporate behaviour and strategies are essential for understanding the dynamics of production networks. However, if we are to understand the role that networks play in growth then we cannot abstract from the wider relations in which corporate decisions are taken. The dynamics of integration are determined by a complex interplay of forces, and understanding them requires going beyond economic approaches and introducing political governance approaches.

Our conceptual approach

If we want to understand the emerging industrial architecture of the wider Europe then industrial organization perspectives will have to merge with political economy perspectives. The basic difficulty with an integrated political economy–industrial organization perspective is to define which variables should be taken into account (Hall 1997). As Lundvall points out, '[I]industrial dynamics is not linked to one specific level of aggregation in terms of micro-, meso-, and macro-analysis... [b]ut presents a specific perspective on the firm as an open system that is affected by and affects wider systems' (Lundvall 1998: 2–3, cited in Ernst 1998). Alongside the multi-level nature of the problem an additional issue is multi-dimensionality. The intersection between different networks is either nationally or sectorally specific and involves a variety of the political and corporate governance and organizational aspects that hinder or enable the alignment of different networks.

We do not have a specific or comprehensive view regarding the factors that shape industrial networks. In this respect, we implicitly accept a contingency-based view of alliances or industrial networks as argued by Lorange and Roos (1992). This assumes that no particular type of network is better, nor universally more correct, than any another (Britto 1998); the choice of networks is dependent on the particular conditions pertaining. Furthermore, unlike the international business literature, which finds contingency considerations only within the set of strategic features related to partner firms, we propose a framework in which variables that influence the formation of networks are broader in scope and relate to CEE state actions, sectoral features and EU policies. This need for the inclusion of different levels comes also from the proliferation of actors which today influence the shaping of international production networks.

As Strange argues very persuasively, we live a in a world of diffused power.

> [T]he power had shifted upward from weak states to stronger ones with global or regional reach beyond their frontiers, that power had shifted sideways from states to markets and thus to non-state authorities deriving power from their market shares, and some power has 'evaporated', in that no one was exercising it.
>
> (Strange 1996: 189)

Taking a similar view, Dunning (1997) argues that contemporary capitalism has changed towards alliance capitalism where the relationship between governments and MNCs has become more cooperative and interdependent. If this is so, then we have to take into account the actions of many more actors (MNCs, international organizations, national and local governments, non-governmental organizations (NGOs)) if we are to understand the patterns of international production and knowledge linkages. Each level (national, global, local or firm) plays a role in the process of shaping global industrial networks. For example, country factors in CEE can explain functional types of FDI but not the extent, volume and structure of FDI (Lankes and Venables 1996). The level of FDI is not explicable by country-specific factors, or at least not only by them: sectoral, firm and other institutional variables play a role.

The strategies of large firms may often be more decisive than country-specific variables in shaping sectoral patterns of international production networks. As von Tunzelmann (1995: 10) points out, 'by endogenously changing their circumstances through technological accumulation, firms may ultimately alter the national system itself'. New systems of innovation in CEE will be strongly shaped by the way enterprises develop and integrate their business functions. This points to a need to incorporate an individual–firm level into the analysis, especially in cases where large foreign investors can change the entire structure of the industry.

All this points to the need for a multi-level analytical framework, which also arises from the nature of globalization. 'Global' does not necessarily mean 'incorporating the whole world'. As Chesnais (1995: 85) put it: 'global markets are exclusively markets where purchasing power and intermediate inputs are effectively located'. This implies that the scope of 'globality' is relative to each specific case.

It differs across different dimensions: financial markets and competition are more globalized than production and sourcing networks. An industry can be global in the sense that industrial competition is global, that is, a situation of 'mutual global market dependence', but this does not imply that production, let alone technology, in that industry is globalized.

We approach the formation of industrial networks as an alignment of various networks. Several scholars have already highlighted this approach. Ernst (1998) points to a 'co-evolution of international and domestic knowledge linkages that explains Korea's extraordinary success in information industries' (p. 32). Kim and von Tunzelmann (1998) point to the alignment of networks as an explanation for the Taiwanese success in information technology (IT). Network alignment comes from effective coupling between the evolution of national specific systems and international (whether global or regional) production networks. In particular, we want to examine the ways in which markets, firms, CEE states and EU actions can bring about the 'alignment' of these networks.

A variety or multiplicity of networks is what drives the process of integrating CEE into global production systems. By plugging themselves into global supply networks domestic firms externalize the problems of accessing markets, technology and finance by surrendering control to foreign owners. Foreign investors then operate as compensating mechanisms for weakened domestic firms. Weak and isolated national networks are likely to have weak growth potential if not aligned to foreign networks.

However, whether an alignment of networks will take place depends not only on their linkages but also on the nature of each individual network. For example, robust industrial networks have developed in a context of effective and complementary structures of political and corporate governance. This has not been the case in CEE. Estrin and Wright's (1999) overview of corporate governance in the former Soviet Union (FSU) shows that slow progress in transition arises from weaknesses in implementing effective corporate governance as well as from weaknesses in the broader economic environment (capital markets; banks; product markets). In this case, weakness of national industrial networks hampers their alignment with global networks.

The more national and local networks are developed, the more sustainable will be their alignment with foreign firms and their networks, provided that their interests are complementary. If local production networks are weak then undeveloped domestic firms can only enter dominant alliances, that is, alliances where local firms are dependent on the foreign partner. In such situations MNCs dominate network alignment, which eventually produces a weak alignment of networks and thus a weak economic position in global production networks.

For the purposes of the network alignment concept, we follow the approach of von Tunzelmann (2002) who defines networks very broadly as 'non-hierarchical linkages between agents, which are other than pure market exchange' (p. 3). This 'negative' definition of networks as everything that is not pure markets and hierarchies is similar to many other basically 'negative' definitions of alliances[1] (see, e.g. the definition of alliances in Dussauge and Garrette 1999). For networks to align, information that is only transmitted through prices is far from sufficient; alignment generally entails network channels of interaction.

Following Kim and von Tunzelmann (1998) the analytical framework should have all three dimensions – global, national and local networks – as well as their interactions. Graphically and in stylized form this framework, when applied to CEE, may look like Figure 3.4 in Chapter 3 in this volume.

The major methodological problem with this framework is how to systematically combine and integrate research on all three levels of networks. A mechanical combination of sector, country and micro studies may not be sufficient. By using the same conceptual framework (network alignment) on all three levels it becomes possible to generate some coherence across the different levels of analysis. We interpret the emergence of a new production location as a multi-dimensional phenomenon, which requires the simultaneous existence of several factors, and complementarities among these factors. Whether complementarities will be realized depends on the governance dimension of international production integration.

This problem has been approached in the literature as a dichotomy: whether it is markets or states that are most important in generating growth through integration in international production networks. In the case of the CEE countries, a market perspective has been dominant throughout transition, which argues that the progress in transition or convergence towards a market economy is both a necessary and sufficient condition for growth.

Hobday *et al.* (2001) point out that underlying both market and state perspectives is the acceptance of a continuum of government–industry relations, typically running through from state-led, to corporatist, to market-driven (Hobday *et al.* 2001: 210). The state vs market dichotomy is unable to account for the strategies of firms and the differences between them. Hobday *et al.* (2001) thus take a significant step forward by bringing company strategies, both local and foreign, into the state–market debate. Even this still omits a variety of other factors that play important roles in CEE countries, such as local governments, EU accession and EU demand. Second, the variety of actors and networks that have to simultaneously align to bring about industrial change requires a conceptual framework that explicitly brings this interaction into focus. The network alignment framework, in our view, offers new opportunities for understanding successes or failures in industrial modernization through international production networks.

Network alignment vs commodity chain perspective

A competing framework for understanding growth via industrial networks in the globalized economy is the concept of commodity chains. This framework was initially developed by Gereffi (1994), and empirical work using this approach has been further extended by Kaplinsky (2000) and Humphrey and Schmitz (2001). Gereffi's original concept of global commodity chains was recently relabelled global value chains.[2]

The commodity chain perspective is a way of linking local and global networks by focusing on design and marketing as well as production. This research has shown the underpinning role of networks in trade, while recognizing the role of global buyers and the opportunities for upgrading via commodity chains. By bringing in governance issues, research has focused on the role of powerful lead firms in organizing global production and distribution networks. The key empirical insight is the emergence of 'manufacturers without factories' (Gereffi 1994) or the large retailers and brand-name companies who are creating global sourcing networks, but do not necessarily own any factories themselves. Global commodity chain research looks at the implications of this organizational form for access to trade and markets, upgrading and incomes.

Both frameworks – global value chains and network alignment – are still largely descriptive constructs that have yet to develop an analytical structure. There are some features common to both frameworks. First, they both include the governance dimension as an integral part of their framework. Second, they are both concerned with issues of upgrading and growth and how these relate to industrial networks. Third, they both take into account the unequal powers of actors and the role that strong actors have in structuring chains or networks.

However, there are also important differences between these two approaches. First, the global commodity chain perspective is greatly concerned with the distribution of rents and how they are distributed throughout the commodity chain.[3] This has not been of concern to network alignment, which looks primarily at the complementarities among networks and agents and how they bring about full or restricted network alignment and therefore growth. From a network alignment perspective the biggest constraint of the commodity chain perspective is its concentration on commodities and resources along a value 'chain'. As von Tunzelmann points out:

> resource flows connect agents with one another, but the actions of aggregated agents can also span across resource flows. There is no one-to-one mapping between resources and agents, and the functions of agents overlap. Demands and supplies need to be resolved in a tensor-like structure, since the resource flows are themselves partly interconnected.
>
> (von Tunzelmann 2002: 12)

From this perspective, the focus on commodity chains in understanding upgrading could be regarded as somewhat simplistic. Technology, finance and other resources tend not to 'align' directly with commodity chains and should be part of the conceptual framework if we are to understand upgrading via industrial networks in a global economy. The focus on vertical linkages omits far too many factors that are shaping the patterns of upgrading under globalization. As Humphrey (2001) points out, by focusing on vertical exchange linkages, research on global commodity chains tends to marginalize local networks, national frameworks, particularly innovation systems, contextual features such as global standards, trade regulations, etc., while its productivist perspective minimizes the role of finance.

Network alignment: from descriptive to analytical concept

Based on the empirical work that has been undertaken within the project that forms the basis for this volume, we have been able to add at least four new analytical dimensions to the network alignment framework.

First, based on the case study of the food industry in this volume, von Tunzelmann has developed a taxonomy of 'network failure'. Network failure is the counterpart of 'market failure', 'corporate failure' etc., which relate to other modes of governance. Such failures can arise because: the network relevant to a particular resource flow is missing; or, the network is present but anti-developmental (inconsistent objectives); or, the networks for differing resource flows are mutually inconsistent. This taxonomy can be applied to case studies that aim to disentangle the reasons behind success or failure of integration of individual sectors into global industrial networks.

Second, whereas the existing literature has examined network alignment mostly in a 'geographical' dimension (local, national and global networks, cf. Figure 3.4 Chapter 3), the analysis in Chapter 3 extends this by clarifying the cross-cutting nature of both functional networks (for finance, technology, etc.) and resource networks. This widening of the focus provides a contrast with commodity chain approaches.

Third, Radosevic (2002a) has tried to give analytical content to the notion of complementarities, which underpin the network alignment concept. By integrating the insights of Milgrom and Roberts (1995) on complementarities he aims to operationalize and analytically develop the notion of alignment into heuristics labelled the 'complementarities-driven alignment of networks'. The notion of complementarity rests on a distinction between a mere evolutionary coincidence of several factors, which jointly produce a fortuitous one-off outcome, and situations where complementarities operate in a systemic fashion. In the latter case, doing more of activity A raises the value of increases in activity B, which then by increasing B also raises the value of increasing A. In the particular case studied, the depth of industry integration into CEE has been dependent on favourable complementarities between management, firm and region (country) specific variables and several external variables. Through changes in company strategy in a context of persistent weakness of the technological environment in CEE some of these complementarities have ceased to exist.

Fourth, the case studies that follow in this book show that the morphology of networks and how they operate can only be understood by examining (i) the content of networking and (ii) the power or control structure within different networks. The unequal resources and capabilities of agents mean that alignment of networks can be understood only if we take into account the content of networking and strategic objectives of agents. Agents with resources and capabilities are those that structure the nature of networks and the scope of network alignment, for example, at regional level (Radosevic 2002b).

Industry vs policy integration

When compared to other market integration projects (like North American Free Trade Agreement (NAFTA)), an important, if not the key specificity of EU enlargement is the extent of institutional integration, complementing market integration. Market integration alone can be thought of as 'shallow' policy integration, as it omits the more profound institutional and policy processes that provide 'depth',

Policy integration	'Shallow' policy integration (trade and finance liberalization; no free movement of labour; some policy cooperation)	'Deep' policy integration (autonomous jurisdiction; direct financial instruments; CAP; single currency regime; movement of capital and labour integrated)
'Shallow' industry integration (spreading of market linkages through trade and finance flows)	**Compatibility** in modes of 'shallow' integration; perhaps limited viability in the long term	**Incompatibility** the lack of industrial integration leads to considerable economic inequalities and cohesion problems
'Deep' industry integration (a variety of production and technology networks)	**Incompatibility** frustration; the lack of political integration leads to tensions and instabilities	**Compatibility**; virtuous circle of policy and network learning through integration and 'catching up'

Figure 2.1 Relationship between policy integration and industry integration.
Source: Authors' own elaboration.

such as the one that EU appears to desire from its accession process. Equally, shallow and deep dimensions can be identified in the case of industry (micro) integration. However, it is important to stress that there is no one-way correspondence between these two forms of integration. 'Deep' policy integration may not necessarily lead to 'deep' industry integration. Equally, 'shallow' policy integration may coexist with 'deep' industry integration and vice versa (see Figure 2.1).

As Figure 2.1 suggests, the key issue is to match the degree of 'integratedness' in the two dimensions. Intuitively we would expect there to be a relationship between the microeconomic architecture (the ongoing state of 'integratedness' of economies) and the degree of political commitment (the extent of agreement on how far policies introduced foster or frustrate that condition).

The challenge for the candidate countries and the EU is to ensure that this relationship is a virtuous one, whereby integration fosters real 'integratedness', which, in turn, helps to promote further integration. The interactions will vary between different CEE countries and sectors and this should create a variety of situations with specific factors of compatibility and incompatibility.

An unexpected conclusion that has emerged from our research is that the *context* and *content* of network alignment are much more important and carry stronger explanatory power than the framework itself. While the framework serves to furnish very useful *heuristics* for analysing firm, sector and country situations, understanding network alignment involves more than presenting the logistic or ordering of different nodes of the network alignment framework. In order to understand how network alignment operates it is necessary to explain both the context in which networking takes place as well as the content of networking. We begin by analysing the content in the next chapter, then enlarge the vision by specific studies in the chapters to follow.

Notes

1 Non-hierarchical in this case means not deploying a hierarchy as the dominant mode of coordination. Networks are often relationships between agents with unequal power, so there is often a strong hierarchical relationship within networks.
2 This approach has been criticized as well as critically developed; see Smith *et al.* (2002).
3 Gereffi (1999) considers that firms in producer-driven chains generate technology rents, which stem from a privileged access to product and process technologies, and organization rents, which refer to intra-organizational process know-how (p. 43). Buyer-driven chains, according to Gereffi (1999) generate relational rents, trade policy rents and brand-name rents. *Relational rents* refer to several forms of inter-firm relationships like links between large assemblers and SMEs, local clusters and strategic alliances. *Trade policy rents* refer to advantages created through protectionist trade policies like quotas. *Brand-name rents* refer to the returns from the product differentiation techniques used to establish brand-name prominence (p. 44).

References

Aghion, P. and Howitt, P. (1998) *Endogenous Growth Theory*, Cambridge MA: The MIT Press.

Baldwin, R. (1989) 'The growth effects of 1992', *Economic Policy*, No. 9, pp. 247–82.

Baldwin, R., Francois, J.F. and Portes, R. (1997) 'The costs and benefits of eastern enlargement: the impact on the EU and Central Europe', *Economic Policy*, No. 24, pp. 125–76.

Birkinshaw, J. (1996) 'How multinational subsidiary mandates are gained and lost', *Journal of International Business Studies*, 27(3): 467–95.

Birkinshaw, J. and Morrison, A.J. (1995) 'Configurations of strategy and structure in subsidiaries of multinational corporations', *Journal of International Business Studies*, 26(4): 729–53.

Britto, J. (1998) 'Technological diversity and industrial networks: an analysis of the *modus operandi* of co-operative arrangements', *SPRU Electronic Working Paper Series*, No. 4, University of Sussex, January.

Casson, M. (2000) *Economics of International Business. A New Research Agenda*, Cheltenham: Edward Elgar.

Chesnais, F. (1995) 'World oligopoly, rivalry between "global" firms and global corporate competitiveness', in J. Molero (ed.) *Technological Innovation, Multinational Corporations and New International Competitiveness: The Case of Intermediate Countries*, Chur: Harwood Academic Publishers, pp. 21–57.

De Mello, R.L. Jr, (1997) 'Foreign direct investment in developing countries and growth: A selective survey', *Journal of Development Studies*, 34(1): 1–34.

Dunning, H.J. (1997) *Alliance Capitalism in Global Business*, London: Routledge.

Dussauge, P. and Garrette, B. (1999) *Co-operative Strategy. Competing Successfully through Strategic Alliances*, Chichester: John Wiley & Sons.

Ernst, D. (1998) 'Catching-up, crisis and truncated industrial upgrading: evolutionary aspects of technological learning in "East" Asia's electronics industry', paper presented at the UNU INTECH Lisboa Conference, September.

Estrin, S. and Wright, R. (1999) 'Corporate governance in the former Soviet Union and central and eastern Europe', *Journal of Comparative Economics*, 27(3): 395–7.

Gereffi, G. (1994) 'The organization of buyer-driven global commodity chains: how US retailers shape overseas production networks', in G. Gereffi and M. Korzeniewicz (eds) *Commodity Chains and Global Capitalism*, London: Praeger, pp. 95–122.

Gereffi, G. (1999) 'International trade and industrial upgrading in the apparel commodity chain', *Journal of International Economics*, 48(1): 37–70.

Guerrieri, P. (1999) 'Technology and structural change in trade of the CEE countries', in D. Dyker and S. Radosevic (eds), *Innovation and Structural Change in Post-Socialism: A Quantitative Approach*, Dordrecht: Kluwer Academic Publishers, pp. 339–84.

Haas, E.B. (1958) *The Uniting of Europe: Political, Social and Economic Forces 1950–1957*, Stanford CA: Stanford University Press.

Hall, P.A. (1997) 'The political economy of Europe in an era of interdependence', Center for European Studies, Harvard University, Cambridge, MA, mimeo.

Helleiner, G.K. (1989) 'Transnational corporations and direct foreign investment', in H. Chenery and T.N. Srinivasan (eds), *Handbook of Development Economics*, Vol. II, Amsterdam: North Holland, pp. 1442–80.

Hix, S. (1999) *The Political System of the European Union*, London: Macmillan.

Hobday, M., Cawson, A. and Kim, S. R. (2001) 'Governance of technology in the electronics industries of East and South-East Asia', *Technovation*, 21: 209–26.

Hoekman, B. and Djankov, S. (1996) 'Intra-industry trade, foreign direct investment and the reorientation of Eastern European exports', World Bank, March, mimeo.

Hoffmann, S. (1966) 'Obstinate or obsolete? The fate of the nation state and the case of western Europe', *Daedalus*, 95: 862–915.

Holland, D., Sass, M., Benacek, V. and Gronicki, M. (2000) 'The determinants and impact of FDI in Central and Eastern Europe: a comparison of survey and econometric evidence', *Transnational Corporations*, 9(3): 163–213.

Holmstrom B. and Roberts, J. (1998) 'The boundaries of the firm revisited', *Journal of Economic Perspectives*, 12(4): 73–95.

Humphrey, J. (2001) 'Global value chains', presented at 'Industrial upgrading through global industrial networks: three competing or complementary frameworks?' workshop, University of Sussex, 28 June.

Humphrey, J. and Schmitz, H. (2001) 'Governance and upgrading: linking industrial clusters and global value chains', Working Paper No. 120, Brighton: Institute of Development Studies, University of Sussex.

Hunya, G. (2000a) 'International competitiveness impacts of FDI in CEECs', Paper presented at the 6th EACES Conference, Barcelona, 7–9 September 2000, http://eu-enlargement.org/

Hunya, G. (ed.) (2000b) *European Integration through FDI: Making Central European Industries Competitive*, Cheltenham Edward Elgar.

Kaminski, B. and Ng, F. (2001) 'Trade and production fragmentation: Central European economies in EU networks of production and marketing', *World Bank Working Paper 2611*, Washington DC: World Bank.

Kaplinsky, R. (2000) 'Spreading the gains from globalization: what can be learned from value chain analysis?' *IDS Working Paper* No. 110, Brighton: Institute of Development Studies, University of Sussex.

Kim, S.R. and von Tunzelmann, G.N. (1998) 'Aligning internal and external networks: Taiwan's specialization in IT', *SPRU Electronic Working Paper Series* No. 17, May.

Konings, J. (2001) 'The effects of FDI on domestic firms', *Economics of Transition*, 9(5): 619–33.

Kokko, A. (1995) 'Policies to encourage inflows of technology through foreign multinationals', *World Development*, 23(3): 459–68.

Kubielas, S. (1999) 'Transformation of technology patterns of trade in the CEE countries', in D. Dyker and S. Radosevic (eds), *Innovation and Structural Change in Post-Socialist Countries: A Quantitative Approach*, Dordrecht: Kluwer Academic Publishers, pp. 385–410.

Landesmann, M. (1997) 'Emerging patterns of European industrial specialization: implications for labour market dynamics in eastern and western Europe', Research Reports No. 230, Vienna Institute for Comparative Economic Studies.

Landesmann, M. (2000) 'Structural change in the transition economies 1989 to 1999', *Economic Survey of Europe*, No. 2/3, chapter 4, www.unece.org/ead/ead-h-htm (also: (2000) Vienna Institute for International Economic Studies, Research Reports, September, No. 269).

Lankes, H.P. and Venables, A.J. (1996) 'Foreign direct investment in economic transition: the changing pattern of investments', *Economics of Transition*, 4: 331–47.

Lindberg, L. and Scheingold, S. (1970) *Europe's Would-be Polity: Patterns of Change in the European Community*, New Jersey: Prentice-Hall.

Lorange, P. and Roos, J. (1992) *Strategic Alliances: Formation, Implementation, and Evolution*, Oxford: Blackwell.

Lundvall, B.-Å. (1998) 'Defining industrial dynamics and its research agenda', paper presented at DRUID Winter Conference, Aalborg, January.

Metcalfe, L. (1996) 'The European Commission as a network organisation', *Publius*, 26: 43–62.

Meyer, K. (1998) *Direct Investment in Economies in Transition*, Cheltenham: Edward Elgar.

Miles, L., Redmond, J. and Schwok, R. (1995) 'Integration theory and the enlargement of the European Union', in C. Rhodes and S. Mazey (eds), *The State of the European Union, Vol. 3; Building a European Polity*, London: Longman, pp. 177–94.

Milgrom, P. and Roberts, J. (1992) *Economics, Organization and Management*, New Jersey: Prentice-Hall.

Milgrom, P. and Roberts, J. (1995) 'Complementarities and fit: strategy, structure and organizational change in manufacturing', *Journal of Accounting and Economics*, 19: 179–208.

Molle, W. (2001) *The Economics of European Integration. Theory, Practice and Policy*, 4th Edition, Aldershot: Ashgate.

Moravcsik, A. (1991) 'Negotiating the single European act', *International Organization*, 45: 19–56.

Ozawa, T. and Castello, S. (2001) 'Multinational companies and endogenous growth: an eclectic – paradigmatic approach', Working Paper No. 27, Economics series, Honolulu: East–West Center, May.

Radosevic, S. (1999) *International Technology Transfer and 'Catch Up' in Economic Development*, Cheltenham: Edward Elgar.

Radosevic, S. (2002a) 'European integration and complementarities driven network alignment: the case of ABB in central and eastern Europe', Working paper No. 11. Available HTTP: <http://www.ssees.ac.uk/economic.htm> (accessed 15.09.03).

Radosevic, S. (2002b) 'Regional innovation systems in central and eastern Europe: determinants, organizers and alignments', *Journal of Technology Transfer*, 27, 87–96.

Radosevic, S. (2004) 'Corporate growth through alliances in Central Europe: the issues in controlling access to technology, market and finance', in S. Radosevic and B. Sadowski (eds), *International industrial networks and industrial restructuring in Central Europe, Russia* and Ukraine, Dordrecht: Kluwer.

Radosevic, S. and Hotopp, U. (1999) 'The product structure of central and eastern European trade: the emerging patterns of change and learning', *MOST – MOCT*, 9, 171–99.

Resmini, L. (2000) 'The determinants of foreign direct investment in the CEECs. New evidence from sectoral patterns', *Economics of Transition*, 8(3): 665–89.

Richardson, J. (ed.) (1996) *European Union. Power and Policy Making*, London: Routledge.

Rodrigo, G.C. (2001) *Technology, Economic Growth and Crises in East Asia*, Cheltenham: Edward Elgar.

Ruigrok, W. and van Tulder, R. (1995) *The Logic of International Restructuring*, London and New York: Routledge.

Sandholtz, W. and Zysman, J. (1989) '1992 – recasting the European bargain', *World Politics*, 42: 1–18.

Slaughter, M. (1997) Per capita income convergence and the role of international trade, *NBER, Working Paper*, No. 5897.

Smith, A., Rainnie, A., Dunford, M., Hardy, J., Hudson, R. and Sadler, D. (2002) 'Networks of value, commodities and regions: reworking divisions of labour in macro-regional economies', *Progress in Human Geography*, 26: 41–63.

Strange, S. (1996) *The Retreat of the State. The Diffusion of Power in the World Economy*, Cambridge: Cambridge University Press.

von Tunzelmann, G.N. (1995) *Technology and Industrial Progress: The Foundations of Economic Growth*, Cheltenham: Edward Elgar.

von Tunzelmann, G.N. (2002) 'Network alignment and innovation in transition economies', SPRU, March, mimeo.

UNCTAD (2000) *World Investment Report 2000*, New York and Geneva: United Nations.

3 Network alignment in the catching-up economies of Europe

Nick von Tunzelmann

At the analytical heart of this book lies the concept of 'network alignment'. This in turn is premised on the notion that catching-up processes involve much more than the 'invisible hand' of the market, or indeed the 'visible hand' of the management of corporate hierarchies.

Equally, they may involve much more than a choice between the state and the market as the vehicle for transition and development. The 'network' component of network alignment supposes that modes of governance are in reality nowadays more complex than the polar extremes of markets, hierarchies and states, while the 'alignment' component brings in the additional complexity of linking not just within networks but between networks developed for different purposes. Network alignment in brief means that different elements are pulling in similar directions, even when their purposes differ, but with the frequent case of network misalignment, the various elements will be pulling in contrasting and often contradictory directions.

While the argument is more general than for the transition countries, and can be applied to catching-up in Western Europe as well as Central and Eastern Europe (CEE), it is the transition process which brings out the issues at their starkest. Transition is most often looked upon as a sideways movement to create the bases for sustained catching-up by formerly centrally planned economies, in which market-based systems will come to dominate. With freer markets, catching-up has been expected to follow semi-automatically, with the catching-up itself being a linear process of more or less imitating what western countries have already undergone. This chapter makes two basic objections to that stylization. First, it argues that market-based systems will not be sufficient to induce semi-automatic sustained growth. Second, it argues that the development process is multilateral and multi-dimensioned rather than linear. This leads ultimately to the conclusion that national policies cannot rest content with instituting markets, if development is to be the real objective.

Theoretical background: governance approaches

The main theoretical contexts for studying networked systems involve theories of economic growth and transition, structural change and complexity. However, the main element considered here comes from theories of 'governance'. These have come out of a variety of social sciences, in somewhat different ways. Because the concept is elusive and often undefined, it needs first to be clarified.

Governance can be usefully defined as 'organizing collective action' (Prakash and Hart 2000). It is perhaps best approached through what it attempts to cover, which can be summarized as (i) structure (the forms in which collective action is organized), (ii) control (how power relations affect these structures) and (iii) process (how it is implemented and changed). Conventionally, the modes of governance are regarded as markets, corporate hierarchies, political hierarchies (states) and networks. In a strict sense, networks are here seen as all kinds of interrelations (among individuals, organizations, etc.) without market exchange or the *direct* exercise of power. In practice, most networks that are of concern to this book also involve some market relations and some power relations, so the term will be used here in a very broad sense.[1]

Just as there are many approaches to networks from different disciplinary backgrounds, so the analytical contexts of theories of governance – most of quite recent origin again – are diversified across the social sciences. For our purposes, they are generally too partial to convey the concept of network alignment in full. An extremely terse and unduly bald statement of some of these would include the following:[2]

1   Economic theories of governance (e.g. 'transaction costs'), mainly distinguishing markets and corporate hierarchies at the micro level, especially for decisions over 'make or buy';
2   'Public choice' approaches, applying neoclassical profit maximization to governments, so primarily relating states to corporate hierarchies but through micro mechanisms, especially for evaluating 'bureaucratic capture' of states;
3   'New institutionalist' views, distinguishing institutions from organizations, and emphasizing for example that markets are themselves institutional innovations and arise in different ways;
4   Political economy approaches, usually to contrast the state and the market at a macro level in the development process, related in kind to discussions of 'national systems of innovation';
5   'Political governance' approaches (developed mainly by political scientists), often analysing the role of government at various levels for sectoral (meso) development, related in kind to 'sectoral systems of innovation';
6   'Régulation' approaches, assessing the 'tuning' between micro and macro levels from both demand and supply sides, especially in labour markets but also more generally in 'social systems of accumulation'.

All of the above (with the possible exception of variants of the régulation school) are thus partial. Some deal with the micro, some with the meso, some with the macro level or any two of these, but rarely all three together. Some deal with states versus markets, some with markets versus corporate hierarchies, etc., but again rarely with all four modes of governance together. Hence, the need to take a more encompassing view in this book. Without being too specific, this chapter will draw upon all of them.

Each mode of governance can be associated with a certain type of failure: markets with 'market failure', corporate hierarchies with 'corporate failure', political hierarchies with 'government failure' and networks with what will be dubbed here as 'network failure'. The above schools can often be identified with one particular type of failure. The political economy school thus saw 'market failure' in the years after the Second World War as the justification for government to take an active role in heading economic development. Conversely, the public choice school emphasized 'government failure' and stressed finding salvation in markets – some form of which was of course imposed on the transition process in the CEE countries (CEECs). However, as Chang and Rowthorn (1995) emphasize, strong assumptions are made in each case. The existence of market failures does not by itself prove that governments are capable of providing an alternative leadership for development. Equally, and particularly relevant here, the existence of government failures, such as those that the socialist period in CEECs undoubtedly saw, does not by itself guarantee that markets will overcome the problems.

Instead, I argue that the basic failings now in transition countries are pervasive 'network failures'. These can be thought of as of three kinds:

(i)   the network relevant to a particular resource flow is missing;
(ii)   the network is present but is anti-developmental (e.g. 'nomenklatura'-based);
(iii) the networks for different resource flows are mutually inconsistent.

Varieties of networks

Most individuals as well as organizations are, in practice, located in a multiplicity of what we call networks. With some of them they may be close to the hub, with others at or near the periphery. Typically, a firm will find itself involved in networks of at least three types.

1   Functional networks relate to the 'functions' carried out by all productive enterprises – particularly technology, production, finance, products (marketing) and management or entrepreneurship (von Tunzelmann 1989, 1995).
2   Resource networks relate to chain-like flows of resources through production or other systems – as shown below there are eight key types of resource, each of which is first associated with a different type of supplying agent, which flow into and out of the above functions of firms.
3   Geographical networks have several levels depending on the extent of territory involved. Narrowest are the local and sub-regional networks, which operate in the immediate vicinity (the precise geographical extent may vary); broader are the national networks, defined by the boundaries of the nation state; and broader still are international networks spanning national boundaries, often referred to below as global networks though they may be sub-groups of countries rather than truly global.

In *functional* networks, the 'networking' involves both external and internal links associated with any or all of the kinds of functions mentioned above. In the centrally planned economy, the functions were in principle carried out in separate enterprises – technology in research institutes and design bureaux, marketing in state monopolies, etc. In the capitalist economy, and some versions of socialism such as 'market socialism', most enterprises carry out all of these functions internally, even when quite small, though there appears to be a growing trend in western economies towards 'outsourcing' of some functions. When all the functions are undertaken within the enterprise, it is the role of managers to integrate the other functions in order to get the best possible out of the resources available to them. In a dynamic situation, it is the role of 'entrepreneurs' to change the context, rather than simply getting the maximum out of the existing context.

The nature of functional relations is expressed schematically in Figure 3.1 (adapted from von Tunzelmann 1995). The rectangles within the figure show the four principal functions of firms as already defined, that is, techniques (the firm's application of technologies), production (processes), products (for marketing) and administration (for finance etc.). These are interlinked by 'horizontal' interrelations shown by the diagonal arrows, and by 'vertical' relations through management (in a static context) and entrepreneurship (in a dynamic context).[3] The four key functions of firms are also connected to analogous functions of the 'national system of innovation' (Lundvall 1992) shown in the surrounding circles – or more exactly the 'social system of production' of the kind discussed in the régulation school approach. To simplify the diagram, each function of the firm is linked to just the function of the national system to which it is most immediately related. Change takes place not only internally through the exercise of entrepreneurship but also at the interface between elements that are internal and external to the firm. These are shown as diamond shapes, reflecting change in terms of each function. These interfaces suggest the main role of networks.

These functional networks as depicted in Figure 3.1 make no explicit reference to the *resources* of various kinds flowing through the system to generate 'production, distribution and exchange'. For a developing or transition country, as well as for an advanced industrial country, at least eight types of resources need to be distinguished: unskilled labour, skilled labour, research labour, managerial labour, physical capital, intangible capital, infrastructural capital and working capital. Indeed, each of these (and any others) has a different 'production process' associated with generating it, together with a different form of organization responsible for each of these production processes (equivalent to the institution dimension in Figure 3.1).

The simplest way of representing the resource flows is as parallel series of individual resources, seen as flowing into Enterprise x, chosen for the sake of argument to be located in Industry y. Figure 3.2 shows the simplest situation, in which each resource flows into Enterprise x and then Distributor z as a linear process, which can be taken as crude 'supply-push'. Enterprise x is theoretically the passive recipient of these linear – and probably uncoordinated – resource flows. This, albeit in an oversimplified way, formalizes the structure of resource flows under central

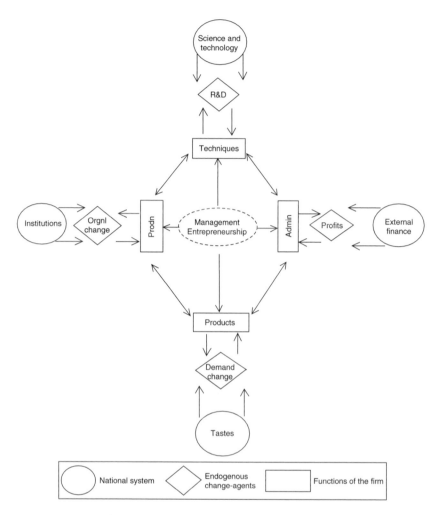

Figure 3.1 Functional networks at the micro and macro levels.

Source: Author.

planning, which stipulated targets for the output of the enterprise and also for many of the resource suppliers through 'material balances'. Distinctively important roles in regard to certain resources included the role of academies in producing research labour (universities were limited to being teaching institutions), and that of trade unions in overseeing unskilled and skilled labour. As noted below, such a structure imposed impossible burdens of information processing on the central planner and, in practice, was leavened by a degree of discretion being exercised by the enterprise in the resources it actually deployed.

The western 'firm' however moves much further in this direction. Figure 3.3 depicts a stylization of how its resource flows operate. The most obvious difference

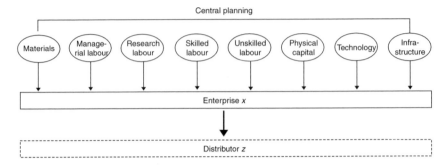

Figure 3.2 Resource flows into the enterprise: the linear model.

Source: Author.

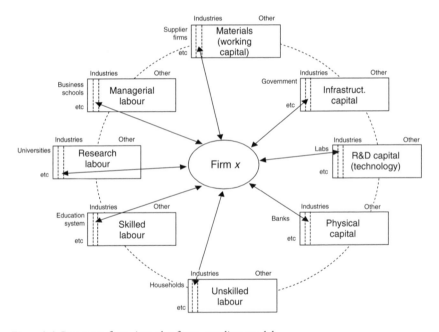

Figure 3.3 Resource flows into the firm: coupling model.

Source: Author.

Notes
Each rectangle (box) represents an input–output relationship for the resource specified. Input agents (suppliers) are listed down the vertical axis of each box. Directions of output (demands) are listed across the boxes (same in each case). The industry relevant to firm x is shown as the dotted column.

is that, rather than the top-down and linearized flows of the soviet-era enterprise, the causal relationships run in both directions: not just supply-push but 'demand-pull', originating in market forces (not shown). This demand-pull flows upwards into the 'production' of the resources themselves. This is represented by characterizing each resource process as input/output tables, extending the standard input/output tables which show the flow of products from the enterprises in the industry which produce them to enterprises in the same or other industries which use them, as well as the flows into 'final demand' (consumption, etc.). The orthodox input/output table considers only these product flows in depth – other resources such as labour flow 'exogenously' into the system.[4] Yet, there are equivalent inter-flows for each of the resources, which are shown here in all eight of the boxes.

It is the case that firms often produce more than one of these resources 'in house': they may do their own training of skilled labour, their own R&D for intangible capital, their own physical capital formation through ploughing back profits, etc. But, in principle, each production process remains different, and the firm somehow has to align all these resources for its production. Very rarely, for instance, is the 'supply chain' for technology the same as that for the materials (working capital). Thus these 'supply chains' are much more complex than the linear flows of materials indicated in the existing literature on strategic management (e.g. Porter 1990) or the recent research on commodity chains in developing countries (e.g. Gereffi and Korzeniewicz 1994; Gereffi 1999; Kaplinsky 2000; Humphrey and Schmitz 2000). Hence, again there are alignment problems, which in a corporate hierarchy are usually internalized as it horizontally relates its various functions (from Figure 3.1).

There is no particular significance about the order in which the resources are laid out as, in the end, there is a classical 'circular flow' of production and reproduction seen from the supply side, or equivalently of production and consumption seen from the demand side.[5] There are therefore 'vertical' cross-connections between the matrices, reflected in two-way links between pairs of agents which are suppressed from the diagram for reasons of simplicity (all that is shown to represent this is the dashed circle); for example the role of the government in furnishing universities and the educational and training system. These imply indirect as well as direct linkages from each type of agent to the producer firm. The complexity of the alignment process even at the firm level begins to become apparent when envisaged in this multi-dimensional way. Rarely, for instance, are the suppliers of technologies the same as the suppliers of intermediate materials. And these various supplies have of course to be matched against demand pressures from product markets.

To an extent, these resource interflows can themselves be undertaken through market mechanisms attempting to balance supply and demand in the same way, or alternatively through hierarchies. The literature on the 'economics of information' that has burgeoned since the 1960s has, however, underlined the likelihood of 'market failures' in these arenas. A particularly significant issue for the transition countries has been that of 'quality' as opposed to quantity – low prices could equally signify poor quality and a good bargain. As many of the case studies to follow indicate, foreign direct investment (FDI) in the CEE countries has been extensively directed at raising quality (of resource inputs, or outputs) and not just quantity. Networks then become particularly important for agreeing quality standards.

Finally, in terms of *geography*, there is a recent thread in the governance literature which refers to 'multi-level governance' essentially in these geographical

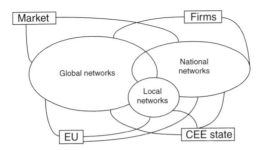

Figure 3.4 Geographical networks for European catching-up.

Source: Radosevic (2003: 18).

terms (local government, national government, supranational government, e.g. the EU). Implicit and sometimes explicit in this literature is the point that the kinds of decisions – and not just their territorial extent – may differ between these levels. One of the impacts of the 'national systems of innovation' literature has been to demonstrate how many of the decisions crucial to innovation are in fact made at the national (macro) level, while not losing sight of the point that technologies are in the last resort generated at the micro level.

An attempt to depict a structure of geographical networks pertinent to European catching-up countries is shown in Figure 3.4, which is a key diagram for this book. Figure 3.4 can be used for catching-up processes in Western Europe (Ireland and Spain) as well as transition in the CEE countries. Its original use was to study successful examples of catching up, such as Taiwan (Kim and von Tunzelmann 1998).

Alignment and misalignment in national transitions

The orthodox discussions of the roles of trade, foreign investment and growth, familiar to the debate on transition and self-sustaining growth, can be enriched by placing them in a network alignment context. The basic argument implicit in what follows is that the same extensions of trade or foreign investment may have different impacts on growth depending on the degree of network alignment. Even more seriously, transition in its sideways form may not turn into self-sustaining growth in due course unless there is some degree of alignment to link the various determinants of the growth path.

The above methodology can be applied to the CEE transition process, as in Figure 3.5. The nodes and networks reproduce those used in Figure 3.4. In the upper panel the situation for the socialist period up to 1989 is set out. In the upper-left segment, the weakness of global networks is apparent. With trade and payments links with non-socialist countries severely restricted because of 'socialism in one country' (or at least 'one bloc of countries'), the international flows were predominantly within the Council for Mutual Economic Assistance (CMEA).

(a) Communist era

(b) Transition era

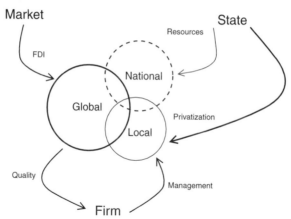

Figure 3.5 Geographical networks under socialism and transition.

Source: Author.

While often crucial, especially to smaller countries in the bloc, the exchanges became increasingly inferior to the potentialities of western commerce, leading ultimately to intense pressures for change. The Former Soviet Union drew upon the resources of other members of Comecon for some key inputs, and probably exploited them, in exchange for military protection.

In the upper-right section of the diagram, the offsetting element was the great power of national structures under central planning. These set national targets for output and for technology and dictated the scale and scope of operations, as is well understood. It can be objected that these were scarcely 'networks' in the genuine sense, since the role of hierarchies was dominant, and there were some concessions to market exchange as well. However, they acted as – or instead of – networks in the broad definition, since they effectively determined the interrelationships among elements of the national system, through the rather unbalanced mixture of hierarchies, 'markets' and networking (knowledge flows, etc.). Local networks were intended to be subservient to national targets, but in practice the production enterprises were left to their own devices to make many of the required managerial decisions, and indeed the system depended on their doing so (von Tunzelmann 1995, ch. 11).

The strong power exercised by the national element relative to the other two does not in any way imply that these were efficient. The opposite was generally the case. For the technology flows specifically, the evidence for the Former Soviet Union shows just how inefficient the system was. The generation of technologies was entrusted to centrally planned R&D institutes, design bureaux and so on, whose targets were to create defined quantities of new technologies. These new technologies were then intended to be the main source of technological diffusion in the enterprises that were responsible for actual production. In practice, the disconnection of function between technology production and technology use meant that very few of these technologies were taken up by the production units. Moreover, the enterprises for technology creation were often far distant from those for production measured in geographical terms (Hirschhausen and Bitzer 2000). The knowledge flows between the production and the use of the technology were exceedingly restricted, essentially because the nature of 'knowledge' was not comprehended in the centrally planned system of the Former Soviet Union. In actuality, the production enterprises came to rely largely on the 'dwarf workshops' within their factories to maintain and even to create their technologies. The limited capacity of such undertakings is represented in the diagram in the very moderate power of local 'networks'.

The overlap between national structures and local networks, seen as the *geographical* representation of networks, was therefore rather marginal because of the lack of alignment of *resource* networks – in this case the flows of technological resources, though also in some other resource flows – and equally the lack of alignment of *functional* networks – here between technology and production processes or products. Later in the chapter it will be concluded that the efficiency of a network structure, such as that in these diagrams, generally depends on the weakest link. Substantial power exercised by one of the networks may be to little avail if another network essential to the overall structure is disproportionately weak.

Figure 3.5b shows the current situation, reflecting the outcome of studies conducted for the project underlying this book. The comparison with the upper panel immediately makes it clear how dramatic a change there has been in the governance structures of transition countries, at least in principle. In the first place, the global networks, kept weak in the socialist era, open up. The main vehicles for the re-establishment of these networks are trade and FDI. The trade links generally involve rather 'shallow' integration into the global economy, but surges of FDI – especially to the most favoured CEE countries – can lead to 'deeper' integration. As detailed throughout this book, FDI can bring knowledge flows relating to technology, product quality, skills, management, etc. – in effect potentially for all the functions of enterprises. It is no surprise that CEE countries hanker after whatever inflows of FDI they are able to attract. At the same time the western markets rapidly replace CMEA markets in CEE trade patterns, in principle providing a demand to match the supply-side contribution. The local networks are boosted to a degree by their new responsibility for helping to determine what is to be produced and where, enhancing the implicit powers of management under the socialist system into a more explicit and sometimes more entrepreneurial role. It is here that the state under transition makes its biggest contribution, through privatization. The network-based links between local functions and supply chains however have not yet become very strong, while privatization alone raises almost as many problems of coordination as it solves, as many of the chapters detail.

The counterpart of the rise of the globally oriented networks is the implosion and semi-collapse of the old national networks. For the technology function, the old R&D institutes and other nationally based R&D operations are left isolated, with not much, if any, demand for their services. The foreign manufacturers and producers coming in through FDI have little time for or patience with the domestic efforts towards R&D. As far as they can, they simply bypass this component of the former socialist system.

Given the low efficiency of the old national 'networks' one might think that it was not surprising that they were now brought to such a parlous condition. However, the new pattern as depicted in Figure 3.5b has its own problems of severe imbalance. In the first place, the admittedly and somewhat limited areas for new growth from domestic sources are especially crippled by the transition – it is business enterprise R&D (BERD) and applied research rather than government or higher-education R&D (GOVERD and HERD) and basic research which receive the most severe cuts. Second, and partly reflecting this, many of the old informal networking linkages survive, even where they are not pro-developmental; only a partial reconstruction of the networked flows is achieved.

The outcome is thus that a new form of misalignment arises. The literature on 'national systems of innovation' has shown the critical nature of the national aspect of the overall system, but here this has largely disappeared or been edged to the side. The national aspect, as I shall argue further below, is perhaps the main base for indigenous growth. From here comes the primary impetus for 'absorptive capacity'. Losing the national system may imply losing the opportunity for self-sustaining growth beyond the transition process. It also leaves the economy highly vulnerable to the caprices of the global economy, as will also be argued below.

Discussion

These considerations of alignment carry some serious implications, some positive but also many negative connotations that are not stressed often enough in this context.

A first implication is that, while FDI is likely to bring considerable short-term gains, it is less clear that its long-term impact will lead to sustained growth, unless it can somehow be harnessed to the bolstering of national and local networks. To do so requires a shift from market-seeking to efficiency-seeking objectives by the MNCs. So long as FDI remains mostly market-seeking, it runs out of purpose after making the once-for-all gains from entry. Indeed, there is some evidence already building up that the productivity impact can be sharp at first, but then may level off. What is needed is learning in the host country to become cumulative. So long as the principal learning processes are largely confined to the home country of the MNCs, such long-term accumulation of knowledge in the CEE countries is likely to be restricted, and so eventually will be their growth processes.

One of the key consequences of weaknesses in connecting domestic sources of knowledge accumulation to the foreign sources is the lack of impetus for skilled younger people to remain in their country of birth. What is already visible and very marked is a brain drain of younger people, equipped with the intellectual and often technical training necessary, but without enriching demands for their talents in their own country. Naturally they go to the MNC home countries, not only because of a demand-pull of higher incomes there, but also because of a supply-push of lack of challenge in the host countries from which they come. Historical studies of migration patterns show very consistently that nearly all major migratory flows reflect a compound of demand-pull and supply-push elements, including the huge outflows from CEE countries to the United States about a century ago (Easterlin 1961). So long as there remains a network misalignment between foreign and domestic technological accumulation, it is difficult to foresee anything else happening, especially as EU accession looms nearer.

Once it has taken command of a CEE market in a relevant product, what does the MNC do?

In a process that recalls the product cycle in international trade identified by Vernon (1966), FDI began by targeting the largest, most stable and comparatively well-off markets, such as Poland. The desired shift to other countries has had to await the extension of those market conditions to the prospective recipients of the FDI. It is then conceivable that, having done its job in the early countries, the FDI will then simply displace itself to the new country and abandon the old so far as production is concerned. The short-term gains of lower wages will act as a temporary attraction to the new country. Some evidence for this sort of cycle appears in several of the industry studies in this book, for instance food-processing, electronics and automobiles.

An alternative strategy for the MNC apart from simply moving on to the next market is intensifying its control of its existing markets. There is a strong and often pursued incentive to buy up domestic plants in order to close them down. As a result, the capacity within the host country may decline rather than grow. Additionally, as the dominant shares of relevant CEE markets fall under MNC control, they may have to outcompete or take over the subsidiaries of other MNCs. There are already some indications of CEE countries unwittingly becoming pawns in global capitalism and its struggles. In what Lenin (1915) called a 'redivision' of markets among warring global players, the CEE countries may become – as he feared – hapless victims. Again it is not clear just how substantial the gains will be for these countries in the long term. For sustained growth, there has to be sustained interaction between the foreign and the domestic functions, and between the macro, the meso and micro levels of the relevant networks.

Conclusions

It must be concluded, therefore, that network alignment is far from automatic.

1   The CEE pattern has involved a shift in *functional* terms from domestic to foreign sources of several key resources, especially finance, management and technology. However, it has not fully hooked in those resources which will continue to be domestically supplied for the foreseeable future, such as production skills, domestic capital and, above all, domestic technology. The functional interrelations are in some crucial areas weakly coupled.
2   In *resource* terms, the supply chains are being reorganized in accord with the needs of MNCs, but problems remain. In the first place, even under transition they often still reflect predominantly 'supply-push' patterns of hierarchy. Second, they are excessively linear in the sense of Figure 3.2 and do not recognize the interactive and jointly determined resource flows indicated by a network alignment perspective – this is another way of representing the lack of consideration of nationally based resources.
3   In *geographical* terms, the old socialist axis of national networks dominating local networks virtually to the exclusion of global networks has been replaced with a transition one in which global networks dominate local networks virtually to the exclusion of the imploded national networks (Figure 3.5). This runs a heavy risk of making the sideways move of transition into an end in itself, and of restricting possibilities for turning this into longer term self-sustained growth.

The existing theoretical approaches to governance set out earlier in this chapter reflect similar limitations. Most focus on simple dualities (states vs markets, markets vs hierarchies, …) and imply either/or choices. In practice, one must consider all dimensions of governance and envisage them not just as choices, but as conjoined. As for Taiwan, or indeed the successful cases of western catching-up, it is the combined and interrelated roles of markets and firms and states, particularly as intercoupled through various levels of networking, that account for successful growth. To enumerate again, the contributions of the varying theories can be illustrated by the following:

1   Economic theories of governance are at the heart of the shift of technology production from 'make' to 'buy' (from MNCs).
2   Public choice approaches show up especially in privatization, which however I would argue is by itself insufficient.
3   'New institutionalist' views would thus warn against the undue reliance on markets, unless there is an attendant process of thoroughgoing institutional innovation.
4   Political economy approaches demonstrate the need to re-establish state-market systems at the national and regional level.
5   Political governance approaches denote the role of 'sectoral systems of innovation' as in Figure 3.3 and as exhibited in case studies throughout this book.

6   Régulation approaches, generalized into 'social systems of accumulation', amalgamate the range of elements of the system into one where network alignment ought to prevail.

This perspective allows a refocus on the role of the state and its policies from a network alignment viewpoint, although the full policy implications cannot be detailed here. The main conclusion is that the exercise of policy has swung from being too interventionist in the socialist period to not interventionist enough in transition. The consequence has been the implosion of national networks. At the more micro level, the complete reliance on privatization as a way of fixing the national production system is equally limited: the emphasis needs to shift from ownership issues to issues of management and governance. Much more thought also needs to be paid to the meso level of the evolution of industrial sectors, to move from a fixation on 'sunset industries' to building the industries of future growth. In terms of resources, the 'linear model' in which science feeds forward into new technologies for production still prevails, in a world in which the need is pressing for demand-pull influences to orient technological change.

As Radosevic (2003) emphasizes, the success of policy depends on the 'weakest link'. Under the socialist system (see Figure 3.5) the national structures were ostensibly powerful but they were in the end not effective, because of the poverty of the local and especially the global networks. Under transition, global networks have become powerful in their place, but these too may turn out to be ineffective unless they are aligned with the local and the weakened national networks. CEE governments cannot afford to sit back and let global markets and global networks take all the responsibility – not only will they lose a control base by doing so, but eventually the efficiency gains may desert them as well.

Notes

1 Sociologists tend to define networks in a positive way, circumscribing what sorts of organizational structures can be legitimately called networks. Here we follow the usual practice in other social sciences of defining networks 'negatively', that is, as what they are not (neither hierarchies nor markets). This leads to a much broader conceptualization of what networks might comprise. For a survey of applications to the modern economy, see Cooke and Morgan (2000).
2 A slightly fuller account of each of these and their overall role is given in von Tunzelmann (2003).
3 For the horizontal/vertical distinction employed here, see, for example Aoki (1984).
4 In the 'dynamic input/output' approaches physical capital is however analysed in a similar way to products or working capital.
5 A 'labour theory of value' would envisage a more layered pattern in which (unskilled) labour was the fundamental resource, but equally one could have a technology or other 'theory of value'.

References

Aoki, M. (ed.) (1984) *The Economic Analysis of the Japanese Firm*, Amsterdam: Elsevier.
Chang, H.-J. and Rowthorn, R.E. (1995) *The Role of the State in Economic Change*, Oxford: Clarendon Press.

Cooke, P. and Morgan, K. (2000) *The Associational Economy: Firms, Regions and Innovation*, Oxford: Oxford University Press.

Easterlin, R.A. (1961) 'Influences in European overseas emigration before World War I', *Economic Development and Cultural Change*, 9: 331–51.

Gereffi, G. (1999) 'International trade and industrial upgrading in the apparel commodity chain', *Journal of International Economics*, 48: 37–70.

Gereffi, G. and Korzeniewicz, M. (eds) (1994) *Commodity Chains and Global Capitalism*, Westport VA: Praeger.

Hirschhausen, C. von and Bitzer, J. (eds) (2000) *The Globalization of Industry and Innovation in Eastern Europe: From Post-socialist Restructuring to International Competitiveness*, Cheltenham: Edward Elgar.

Humphrey, J. and Schmitz, H. (2000) 'Governance and upgrading: linking industrial cluster and global value chain research', *IDS Working Paper* No. 120, Brighton: Institute of Development Studies, University of Sussex.

Kaplinsky, R. (2000) 'Spreading the gains from globalization: what can be learned from value chain analysis?', *IDS Working Paper* No. 110, Brighton: Institute of Development Studies, University of Sussex.

Kim, S.-R. and von Tunzelmann, N. (1998) 'The dynamics and alignment of "networks of networks": explaining Taiwan's successful IT specialization', *SEWPS* No. 17, Brighton: SPRU, University of Sussex (http://www.sussex.ac.uk/spru/publications/imprint/sewps/sewp17/sewp17.pdf).

Lenin, V.I. (1915) *Imperialism: The Highest Stage of Capitalism*, New York: International Publishers, 1939 edn.

Lundvall, B.-Å. (ed.) (1992) *National Systems of Innovation: Towards a Theory of Innovation and Interactive Learning*, London: Pinter.

Porter, M.E. (1990) *The Competitive Advantage of Nations*, London: Macmillan.

Prakash, A. and Hart, J.A. (eds) (2000) *Coping with Governance*, London: Routledge.

Radosevic, S. (2003) 'The emerging industrial architecture of the wider Europe: the co-evolution of industrial and political structures', *Working Paper* No. 29, London: Centre for the Study of Economic and Social Change in Europe, SSEES.

von Tunzelmann, G.N. (1989) 'The supply side: technology and history', in B. Carlsson (ed.) *Industrial Dynamics*, Boston MA: Kluwer Academic Press, pp. 55–84.

von Tunzelmann, G.N. (1995) *Technology and Industrial Progress: The Foundations of Economic Growth*, Aldershot: Edward Elgar.

von Tunzelmann, G.N. (2003) 'Historical coevolution of governance and technology', *Structural Change and Economic Dynamics*, 14: 365–84.

Vernon, R. (1966) 'International investment and international trade in the product cycle', *Quarterly Journal of Economics*, 80: 190–207.

4 State strategy and regional integration

The EU and enlargement

Francis McGowan

Introduction

In Chapter 2, we noted the interrelationship between policy and production integration. Here we look more closely at the dynamics of policy integration and in particular how the process of enlargement has affected 'state strategies' of the candidate Central and Eastern European Countries (CEECs). Given the nature of the European Union (EU) integration and enlargement process one might have expected a relatively clear-cut shift in state strategy – in terms of both the *orientation* of policies that states can adopt and their *capacity* to pursue such policies. Alignment with EU rules would tend to narrow the scope of policy orientation, pushing CEECs towards a predominantly 'regulatory' rather than a 'developmental' mode of governance, and reinforce administrative capacity. In fact, the picture is more ambiguous, with incumbent as well as candidate states not always able or willing to adapt to the apparent logic of integration.

We begin by outlining the concept of state strategy, borrowing from the wider literature on the political economy of development to explore the two aspects of 'orientation' and 'capacity': the analysis of orientation builds upon the debate concerning developmental and regulatory states, while capacity is considered on the basis of ideas of strong and weak states.[1] We then consider how these factors are affected by the context of regional integration, touching on the contrast between policy and production integration developed within the context of this project. How do national policy orientations and administrative capacities interact with commitments to cooperate regionally? Do such regional arrangements constrain state strategies? Are some policies and practices more compatible with regional cooperation than others?

In our discussion of the EU and state strategy we focus on how far the EU is predisposed more towards some modes of governance than others, constraining the orientations of states at the national level, while the legal and policy obligations of membership oblige states to develop effective administrative and judicial machinery. Although the evidence is not conclusive, member states do seem on the whole to be adapting their national economic policies to those agreed in the EU; nonetheless within the EU there are 'persisting anomalies' of member states that are relatively less willing or able to reform, thereby constituting potential 'precedents' for prospective member states.

The enlargement and CEEC state strategies section extends this analysis of the EU's impact on orientation and capacity to the CEECs themselves. After highlighting the scale of the challenge facing the candidate states, this section draws upon the EU's own surveys of the accession process and other international agency reports on institutional reforms, to examine how far the candidate states are reorientating towards an EU model of economic policy and to consider the changes that have taken place in national administrative and judicial structures and practices. The last section provides some conclusions.

State strategy: the interaction between orientation and capacity

The history of the modern state has been generally characterized by both an increased administrative capability and extended oversight of economic activity (Gerschenkron 1962). How governments have intervened and for what purposes have, of course, varied across time and territory along with changes in the mechanisms chosen. Governments have been able to deploy their powers to own, tax, spend, buy, protect, promote, regulate, etc. (Grant 1993) in the pursuit of a variety of economic objectives (though equally it is true that the effects have not necessarily been those that were intended). At the risk of oversimplification we have synthesized various insights on the nature of policy-making (Johnson 1982; Lowi 1964; Majone 1996; Weiss 1998) and have aggregated these instruments and intentions into three broad categories of governance: developmental, distributive and regulatory.[2]

The *developmental state* (i.e. where developmental modes of governance are predominant) is one where the state is involved in targeting sectors for rapid and/or focused development and directing foreign investment, trade policy, domestic finance and firms accordingly (White 1988). However, while the developmental state is one in which bureaucrats play a key directive role through planning and coordination activities, it is not the same as the former command economies of the socialist bloc. It is not by definition dominated by state activities (though in some – such as Korea and Taiwan – the scope of public enterprise has been relatively extensive), nor is it closed to foreign competition or investment (on the contrary they are characterized by their export-orientation) (Wade 1990). Nonetheless, the state does play a central role, coordinating banks, firms, universities and other actors to enhance competitiveness.

Industrial economies have tended to be the main focus for debates over the *regulatory state*. Most accounts tend to take development for granted and focus on a set of what are envisaged as 'post-industrial' problems. The regulatory state is one where rule-making prevails, with a strong attachment to the rule of law and a predilection for judicial or quasi-judicial solutions over direct intervention (Majone 1996). Just as the developmental state should not be seen as equivalent to a maximal state along the lines of the Former Soviet Union, so we should be careful not to equate the regulatory state with a minimal or 'night-watchman' state: aspects of the developmental mode of governance are at work in all states, even those that are a predisposed towards a regulatory mode (McGowan and Wallace 1996).

The *distributive state* is one where government is engaged in an extensive process of redistribution through fiscal mechanisms, and where a broadly defined and inclusive welfare system has developed. Thus, whereas the United States and Japan have welfare systems entailing extensive transfers of resources, the relative share of public expenditure in the economy is much lower than in most west European states. Within Europe it would be the Scandinavian states – even after a period of retrenchment – that we would highlight as 'distributive' (Weiss 1998).

Given these characteristics, the three modes can be contrasted in a number of important ways. Whereas the regulatory state is one where rule-making is the central activity of government, the activities of the developmental state are more extensive and the role of law is arguably secondary to other ways of intervening, as is the case with the distributive state where budgetary transfers are the main mechanism. The relative neutrality of the regulatory state is another possible difference from the other two – the state is concerned with keeping the playing field level and enforcing the rules of the game rather than with 'picking winners' or providing an extensive range of entitlements.

Whatever the balance of those commitments, governments have to be able to follow them through on the basis of effective administrative capabilities, relative autonomy *vis à vis* other actors. In the first respect, the bureaucracy has to be sufficiently resourced and trained to be able to carry out policy. In the second, it needs to enjoy sufficient independence from firms and other actors to pursue wider public interests while at the same time engaging with those groups in order to define and follow up those wider goals (Evans 1995). Thus, in order to understand the characteristics and the effectiveness of state strategies it is as important to examine state *capacity* as its *orientation*.

These questions of administrative effectiveness and state autonomy are at the heart of two distinct but overlapping understandings of 'state strength'. In the first 'commonsense' definition, a strong state is one that possesses a professional and expert bureaucracy backed up by an independent judiciary, with both mechanisms applied in a procedurally clear and disinterested manner, while a weak one will be where the bureaucracy's competence and the judiciary's independence are questionable. The second sense – which has developed within the political science literature – refers to the relationship between the state and society and the ability of the state to pursue public interests independently of, and over, private groups (Migdal 1987).

These two aspects of state capacity – effective administrative and judicial capabilities on the one hand and relative autonomy from special interests and political groups on the other – tend to converge. In most cases, the very fact of institutional development seems to be associated with a high degree of autonomy; conversely, those states with poorly developed administrative and legal systems tend to be prone to the most extensive forms of corruption and cronyism. However, there are some cases where the two do not quite match up. The United States is often characterized as a 'weak state' (Gourevitch 1978) on account of its openness to special interests – and some have argued regulatory capture – yet it possesses an effective administrative and legal system.

How do these issues of capacity and orientation interact? It might be argued that for a state to have an orientation presupposes a certain capacity. Where developmental, distributive and regulatory states are effective it is because they have the capacity to govern, enjoying the autonomy, skills and ethos that permit effective policy formulation, and engaging with society in ways that allow them to consult, communicate and ensure compliance from other groups. By contrast the weakest states may well have no orientation beyond the enrichment of officials, clients and vested interests (Evans 1995).

Regional integration and state strategy

How might the state's role be affected by regional integration? In order to understand this it might be useful to consider certain aspects of the theory of integration. According to Pinder, economic integration can take two forms 'the removal of discrimination as between the economic agents of the member countries and the formation and application of co-ordinated and common policies on a sufficient scale to ensure that major economic and welfare objectives are fulfilled' (Pinder 1973: 126), respectively *negative* and *positive* integration. While both aspects are possible, in practice positive integration has been much more difficult to achieve and most effective regional integration schemes have been driven primarily by negative integration (Hayek 1949; Holland 1980; Pinder 1973: 135). It seems that the parties to integration find it relatively easier to commit themselves to the removal of barriers than to agree to new policies (which would usually entail more visible transfers of finance and sovereignty).

What are the implications of this bias for state strategies? It may be that more interventionist models of development are harder to reconcile with – let alone advance within – regional integration. Historically this has led to the breakdown of the integration schemes themselves: where regional integration conflicted with ISI development strategies in the 1960s and 1970s, it was regional integration that suffered (e.g. in Latin America). Moreover, it is noteworthy that some of the most dynamic developmental states appear to have been among the least engaged in regional integration (e.g. in North East Asia). It could be argued that, as the commitment to regional integration increases, it becomes harder to deploy the instruments associated with the developmental state or the distributive state. By contrast it could be argued, from the recent experience of the EU and some 'new regionalisms' that a less interventionist state is relatively compatible with integration.

If regional integration constrains the orientation of state strategy, what does it do to state capacity? Clearly this has been a problem in the past where states unable to resist societal pressures shirked their commitments under integration. To the extent that states become reconciled to integration this requires a greater degree of compliance. Nonetheless, it is still possible that, notwithstanding the best intentions of governments, they remain unable to fulfil such commitments due to weak administrative/legal mechanisms.

The EU and European state strategies

Increasingly, a version of the regulatory model has come to characterize the EU approach to policy-making. Because of the particular character of European economic integration the EU has more powers to regulate than to use other forms of public policy; its efforts to develop other forms of public policy (i.e. to adopt developmental or distributive modes of governance) are much more heavily constrained and likely to remain so. The emphasis on market liberalization in the Treaties provides a good basis for the extension of a regulatory approach. It is not, however, the case that the EU dimension translates into a perfect convergence of member states' policies and policy styles: on the contrary there are persisting divergences, reflected in 'implementation gaps' between policies agreed in the EU and policies carried out by national authorities. These gaps are indicative of variations in the regulatory model across the Union (reflecting perhaps the difficulties – political as well as economic – of adjustment in some member states). These differences have affected not only the timing and content of emerging European regulatory regimes, but also their subsequent implementation.

The impact of the EU on state strategy – in principle

In distinguishing the experience of European integration from other experiments in regionalism, the characteristic that commentators almost always address is the existence of a robust legal order to underpin the various rules and regimes agreed within the EU. From the very beginning, European integration was characterized by a system of decision-making which combined an activist bureaucracy and system of law with the involvement and subsequent support of member state governments in the decision-making process: the European Commission took on the role of policy initiator with oversight of compliance with policy; the European Court of Justice asserted the primacy of the Community legal order; and the member states agreed to be bound by these principles (Hix 1999).

This rule-based system of integration permeates most areas of policy-making, though some such as Wallace (2000) argue that this is only one set of governance mechanisms in EU policy-making and one that is less and less relied upon in both new areas and, to a degree, the extension of existing competences. However, it remains particularly relevant in 'microeconomic governance', that is, in the regulatory infrastructure that underpins both the single market and the system of competition policy that sets rules on what firms and governments can do within that market. Moreover, the extent to which other 'orientations' are present at EU level is quite limited. Figure 4.1 attempts to map out some of the key areas of EU policy-making against our taxonomy of state orientations. The distributive aspect has a limited though (for some states and regions) still significant impact in the form of the Common Agricultural Policy (CAP) and Structural Funds. The developmental aspect might be regarded as manifest in the policies towards R&D and the attempts to develop an industrial policy within the EU. However, while its efforts in this respect are relatively longstanding – and indeed there has been a recent initiative in this area – the actual powers enjoyed and results achieved have been rather limited

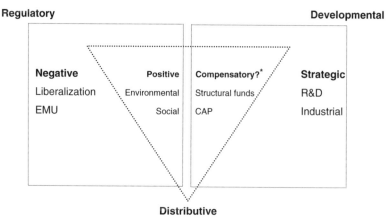

Figure 4.1 The EU and 'state' roles.

Source: Author.

Note

★ Author's own elaboration.

(European Commission 1970; European Commission 2002b; Hodges 1983; Pearce and Sutton 1985). By contrast, through initiatives such as the single market and its agenda of regulatory reform in many sectors, the regulatory mode has prevailed.

While the reliance on a rule-based system of integration implies obligations to develop state capacity, the substance of those rules may constrain the orientation of policy pursued by member states. It is clear that the character of the EU's rules could be regarded as requiring member states to follow particular policies (and precluding them from following others). Thus, the content of the single market programme and the constraints imposed by regimes such as competition policy are designed to lock states into certain commitments on how they intervene in the economy (refraining from certain types of financial support or preferential policies towards local suppliers, etc.). The effect of these legal constraints in locking member states into a relatively narrow range of policies appears to be reinforced by the development of non-binding but influential policy recommendations in recent European Councils – most notably the 'Lisbon commitments' agreed in 2000 – and in published guidelines on overall direction of economic policy (European Commission 2001a,b).

To the extent that member states follow these guidelines and abide by their legislative commitments, it could be argued that they are obliged to converge upon a particular economic orientation or at least to narrow their own policy preferences. There seems to be some substance in the claim that the model of the regulatory state is applicable at both national and EU levels – even that there is a degree of reinforcement between levels in this respect.

The impact of the EU on state strategy: in practice

If the effect of European integration in principle is to impose quite substantial constraints on what states can do, what happens in practice? In capacity terms, how have states adapted their administrative and legal practices to membership? In terms of orientation how far has the room for manoeuvre for states been constrained? Overall, it appears that while convergence of both administrative capacity and policy orientation has taken place, it is incomplete, though in some respects there is a blurring of the capacity and orientation factors. One place to start an assessment of the practical impact of integration is with those formal measures of adaptation, principally in terms of legislative output, also in terms of compliance with other policies.

Competition policy/state aid

Competition policy – with its constraints not only upon firm conduct, but also on the policies of government – might offer a better sense of how orientations have changed. In many key areas of competition law – notably merger control – the degree to which states intervene either to encourage firms to collaborate or to defend national champions is relatively limited: while historically national authorities tolerated and even encouraged cartels, EU antitrust policy has contributed to a major shift in most states' perspectives (the creation of a 'competition culture').

The area of European competition policy where the impact is most obviously felt is that of state aid. This traditional instrument of government support for industry has been targeted by the Commission as a market distortion to be exposed and phased out. The overall level of government aid appears to be in decline, down from 1.45 per cent of GDP in 1996 to 0.99 per cent in 2001. While there appears to be some variation in the levels of aid from state to state, the trend to lower levels is uniform (though there are year-to-year fluctuations – see Table 4.1). This, it

Table 4.1 State aid as a percentage of GDP

	1996	1997	1998	1999	2000	2001
EU	1.45	1.30	1.18	1.04	1.00	0.99
B	1.63	1.42	1.41	1.39	1.34	1.34
DK	1.14	1.07	1.21	1.26	1.51	1.36
D	1.72	1.54	1.43	1.33	1.23	1.14
EL	1.50	1.78	1.19	1.05	1.06	1.02
E	1.37	1.08	1.10	0.90	0.85	0.74
F	1.52	1.59	1.37	1.23	1.18	1.10
IRL	0.82	0.82	1.31	1.35	1.31	1.20
I	1.79	1.61	1.35	0.97	1.04	1.01
L	1.06	0.61	1.44	1.37	1.38	1.30
NL	0.86	0.67	0.85	0.99	0.95	0.98
A	1.32	1.26	1.14	1.06	0.96	0.99
P	1.61	2.21	1.38	1.24	1.13	1.04
FIN	1.99	2.24	2.09	1.89	1.73	1.58
S	1.03	0.81	0.86	0.75	0.71	0.71
UK	0.79	0.67	0.60	0.45	0.40	0.66

Source: European Commission State Aid Scoreboard (European Commission 2003c).

could be argued, appears to support the conclusion that there is a steady convergence of economic practice in member states. Even so there are instances and sectors where certain member states sustain large programmes of support, reflecting divergences in policy preferences across the EU.

Another gauge of how far member states are locked into the process of integration is their adoption of the Single Market acquis. The Commission publishes a regular 'Single Market Scoreboard' (European Commission 2003a) that monitors progress in transposing such legislation (see Table 4.2). While there has been a steady improvement over the years in reducing the 'transposition deficit' (the proportion of directives that have not yet been transposed into national legislation, the first step towards implementation), in late 2002 that trend was reversed. By 2003, the overall deficit stood at 2.4 per cent, down from 6.3 per cent in 1997 but up slightly from previous lows. This average conceals considerable disparity in performance of member states; while some states have low deficits (such as Denmark's 0.6 per cent) others have much poorer records (notably Italy's 3.9 per cent). While the overall effect of such disparities may mean that the internal market remains fragmented, the fact that most states have followed through the legislative process seems to indicate at least a formal alignment with the acquis and a corresponding narrowing of policy preferences.

It is true, however, that transposition only reveals the translation of EU rules into national contexts; it tells us little about implementation or compliance. In this respect, the evidence of 'infringement procedures' (again monitored by the Commission in its 'Single Market Scoreboard') provides a different perspective. Not including cases of late transposition the Commission was dealing with nearly 1,600 cases of breaches of Internal Market law, such as failure to implement directives properly or non-conformity with the rules (see Table 4.3). Such failures of transposition and implementation may reflect member states' policy preferences (or unwillingness to adapt) or they may reflect administrative shortcomings and lack of autonomy. Whichever is

Table 4.2 Implementation of Internal Market Directives

I	P	IRL	A	EL	F	L	D	NL	B	UK	E	FIN	S	DK
3.9	3.7	3.5	3.4	3.3	3.3	3.2	3.0	2.0	1.8	1.5	1.2	1.0	1.0	0.6

Source: European Commission, Single Market Scoreboard.

Note
Member State implementation deficits as on 1 April 2003 (percentage).

Table 4.3 Infringement cases

F	I	E	EL	B	D	IRL	UK	A	NL	P	FIN	DK	L	S
220	200	153	144	138	136	132	121	79	68	57	47	36	34	32

Source: European Commission, Single Market Scoreboard.

Note
Open Internal Market infringement cases per Member State, February 2003.

the case, it is clear that the impact of European integration upon member state strategies is ambiguous (European Commission 2002a).

Enlargement and CEEC state strategies

Having looked at the impact of the EU upon existing member states, how has it affected new entrants? Table 4.4 summarizes the enlargement phases and their main phases. Compared with the current 'eastern' enlargement, previous enlargements have involved countries that were much closer to the EU in terms of both their system of economic governance and their level of economic development, and they occurred earlier in the evolution of European integration.

The reorientation of the CEEC economies and economic policies after 1989 was clearly influenced by the prospect of European integration. Many of the important decisions on the nature of economic policy and many of the assumptions about the

Table 4.4 Enlargement phases

	Extent of European integration	*Economic context*	*Political context*	*Enlargement 'gap'*
Denmark, Eire, UK (1973)	Relatively undeveloped	UK/Denmark close to '6' average; Eire underdeveloped. Mixed economies and established economic institutions	Established democracies and independent administrative-legal machinery	Low
Greece (1980), Portugal, Spain, (1986)	Some progress but obstacles in wake of 1970s/1980s recessions. Membership coincides with new activism (Single Market)	All three well below '9' average. Mixed economy but relatively statist and some institutions underdeveloped	Recently re-established democracies. Some administrative-legal 'gaps'	Moderate
Austria, Finland, Sweden (1995)	Post Maastricht	All three above '12' average. Mixed economies and established economic institutions	Established democracies and independent administrative-legal machinery	Low (especially post EEA)
CEECs (2004), Cyprus, Malta	Further advances (post EMU)	All three well below '15' average. Emerging from planned economy with many institutions underdeveloped	Recently established democracies. Extensive administrative-legal 'gaps'	High

Source: Author.

quality of those policies were taken in both a broader and a narrower context than that of EU membership. The broader context was, of course, the more general transition to capitalism, which was informed by a variation of the Washington Consensus (a pro-market and private-sector package of macro and microeconomic reforms), which provided the principal developmental model for developing and transition economies (Roland 2000), and by trade liberalization (Bacchetta and Drabek 2002). The narrower context was the variety of specific national environments, which proved to be an important determinant of the way in which such reform commitments were pursued. Some authors have gone so far as to argue that the varied approaches to such issues as privatization, financial and stock market reform and investment reflected different 'implicit development strategies' (Comisso 1998). Despite these differences, for most CEECs, substantial reform (or at least the commitment to it) had been agreed by the time the enlargement process was formally initiated.

In tandem with the shift in the orientation of policy following 1989 came a series of reforms of state capacity (Nunberg 1999). The process of democratization and the recognition of a need to restructure the state machinery prompted most CEECs to begin the adaptation of their administrative and legal systems (Ahrens and Meurers 2002; Johannsen and Norgaard 2001; Vilpisauskas 2002). However, as with economic reforms, the degree of commitment to such changes and the effectiveness of the reforms varied considerably. Political cronyism and capture restricted the effective formulation of policy, while competing claims for resources further constrained what CEEC governments could do (Amsden *et al.* 1994: 194–8). Relatively speaking, state capacity in the bulk of the CEECs was much improved as the enlargement process got under way and was much better than was seen in the CIS: in surveys of corruption and capture in the transition economies, the problems were considerably more limited in CEECs than in the CIS (Hellman and Schankerman 2000; Hellman *et al.* 2000a,b).

The capacity of the CEEC governments depends on the interaction between pre-existing institutions, attitudes and resources, on the one hand, and administrative reforms, on the other. It is clear that, as with the actual outcomes of policies, there are considerable differences among the CEECs in these respects. Nonetheless, there have been some general similarities in terms of the starting points, the institutions and the pressures that these regimes have faced.

How have the orientation and capacity of candidate states been affected as the accession process has intensified? Here we review changes on the basis of the Commission's own assessment of progress as well as other analyses. One is the regular review by the European Bank for Reconstruction and Development (EBRD) (2000, 2002) on 'Transition Indicators' (which identify progress in economic policy reform and effectively match our concern with state orientation). The other is the World Bank's survey (Hellman *et al.* 2000a) of changes in the 'Business Environment' (which, *inter alia*, covers the questions of legal and administrative capabilities and of corruption and capture that match up with our concern regarding state capacity). We consider the types of change that have taken place within the candidate countries themselves and compare them with other transition economies to see whether it is possible to identify an accession effect.

One of the main guides to the impact of enlargement upon the candidate countries' policy orientation is the Commission's own assessment of their progress in the enlargement negotiations (European Commission 2000). To the extent that governments are adapting their policies in line with both the detailed acquis and the Copenhagen criteria of a functioning market economy, and the ability to withstand competitive pressures and market forces, such adjustments can be interpreted as successful reorientation in line with the liberal economic policies pursued by existing member states.

Analysis of the progress made by candidate countries shows that there are a number of areas of concern in liberalizing economies. The Commission notes that while the candidates have been transposing the acquis in areas such as the internal market and sectoral liberalization, there remain some problematic areas, notably public procurement and financial services (European Commission 2003b). It is, of course, worth recalling that such areas continue to pose problems for existing member states (procurement in particular is one of the areas where transposition has been most difficult).

One of the principal indicators – and perhaps the guarantor – of a 'reoriented' strategy is competition policy. Often seen as a core element of the regulatory state, competition policy takes on a particular significance for countries in transition. Given the initial conditions under transition, in particular the market power of incumbents and the absence of competition, competition policy has had the potential to play a 'market-making' role, tackling the particular distortions in transition economies and playing a wider advocacy role. While some argue that the policy is unnecessary or even counterproductive – serving as an obstacle to rather than a catalyst of market forces – most accounts see the policy as having a broadly positive effect (Dutz and Vagliasindi 1999; Fingleton *et al.* 1996).

The overall impact of the enlargement process has been to raise the profile of competition policy within the CEECs, though as noted for a number of states the policies were functioning in advance of the process – in terms of the orientation and capacity these states were already moving in the right direction. The principal problem identified is related to influence, in terms of both how much is exercised by the competition authorities themselves and how much is exercised upon them. In the first instance, the problem is generally seen as being that the authorities do not enjoy enough influence: although they play an advocacy role for competition, they have often been rather isolated in that position, with other interests – economic and political – prevailing in economic policy-making. Those other interests have in turn sought to shape the conduct of competition policy itself: perhaps the most commonly voiced concern is that of politicization – that the independence of the authorities on particular cases will be eroded by the political priorities of the government in power (Dutz and Vagliasindi 1999). However, for the Central European states at least, the problems seem to be more related to the former than the latter condition – competition authorities seem to have retained their independence and worked effectively but their influence has been less apparent. This is not a problem unique to these countries, however; there are many shortcomings regarding the influence of competition policy within existing member states.

The principal substantive cause for concern in competition policy is control over state aid (Monti 2002). However, the problem does not appear to be acute: the overall levels of state aid are running at around €5 billion compared with €70 billion in the EU 15, and the per capita levels are just over half those in the EU. On a gross domestic product (GDP) basis however, the levels are relatively higher than those in the EU: 1.3 per cent compared to 0.8 per cent of GDP. Moreover, the aid is concentrated in the industrial sector (46 per cent compared to 35 per cent, often in sensitive sectors) and is bestowed on the basis of tax exemptions rather than direct aids (European Commission 2002c).

While the overall effect of regulatory policies is likely to be significant for the new members, other policies may be less significant. As noted earlier, the EU's role in areas such as industrial (or 'enterprise') policy is relatively modest. The 1998 'Action Plan to Promote Entrepreneurship and Competitiveness' identified a series of measures that governments could adopt to encourage the development of business in the EU. Since then the Commission has sought to encourage member states to coordinate – rather than harmonize – their enterprise policies: the aim has been to foster best practice in the main areas of education, access to finance, innovation, support services, public administration and employment. As part of the enlargement discussions, candidate countries agreed to map their progress in enterprise. The results of this assessment showed that candidate countries were engaged in most areas but with mixed commitment. On the one hand, governments appear to have developed policies to support enterprises, particularly small and medium sized enterprises (SMEs), and to have enhanced links between education and business. On the other hand, they have been less effective in improving access to finance for enterprises and providing back-up in areas of innovation policy (particularly patents) while there remain serious bureaucratic obstacles to enterprise development in a number of states. Interestingly, one of the principal rationales for the revisiting of industrial policy noted earlier in the chapter is precisely to address questions of enlargement and of the condition of industrial sectors in the candidate countries. However, the effects of such developmental interventions is likely to be less substantial for new member states than was the case for regulatory or even distributive initiatives (European Commission 2001c).

Overall, therefore, there appears to have been substantial alignment of CEEC economic policies with those in the EU. How far can we discern an accession effect distinct from the broader process of economic reforms in these countries? In a sense the clearest distinction is in the formal alignment with the acquis communautaire and the adaptation of national legislation and practices to EU requirements. Another measure that provides some indication of the progress of candidate and other transition economies is the EBRD's transition indicators. Table 4.5 compares these indicators for various groups of transition countries for the years 1995 and 2001 (1995 being the earliest year where a more or less comprehensive coverage was available and also relatively early in the accession process). This shows that the candidate countries were performing better than others in both 1995 and 2001 but that the extent of progress made in the interim has not outpaced improvements in other regions. On the contrary, it has been the countries of

Table 4.5 EBRD transition indicators, 1995 and 2001

	Large-scale privatization	Small-scale privatization	Enterprise reform	Price liberalization	Trade liberalization	Competition policy	Bank reform	Securities reform	Infrastructure reform	Overall
2001										
CC	4–	4+	3	3	4+	3	4–	3	3	3+
SEE	3–	4–	2	3	4–	2–	3–	2	2+	3–
CIS	3–	3+	2	3–	3+	2	2	2–	2	2+
1995										
CC	3+	4	3–	3	4	3–	3	3–		3
SEE	2–	3–	2–	2+	3	1+	2	1+		2
CIS	2+	2+	2–	3	3–	2–	2	2–		2

Source: EBRD Transition Reports, various years.

South-eastern Europe that have made the biggest improvements. This may reflect some combination of the effect of political changes in that region and the relative ease of achieving some of the initial reforms.

How has the EU affected the prospective member state capacities? It is clear that the prospect of membership has concentrated the minds and resources of administrative elites in the Central European states: there has been a streamlining of consolidation of the coordination function and of relations with the European institutions, as manifest in the development of offices of European integration in most national executives. Indeed, it has been argued that European integration has strengthened the development of core executives in the member states. However, while linkages between the candidates and the EU have become well developed it is less clear how well established is the European dimension in the overall bureaucratic network, with many commentators warning of enclaves of expertise and attitudes that do not necessarily impact on the rest of the administrative infrastructure (Goetz 2001; Grabbe 2001; Lippert *et al.* 2001).

Yet, it is also true that the adaptation of the acquis has impacted on state capacity. While this is clearest in areas where financial transfers will be significant it has also influenced other areas of the acquis, for example, market liberalization. However, there is a question over the interaction between wider processes of administrative reform and the effects of enlargement. While the Commission records progress in a number of areas, other accounts have been more pessimistic about change, highlighting the resistance of existing structures and personnel to reform (Nunberg 2000).

The resistance to reform is also manifest in the persistence of corruption: according to World Bank research the levels of corruption remain relatively higher in the candidate countries than in the OECD, though levels are lowest in the Central European and Baltic states compared with South-east Europe and in particular the Former Soviet Union. To some extent the question of corruption raises issues of how state capacity can be improved; indeed there appears to be a vicious circle between the persistence of corruption and the failure of state reforms to be implemented, reforms that would otherwise help to reduce the possibilities for corruption.

Changes in the legal infrastructure and its implementation are generally regarded as an important component of state capacity (and a particularly important element in underpinning the 'reorientation' of economic policies). Generally, the EU Accession Reports highlight progress in this area (with some caveats) and these conclusions are broadly supported by the EBRD's index of commercial law reform (summarized in Table 4.6), a measure of both the extent of reform and the degree to which it is effectively implemented. Interestingly, however, the EBRD index notes some variation and even reversal of trends for some candidate countries (leading in aggregate terms to no overall improvement in the index).

A more wideranging set of indicators of state capacity in CEE states can be found in the Business Environment and Enterprise Performance Survey (BEEPS) carried out by the EBRD. This covers businesses across the transition economies and questions them on their attitudes to the performance of government across

Table 4.6 Legal transition indicator

	1997 extensiveness	*1997 effectiveness*	*2002 extensiveness*	*2002 effectiveness*
Candidate country states	4−	4−	4−	4−
South-eastern European states	3−	3−	3+	4−
CIS states	3−	2+	3	3−

Source: EBRD Transition Reports, various years.

Table 4.7 BEEPS indicators

Country	*Governance obstacles index*	*State capture index*
CCs	2.299	0.139
SEE	2.819	0.230
CIS	2.744	0.230

Source: Based on Hellman and Schankerman (2000).

a range of indicators (including macroeconomic performance, access to finance, taxation, regulation, crime, corruption and judiciary), ranked from 1 (low obstacles) to 4 (high obstacles). According to the 1999 survey, obstacles are relatively lowest in the candidate states compared with other transitional economies (see Table 4.7). It also shows that the degree of state capture is lower in these states than in other transition economies.

This tends to show a similar picture to that shown in the transition indicators, that is, that candidate countries have the best records and have sustained that position over time but that other states have caught up. A clearer picture of change can be obtained from a World Bank 'meta-survey' on the quality of governance in developed and developing countries (including the BEEPS survey conducted by EBRD). By way of comparison, the results for existing EU states are also included (see Table 4.8). Countries were ranked from −2.5 (bad) to +2.5 (good) in terms of national perceptions of a variety of indicators. The results broadly mirror those of the EBRD in showing the relatively strong performance of the Central and Eastern European candidate countries relative to other transition countries but a more rapid improvement in those other countries over the two time periods.

Across a range of indicators for both orientation and capacity, the candidate countries appear to be the most advanced of the transition economies. Moreover, they have improved their performance across most indicators over the period of accession. However, the rate of improvement is generally slower than is the case for other transition economies. It may be that this does reflect the relative ease of initial

Table 4.8 Business environment indicators

	Voice and accountability		Political stability		Government effectiveness		Regulatory quality		Rule of law		Control of corruption	
	2000/01	1997/98	2000/01	1997/98	2000/01	1997/98	2000/01	1997/98	2000/01	1997/98	2000/01	1997/98
CEEC Candidates	1.0	0.9	0.7	0.8	0.5	0.4	0.6	0.6	0.6	0.5	0.5	0.4
CIS	-0.6	-0.6	-0.6	-0.4	-0.9	-0.8	-1.1	-0.9	-0.7	-0.6	-0.8	-0.9
SEE	0.2	-0.2	-0.1	-0.5	-0.6	-0.7	-0.3	-0.4	-0.4	-0.5	-0.5	-0.6
EU	1.4	1.4	1.2	1.1	1.4	1.4	1.1	0.9	1.4	1.3	1.5	1.5

Source: Based on Hellman and Schankerman (2000) and Kaufmann et al. (2002).

reforms and that the other states are in some phase of catch-up. It may also reflect the limitations of what are often rather subjective measures. Nonetheless, the persistence of this pattern does raise some important questions for our assessment of the impact of the EU on the orientation and capacity of candidate states. Are these states the best performers because of accession or are they candidates for accession because of their overall performance (or even because of initial conditions in terms of history and geography)? How do we explain the plateauing of change, which seems to affect the best performers, and what does this imply for further reform after membership?

Conclusion

This chapter has examined how the regime of EU integration affects the policy options and administrative capacities of candidate states in Central and Eastern Europe. On the basis of an analysis of the nature of regional integration and its European variant, of the experience of member states within the EU, of previous waves of enlargement and of the accession process itself, it is clear that the prospect of membership and the associated conditions is altering the orientation and capacity of candidate countries. However, the extent of that impact is debatable. It is, for example, difficult to disentangle the adjustments that candidate countries are making in the name of EU membership from those that would have been made in any case in a post-communist transition. Moreover, the experience of existing member states in the EU suggests that the degree of compliance of states with EU rules may be to some extent limited in practice (even though there appears to be a definite long-run impact of membership). Finally, there are ambiguities in the orientation of EU policy which could provide the basis for alternative strategies for existing and candidate states (though again, the relative impact of these is limited both in terms of available resources and in comparison with the overall liberal orientation of economic regulation within the EU regime). Given that there are additional constraints upon the candidate states in terms of domestic pressures, administrative limitations and political choices, the impact of enlargement may not be as clear-cut as is sometimes claimed.

Notes

1 In both respects the chapter draws heavily on Peter Evans's (1995) concept of 'embedded autonomy'.
2 These categories 'synthesize' terms used by political science to analyse state activities in the economy – see, for example, Johnson 1982; Lowi 1964; Majone 1996; and Weiss 1998.

References

Ahrens, J. and Meurers, M. (2002) 'How governance affects the quality of policy reform and economic performance: new evidence from economies in transition', mimeo.
Amsden, A., Kochanowicz, J. and Taylor, L. (1994) *The Market Meets its Match: Restructuring the Economies of Eastern Europe*, Cambridge, MA: Harvard University Press.

Bacchetta, M. and Drabek, Z. (2002) 'Effects of WTO accession on policy making in sovereign states', *WTO Working Paper DERD-2*, Geneva: WTO.

Comisso, E. (1998) 'Implicit development strategies in Central East Europe and cross national production networks', in J. Zysman and A. Schwartz (eds), *Enlarging Europe*, Berkeley: University of California Press, pp. 380–423.

Dutz, M. and Vagliasindi, M. (1999) 'Competition policy: implementation in transition economies', *EBRD Working Paper* 47, Washington: EBRD.

European Bank for Reconstruction and Development (2000) *Transition Report* 1999, Washington: EBRD.

European Bank for Reconstruction and Development (2002) *Transition Report* 2002, Washington: EBRD.

European Commission (1970) *Industrial Policy in the Community*, Brussels: EC.

European Commission (2000) *Enlargement Strategy Paper*, Brussels: EC.

European Commission (2001a) *Economic Reform: Report on the Functioning of Community Product and Capital Markets*, COM (2000) 881, Brussels: EC.

European Commission (2001b) *Recommendation for the 2001 Broad Guidelines of the Economic Policies of the Member States and the Community*, COM (2001) 224, Brussels: EC.

European Commission (2001c) *Report on the Candidate Countries' Measures to Promote Entrepreneurship and Competitiveness*, SEC (2001) 2054, Brussels: EC.

European Commission (2002a) *Economic Reform: report on the Functioning of Community Product and Capital Markets*, COM (2002) 743, Brussels: EC.

European Commission (2002b) *Industrial Policy in an Enlarged Europe*, Brussels: EC.

European Commission (2002c) *State Aid Scoreboard, Autumn 2002 Update, Special Edition on the Candidate Countries*, COM (2002) 638, Brussels: EC.

European Commission (2003a) *Single Market Scoreboard*, Brussels: EC.

European Commission (2003b) *Making a Success of Enlargement – Enlargement Strategy Paper*, Brussels: EC.

European Commission (2003c) *State Aid Scoreboard Spring 2003 Update*, COM (2003) 225, Brussels: EC.

Evans, P. (1995) *Embedded Autonomy*, Princeton NJ: Princeton University Press.

Fingleton, J. et al. (1996) *Competition Policy and the Transformation of Central Europe*, London: CEPR.

Gerschenkron, A. (1962) *Economic Backwardness in Historical Perspective*, Cambridge, MA: Harvard University Press.

Goetz, K. (2001) 'Making sense of post communist central administration', *Journal of European Public Policy*, 8(6): 1032–52.

Gourevitch, P. (1978) 'The second image reversed: the international sources of domestic politics', *International Organization*, 32(4): 881–911.

Grabbe, H. (2001) 'How does Europeanization affect CEE governance', *Journal of European Public Policy*, 8(6): 1013–31.

Grant, W. (1993) *Business and Politics in Britain*, London: Macmillan.

Hayek, F. (1949) 'The economic conditions of interstate federalism' in *Individualism and Economic Order*, London: Routledge, pp. 255–72.

Hellman, J. and Schankerman, M. (2000) 'Intervention, corruption and capture: the nexus between enterprises and the state', *EBRD Working Paper* No. 58, London: EBRD.

Hellman, J., Jones, G. and Kaufmann, D. (2000a) 'Seize the state, seize the day: state capture, corruption and influence in transition', *World Bank Policy Research Working Paper* No. 2444, Washington: World Bank.

Hellman, J., Jones, G., Kaufmann, D. and Schankerman, M. (2000b) 'Measuring governance, corruption and state capture', *World Bank Policy Research Working Paper* No. 2312, Washington: World Bank.

Hix, S. (1999) *The Political System of the European Union*, London: Macmillan.

Hodges, M. (1983) 'Industrial policy', in H. Wallace, W. Wallace and C. Webb (eds), *Policy Making in the European Communities*, London: Wiley, pp. 265–95.

Holland, S. (1980) *UnCommon Market: Capital, Class and Power in the European Community*, London: Macmillan.

Johannsen, L. and Norgaard, O. (2001) 'Governance and state capacity in post communist states' paper presented to ECPR Joint Sessions, Grenoble, 2001.

Johnson, C. (1982) *MITI and the Japanese Miracle*, Stanford CA: Stanford University Press.

Kaufmann, D., Kraay, A. and Zoido-Lobaton, P. (2002) 'Governance matters II', *World Bank Policy Research Working Paper* No. 2772, Washington: World Bank.

Lippert, B., Umbach, G. and Wessels, W. (2001) 'Europeanization of CEE executives', *Journal of European Public Policy*, 8(6): 980–1012.

Lowi, J. (1964) 'American business, public policy, case studies and political theory', *World Politics*, 16(2): 677–715.

McGowan, F. and Wallace, H. (1996) 'Towards a European regulatory state', *Journal of European Public Policy*, 3(4): 560–76.

Majone, G. (1996) *Regulating Europe*, London: Routledge.

Migdal, J. (1987) 'Strong states, weak states: power and accommodation', in M. Weiner and S. Huntington (eds), *Understanding Political Development*, Cambridge, MA: Little Brown, pp. 391–437.

Monti, M. (2002) 'Competition policy in the candidate countries – the accession negotiations and beyond', presentation to the 8th Annual Competition Conference between the Candidate Countries and the European Commission, Vilnius, Lithuania, 16–18 June.

Nunberg, B. (1999) *The State after Communism*, Washington: World Bank.

Nunberg, B. (2000) 'Ready for Europe – public administration reform and European Union accession in Central and Eastern Europe', *World Bank Technical Paper* No. 466, Washington: World Bank.

Pearce, J. and Sutton, J. (1985) *Protection and Industrial Policy in Europe*, London: Routledge.

Pinder, J. (1973) 'Positive integration and negative integration: some problems of economic union in the EC', in M. Hodges (ed.), *European Integration*, London: Penguin, pp. 124–50.

Roland, G. (2000) *Transition and Economics: Politics, Markets and Firms*, Cambridge, MA: MIT Press.

Vilpisauskas, R. (2002) 'The changing role of the state in the Central and East European Countries: patterns of transition and accession into the EU', mimeo.

Wade, R. (1990) *Governing the Market*, Princeton NJ: Princeton University Press.

Wallace, H. (2000) 'The policy process', in H. Wallace and W. Wallace (eds), *Policy Making in the European Union*, Oxford: Oxford University Press.

Weiss, L. (1998) *The Myth of the Powerless State*, Cambridge: Polity Press.

White, G. (ed.) (1988) *Developmental States in East Asia*, London: Macmillan.

5 Industrial networks in central and eastern Europe at the firm level

Summary and overview of ten case studies

Slavo Radosevic and Deniz Eylem Yoruk

Introduction

In contrast to the past, today's globalization is distinctive as a micro-phenomenon that enables production integration and networking and, as such, creates *deep* international integration at firm level. There are high expectations that EU enlargement will lead to deep integration of central and eastern Europe (CEE) into pan-European industrial networks. It is certain that the extent and nature of the linkages that emerge between the east and the west of Europe will strongly shape the competitive dynamics and industrial development not only in CEE, but also in individual sectors in the EU. However, whether east–west industrial networks will act to improve the growth prospects of the enlarged EU or whether they will deepen the differences in levels of development and undermine the prospects for more balanced growth is an open issue.

A proper understanding of the conditions for deep integration demands a better understanding of the extent, factors and nature of production and technology linkages between the existing EU and the CEE countries. In this book, we explore factors that influence the degree of networking between old and new EU members at industry, country and firm level. This chapter summarizes the major issues involved in industrial integration at the firm level. Based on ten in-depth case studies of CEE companies and multinational corporations (MNCs) operating in the CEE, we identify the major factors which either promote or hinder deepening of industrial integration. This case study review uses the alignment of networks perspective to analyse their common features (see Chapter 3, this volume).

The key idea of network alignment is that growth in a globalized context is a complex, multilevel process which requires alignment of different networks to generate a virtuous circle of growth. It is at the micro-level that we can observe how firms interact with other firms and organizations and grow based on networking, that is, on sharing resources, skills and complementing each other's activities. This process is driven by market and non-market interactions and is fraught with different forms of network failure (see Chapter 3).

The essential features of each of the cases are described and compared across several network alignment elements: firms' strategy, local and national networks, EU and government policy. These are actors of network alignment whose activities can match or mismatch with each other. In that respect, our focus is geographic, as referred to in Chapter 3, but by looking at the strategies of the actors involved it also encompasses functional and resources aspects of network alignment.

In the next section, we briefly explain the concepts that form the background of the empirical case study analyses and point to key questions which we try to address. The section 'Overview of firm-level case studies results' summarizes the case studies and compares them. The section 'Determinants of network alignment' generates 'stylized facts' shared by all cases. The final section summarizes the results and provides conclusions.

Concepts and research questions

There are several concepts that inform our comparative analysis and which we explain briefly. Each of the concepts raises respective research questions, which we try to answer in subsequent sections of the chapter.

First, deep or industrial integration includes production and technology integration. Production integration refers to value chain linkages and can be described through buyer–supplier relationships and involves flows of products, parts and materials. Technological integration is the integration of domestic enterprises into a dynamic learning process with foreign partners whereby they become involved as active contributors and recipients in the production of knowledge for generating technical change (Radosevic 1999a,b). We want to find out whether the surveyed companies have been integrated at the level of technological integration or only at the level of production integration.

Second, any firm has three basic strategic choices for growth: to (a) undertake generic expansion, (b) conduct mergers and acquisitions (M&A) and/or (c) develop inter-organizational relationships, that is, networks (Peng and Heath 1996; Peng 2000). Networks help overcome a firm's problem of having insufficient resources to accommodate growth, while avoiding the substantial bureaucratic costs of internalizing operations (Peng 2000: 513). In the period of post-socialist transition, deficiencies in resources have pushed firms to pursue a network strategy. This internal pressure driven by resource deficiencies matched a broader change in production systems towards fragmented value chains. For example, in electronics (see Chapter 7), domestic firms with developed production capabilities were able to meet the requirements of own equipment manufacture (OEM) and contract manufacturers, which were diversifying supply bases. We want to find out what is the dominant mode of growth in our sample.

Third, from a network perspective the biggest problems for post-socialist firms are system integration at product level and process integration at firm level. Production and continuous improvement require integration of different functions (finance, R&D, engineering, procurement, production, sales) whose integration is essential to innovation dynamics. Hence, system integration at product level or the capability to integrate different functions is essential for firms to cooperate in networks. The more developed a firm's range of business functions the better is its position in global (regional) value chains.

Production and innovation have to be organized across several tiers of suppliers which are all involved to different degrees, not only in production, but also in innovation. Hence, process integration at firm level is essential to participate in global networks. Firms called 'network organizers' are those that are able to organize local supply chains.

Socialist firms were only production, not business organizations. This explains why post-socialist firms are the weakest in these two types of capabilities, which require strong linkage capabilities. Lall (1992) defines linkage capabilities as the skills needed to transmit information, skills and technology to, and receive them from, component or raw material suppliers, subcontractors, consultants, service firms and technology institutions. We want to find out if firms in our sample have overcome weaknesses in system integration at product level and process integration at firm level and how strong their linkage capabilities are. These capabilities are essential for CEE firms to be active in the process of network alignment, that is, in plugging themselves in at different stages and levels (functions) of value chains.

Fourth, the key driving mechanisms of network alignment are complementarities in strategies between actors. The notion of complementarity rests on the distinction between a mere evolutionary coincidence of several factors, which jointly produce a fortuitous one-off outcome, and situations where complementarities operate in a systemic fashion. In the latter case, doing more of activity A raises the value of increases in activity B, which then, by increasing B also raises the value of increasing A (Milgrom and Roberts 1995). Firms operate in a context where their growth may be constrained by weak external networks, be they national or local networks, or by weak supporting infrastructures or anti-competitive regulations. On the other hand, organizations in the immediate and indirect environment may be strong and able to support the growth of firms but if their strategies do not match the complementarities are not realized. We want to find out how strong is complementarity-driven network alignment in each of our cases.

Overview of firm-level case studies results

Ten case studies cover three groups of companies: MNC subsidiaries (4), domestic CEE companies with foreign strategic investors (2) and domestically controlled companies (indigenous manufacturers) (4). Table 5.1 shows the main features of the case study firms. Table 5.2 shows the focus of individual case studies.[1] The firms chosen are the 'success stories' and are thus deliberately chosen to explore the relevance of network alignment in their success. We compare individual factors of network alignment (CEE firm, MNC, CEE national and local networks, CEE government and EU market and accession).

MNC subsidiaries

Eridania Beghin-Say (EBS)

EBS is an agri-business multinational company that entered CEE due to competitive pressures in EU markets (push factor) and market opportunities in

Table 5.1 Basic features of firms in the sample

	Multinational companies in CEECs				Domestic companies with strategic foreign investors		Indigenous firms in CEECs			
	EBS – Italy and France	Tesco – the UK	ABB	Soufflet – France	Elektrim SA – Poland	Sokolow SA – Poland	Videoton – Hungary	Dobrogea SA – Romania	Vistula SA – Poland	Braiconf SA – Romania
Industry	Agri-business	Retailer	Power transmission and distribution; automation; oil/gas/petro-chemicals equipment; building technologies	Malt	Telecommunications, power generating equipment and cables	Meat processing	Consumer electronics	Milling and bakery	Men's wear	Men's wear
Year of foundation	1987	1919	1988	1950s	1948	1970s Sokolow, 1991 Farmfood	1938	1961	1945	1950
Year of privatization and/or entry to CEECs	1989	1994	1990	1998	1989	2000 merged Sokolow	1991	1995	1993	1996
Ownership	Holding company – part of Montedison	Share-owned company	Merger of ASEA AB (Sweden) and BBC Brown Boveri Ltd (Switzerland)	100% wholly-owned subsidiary	Share-owned company	A share-owned company with three foreign strategic investors	100% Hungarian capital	100% Romanian capital – MEBO privatization	Share-owned company	Share-owned company
Author(s) of case study	Yoruk and v. Tunzelmann (2001)	Yoruk and Radosevic (2000)	Radosevic (2002)	Yoruk (2002a)	Radosevic, Dornisch and Yoruk (2001)	Yoruk (2002b)	Radosevic and Yoruk (2001)	Yoruk (2002c)	Yoruk (2002d)	Yoruk (2002e)

Source: Authors.

Table 5.2 Focus of individual case studies

MNCs in CEECs	EBS – Italy and France	Establishing and upgrading company network in CEE
	Tesco – UK	Supplier chain development in the CEECs (particularly for own-label products) and adoption of Tesco's business processes
	ABB	Development of production network in CEE and the issue of complementarities
	Soufflet – France	Development of strong local networks at the upstream of the industry
Domestic companies with strategic foreign investors	Elektrim SA – Poland	Transformation from foreign trade organization into conglomerates and then to focused firm
	Sokołow SA – Poland	Growth through M&A and development of local and international networks with help of strategic foreign investor
Indigenous firms in CEECs	Videoton – Hungary	Domestically controlled growth based on networking and contract manufacturing
	Dobrogea SA – Romania	International network as a source of knowledge to the firm
	Vistula SA – Poland	Establishing domestic vertical and horizontal production networks and building firm as a network organizer
	Braiconf SA – Romania	Knowledge acquisition and assimilation through global production networks

Source: Authors.

CEE (pull factor). In the wake of the recession in the world agri-business markets, EBS developed a business strategy based on seeking growth through acquisition in the CEE and improving the productivity of its operations by controlling its costs. EBS is an orthodox multidivisional company with five core businesses in which it established several market-seeking and low risk investments in a number of CEE countries. Its entry has been facilitated by the privatization policies of CEE governments and its orientation towards CEE has been facilitated by EU accession.

EBS has a strong company network among its subsidiaries and affiliates. It has technologically upgraded its CEE subsidiaries, and trained CEE staff in order to improve synergy among the subsidiaries. It has improved its intra-firm network through the use of electronic telecommunication programs that involve CEE subsidiaries. It has managed structural transformation in terms of quality assurance. There is a coordinated linkage between its Western subsidiaries in R&D whose spillovers have been managed through application in the CEE subsidiaries. There is also an experimental centre (research farm) and a training centre in Poland which collaborate closely with the R&D unit in Belgium. EBS appears to be a network organizer within the entire Group.

Its relations with CEE customers are strongly based on feedback for improvements according to the needs of the customers. It tries to develop linkages with local upstream suppliers at both the national and local level to overcome agricultural deficiencies in the East European countries. It prefers to develop strategic partnerships with the multinationals' subsidiaries (e.g. Henkel) in the CEECs. Its presence has a strong indirect impact on local products through competition.

Tesco

Tesco (UK) is one of several European retailers whose entry into Central Europe has changed the local retailing structure. Expansion to Central Europe has been one part of the company's strategic response to globalization in retailing. It grew first through acquisition of local chains and of chains of Western retailers, and then through greenfield investment in new hypermarkets. Government regulations did not present major problems to its expansion, which was also indirectly enabled by EU accession. Yet in some cases its greenfield investments were curbed by bureaucratic pressures from local governments.

Tesco involves local suppliers in its supply chain and strives to operate as a potential network organizer. It tries to overcome the inexperience of local suppliers in business practices by giving them training. With the encouragement of Tesco, British suppliers have established offices in central Europe. Tesco has developed a network of local suppliers/subcontractors for its own-label products which is a new concept for the central European retailing sector. Tesco provides training for these local suppliers according to its requirements for each product. However, its role as network organizer at national and local levels is still limited due to its efficiency-seeking strategy among the central European subsidiaries that complements its main market-seeking motive.

Tesco's presence as well as that of other Western retailers has led to significant restructuring and increased productivity in the central European retailing sector that formerly was unsaturated and largely fragmented. Tesco has introduced an advanced technological infrastructure compatible with point-of-sale, stock control, financial and office systems in central European stores in order to achieve comparable performance with the United Kingdom. Its upgrading activities are the strongest in training and management in its central European stores and in its efforts to develop long-lasting relationships with local suppliers.

ABB

ABB is a global technology and engineering group providing services in power transmission and distribution; automation; oil and gas, petrochemicals; building technologies and financial services. During the 1990s, ABB managed to restructure and integrate its CEE affiliates into its global corporate network. These networks were mainly dyadic, though they involved some additional relationships like contracts with universities or close relationships with big CEE clients. However, local affiliates are fully integrated into the ABB corporate network where their scope for upgrading seems to be quite extensive as some of the Polish affiliates demonstrated.

The ABB network in CEE has developed based on the strong complementarities between management-, firm- and region-specific factors that operated during the 1990s. The vision and commitment of top management complemented by the heterarchical- and matrix-based organizational structure of ABB, which allowed for initiatives from subsidiaries. The management- and firm-specific factors complemented regional needs in finance, technology and access to the export market in heavy engineering. Regional advantages in terms of low cost, skilled labour and a local market complemented ABB's need to compete based on low cost complementary specialization strategies, by combining the diverse cost and technology advantages of different locations.

The dynamics of the competitive process, especially the shift towards knowledge-based services, pushed ABB towards knowledge and service-based businesses and led to the sale of many of its CEE subsidiaries. It seems that in this new period complementarities between ABB and CEE, which operated so well during the 1990s, are much weaker. It is unclear to what extent CEE will be able to complement the shifts of companies like ABB towards 'knowledge based companies'.

Soufflet

Soufflet is the French agri-food MNC which is an important player in the CEE malt industry. Soufflet has revived the once not very profitable and abandoned malting barley production through the long-term guarantee of business with farmers in return for their cooperation to produce quality raw material (malting barley).

Its CEE subsidiaries are successfully integrated into its global network and are aligned with local networks, which are still undeveloped. The hierarchical organizational structure of the mother company is apparent in the generic expansion of subsidiaries through capable managers. The development of the local networks by the CEE subsidiaries is based strongly on trust and mutual understanding between the parties in the networks. The alignment of the global network of the mother company with the local network of the subsidiaries emanates from the fact that the organizer and driver of these networks is Soufflet. However, at the national level, coupling with public sector and other organizations even for powerful MNCs is more complex due to institutional barriers. The cooperation between Soufflet and national R&D organizations is not supported by CEE governments. EU accession and the EU market have not played a significant role in Soufflet's investments as they are predominantly local-market oriented. Potential for export to the EU exists but has not yet been realized. Its overall impact on the sector is strong and is developing.

Table 5.3 summarizes the state of and interaction between different network alignment elements for the four MNCs analysed. First, the effects on local subsidiaries have been profound in terms of increased productivity and close integration into the MNC network. Second, relationships with local partners and firms, apart from some cases with partners in the supply chain (Soufflet with local farmers and partly Tesco), have been limited. Third, local and national networks are weak components for further networking and MNCs would have to cover high fixed costs to improve local networks, which they seem to be unwilling to do

Table 5.3 Comparing network alignment elements in four MNC investors in CEE

	Eridania Beghin-Say (Montedison), EU MNC	Tesco, UK	ABB, central and eastern Europe	Soufflet, France
CEE firm	Upgrading of its CEE subsidiaries	Local suppliers are being involved in supply chain	Full integration of CEE subsidiaries in ABB network	Foreign breweries in CEE are the main customers
MNC	CEE as saviour of some lines of businesses	Expansion as the strategic response to globalization in retailing	Strong complementary interests with CEE countries before shift to knowledge based strategy	Organizer of local supply networks
CEE national networks	Linkages with upstream suppliers under development	Weak; TESCO is the potential organizer	Weak links with other local firms	Weak or non-existent
CEE local networks	Linkages with upstream suppliers under development	Weak; TESCO is the potential organizer	Limited local networking	Weak
CEE government	Privatization enabled a variety of acquisitions and greenfield strategies	Not major problems (cf. greenfields)	Complementary strategic interests during privatization	Governments are not supporting agriculture
EU accession	Enabled wider European strategy	Enabled wider European strategy	Secondary positive effect in pursuing complementary specialization	Potential, but not yet realized, market opportunities in EU markets
Sectoral impact	Strong indirect impact through competition	Restructuring and increased productivity in retail sector	Strong sectoral impact in terms of productivity and technical capability	Strong competition and restructuring effects
Overall assessment of network alignment	Restricted	Weak but developing	Strong but confined to dyadic relationships (before shift to knowledge-based strategy)	Strong and developing

Source: Authors.

unless there proves to be no other option. Fourth, government policies and those of the EU did not directly inhibit or stimulate the operations of MNCs. However, the indirect effects of enlargement and privatization policies have been conducive to industrial integration of the CEE.

Firms with foreign strategic investors

Elektrim

Elektrim is one of the biggest private companies in Poland in terms of market capitalization and the second largest publicly traded company after TPSA, the national telecom company. Elektrim belongs to a group of large domestically controlled CEE enterprises that operated in the socialist period and have managed not only to survive but also to expand in the transition period. What distinguishes Elektrim within this group is that it operated as a foreign trade organization during the socialist period and that it has become a conglomerate in the transition period (with business strategy based on unrelated diversification), and currently is focusing on cables, energy and telecoms (change in business strategy towards concentration). Elektrim experienced significant difficulties when it tried to shift from a conglomeration- to a telecommunications-dominated strategy. The management of its telecom businesses is partly controlled by Vivendi and Deutsche Telekom, which contested each other's control which, in turn, led to serious problems in corporate governance. Hence, the role of strategic partners has not been handled well by the management. Elektrim grew through acquisitions and has been mainly preoccupied with its portfolio. Hence, it did not manage to develop business further so that it could operate as the local network organizer. Relationships with government helped the company in the period of acquisition frenzy but the company did not benefit from government regulations in relation to its telecom business. Privatization of telecom services has transferred EU competition to the Polish market which, as a result of the battle for control in its telecom arm, had temporary negative effects on the growth of the company. Overall, Elektrim did not operate as a restructuring agent or if it did it was confined to intra-firm operations without being able to operate as network organizer in its respective sectors. A lack of complementary interests with foreign partners and weak restructuring activities of Elektrim itself meant that the overall network alignment was weak.

Sokołow

Sokołow, the Polish meat producer, was established through M&A of several local companies that are key players in the Polish meat processing industry. The company grew through the effective use of M&A and the development of raw material supply networks. A foreign strategic investor was highly instrumental in this growth by providing finance and know-how, especially through modernization of breeding centres. There have been strong complementary interests between Sokołow and the foreign investor. The main actor in the development of local network is the breeding centres which train and supervise farmers. The company has no further relations with the MNC network, whereas it is very active and successful in developing the local, and partly national, linkages. The networks at the local level do not appear to be strong, yet the direction of the knowledge transfer is significant for the diffusion of knowledge within the value chain. The national linkages, despite less frequency, appear to allow significant knowledge transfer from the universities and other relevant institutes, strengthening the links that are necessary within the regional and national innovation systems. EU accession has been a strong source of pressure for the company to conform to EU health and safety regulations even before EU accession. Government played no role in the growth of the company and in network alignment, that is, in the development of local, national and international linkages. Sokołów's restructuring and links with breeding centres have had a strong direct impact on competition and restructuring in the sector. However, the restructuring did not go further down the value chain and can be considered to be somewhat restricted.

Table 5.4 summarizes the state of and interaction between different network alignment elements for two domestic firms with foreign strategic investors. A comparison shows how differences in interests between firm and strategic investors play a key role in the restructuring outcome. Moreover, unsettled disputes about control inhibit any networking efforts and restrict any attempt by the company to make

Table 5.4 Comparing network alignment elements in two domestic firms with foreign strategic investors

	Elektrim – Poland	*Sokołów SA – Poland*
CEE firm	Problems in organizational coherence (process vs products)	Strong organizational and technological capabilities
MNC	Strong control interests and conflicts	Main source of finance and know-how
CEE national networks	Acquisitions and competition	Limited links
CEE local networks	Limited networking	Developing links with farmers
CEE government	Rents but also conflicting interests	Irrelevant
EU accession	Attractiveness of domestic market brings oligopolistic competition	Compliance with EU standards as a driver of restructuring
Sectoral impact	Restructuring agent with mixed results	Strong direct impact on competition and restructuring in sector
Overall assessment of network alignment	Weak	Restricted

Source: Authors.

intra-firm productivity improvements (Elektrim). Sokołow, which has been relieved of such problems, has managed with the assistance of foreign strategic investors to restructure its upstream chain. In this respect, it has managed to establish itself as a network organizer and in time may try to restructure the downstream value chain also. Unfortunately, these efforts have not been complemented by government policies or activities at the level of national networks.

Domestically controlled firms

Videoton

Videoton is one of the only few ex-socialist electronics conglomerates that have successfully restructured by becoming a contract manufacturing producer. The successful turnaround of this firm can be greatly but not entirely explained by management entrepreneurship. The presence of foreign demand through MNCs that came to Hungary supported by a stimulative government policy also played an essential role. Strong complementary interests between Videoton and electronics MNCs, who were looking for local firms that can offer manufacturing services and manage parts of supply chain, were also crucial factors. Local initiatives to attract foreign companies and facilitate their establishment through industrial parks further enhanced the actions of other actors. Prospects of EU entry and proximity to EU markets have further stimulated the entry of foreign companies. The simultaneous presence of these factors is essential to understand why Videoton has succeeded. Its success is not only the result of developing individual networks, in particular of Videoton Holding as a restructuring agent, but also of integrating Videoton and local networks with the networks of global companies.

Entrepreneurship alone cannot explain why most of the other ex-socialist electronics companies failed. However, if we take into account the quality of networks and their (non)alignment as factors behind the failures and successes the individual cases become more clear. Videoton shows that domestically controlled modernization is possible. The transformation of Videoton took place without any sizeable foreign direct (equity) investment. Nevertheless, even domestically controlled modernization has to rely on foreign partners for most of its strategic aspects. The Videoton case shows that despite technological lags central European companies can grow based on networking by plugging themselves into global production networks.

Vistula

Vistula is a Polish clothing manufacturer, which managed to grow and restructure through cooperation with the global production networks in the clothing industry. It is engaged in networks with foreign brand manufacturers, retailers and intermediary companies to produce garments to their specifications to be sold under their brand names. In addition, through franchising agreements, it has extended its networking with the foreign brand manufacturers to distribution.

Vistula's capability to learn through these networks has enabled it to become a 'network organizer' for the domestic market. Instead of producing only contracted manufacturing for the foreign customer, it subcontracts to its own four subsidiaries, which have been recently created out of the extensive and successful restructuring. Also, it subcontracts to small-sized Polish companies (with fewer than 100 employees) and treats them in the same way as the foreign customer does, sending the cut pieces to be assembled. It has established a production network with the companies that are on a par with Vistula. These companies produce a complementary garment or accessory for the men's wear collection under an agreement with Vistula, which keeps the intellectual property rights of the brand and sells the products in its own branded shops.

This has resulted in several types of upgrading such as technological and functional. Technologically, Vistula upgraded earlier than any other Polish clothing producers and this has been one of its main advantages. The company is building its own brand status in foreign markets and, in addition to production, has focused on distribution. Its growth has been self-financed.

The company's growth has not been affected by government regulations while the EU accession has further deepened the already complementary interests of Vistula and global distributors/manufacturers to cooperate in low-cost quality garment.

Dobrogea

Dobrogea is one of the biggest Romanian companies in the milling and bakery industry. It has twenty-one production units, 200 distributors and 2,000 clients, which suggests that it has an extensive production and distribution network. Since its privatization through a management–employee buyout (MEBO), Dobrogea has become successful at combining its location advantages (tourist region of Romania) with its organizational capabilities, including the capability to cooperate with foreign partners. It has a 50:50 joint venture with a Danish company. One of the crucial capabilities that Dobrogea has acquired from its involvement with foreign partners is new product development, which gives it competitive edge and makes it a first mover among domestic and sometimes foreign producers in the local market. These external opportunities have been coupled with developments and changes in organizational structure which have been profound and which are jointly responsible for its current very strong competitive position in the domestic market.

Dobrogea has problems in controlling the upstream end of the value chain as the wheat produced by local farmers is of poor quality, which directly affects the quality of its products. However, instead of trying to improve the quality of upstream activities and work with the farmers Dobrogea has developed its own 'correction technology' which it applies to the flour. When the flour is produced, it is treated with some other ingredients measured in computer-controlled doses. In this way, it avoids the risks of operating as network organizer and controller of the upstream part of the value chain. Dobrogea does not try to develop or restructure the local supply network and instead focuses on developing R&D linkages and on its own technology efforts. Government and EU funding for R&D have been instrumental in the firm's product development and product differentiation strategy. Network alignment is strong in relation to the R&D network but is very limited in terms of the production network, which can be explained by the opportunities and constraints that Dobrogea has faced.

Braiconf

Braiconf is a Romanian clothing company that has benefited from being involved in international production networks. Learning from these relationships and integrating them into company strategy has been central to its growth. Effective assimilation of knowledge within the firm is behind its upgrading to the status of original design manufacturer (ODM) in the foreign market and original brand manufacturer (OBM) in the domestic market.[2] Its growth is entirely based on a dyadic relationship with foreign parents and its capability to manage these relationships.

Braiconf has passed through several upgrading stages. First, it improved the quality of its products through successful adaptation of the machinery and equipment, then it improved its design capabilities, which fostered its upgrading to ODM and OBM. In the long term, Braiconf seeks to grow further through development of its own distribution system within Romania.

A successful operations management has enabled it to be self-financing. During the 1990s, Braiconf was involved in a fully export-oriented joint venture with an Italian company which was dissolved after ten years with the sale of shares to its Italian partner. This relationship enabled the company to survive financially during the critical period of the 1990s as a result of tax exemptions on profits that joint ventures could enjoy for 5 + 5 years.

Braiconf's ownership structure is not yet consolidated and is a mixture of passive investors (domestic and foreign), management and employees. However, the management which has been in charge of the company for 20–30 years has retained the real control which has ensured continuity of organizational learning.

Braiconf's gradual development of organizational and technological capabilities has been backed by the complementing interests of foreign partners. However, dyadic relationships have not been in any way complemented by building network relationships at national and local level, except partly through technical contacts with national technical institutes. With the exception of the tax exemptions granted for its joint venture operations, there has been neither positive nor negative interference from government and the EU in its relationships, which are entirely market driven.

Table 5.5 summarizes each of the nodes of the network alignment for the four domestically controlled companies. These cases share four common features. First, when compared to other local companies their growth has been excellent based on networking or cooperation with foreign partners. These relationships range from the dyadic relationships of Romanian companies to the extensive network relationships of Videoton and Vistula. However, essential to the company's growth is the management capability necessary to exploit these relationships to produce learning benefits additional to the benefits that all such companies enjoy such as

Table 5.5 Comparing network alignment elements in four domestically controlled firms

	Videoton – Hungary	*Vistula – Poland*	*Dobrogea SA – Romania*	*Braiconf SA – Romania*
CEE firm	Good organizational coherence	Developed organizational capabilities	Fast building of business functions and capabilities	Gradually improving organizational capabilities
MNC	Complementary interests	Complementary interests	Competition and partnership with MNCs in domestic market	Complementary interests with foreign buyers
CEE national networks	Organizer of subcontracting network	Organizer of production and distribution network	R&D links under development	Weak, restricted to R&D
CEE local networks	Organizer of industrial parks	Non-existent	Limited	Very weak
CEE government	Rents during privatization used productively	Irrelevant	Facilitating international R&D projects of company	Irrelevant, except tax exemptions for joint ventures
EU accession	Proximity to EU enables flexible sourcing for MNCs	Increased competition	Prospects for further R&D cooperation	Market access
Sectoral impact	Contributed to extensive restructuring in electronics	Vistula developed domestic production network	Strong competition in national market based on product differentiation	Successful restructuring; strong competition
Overall assessment of network alignment	Strong	Strong	Strong but only in R&D	Weak but developing

Source: Authors.

access to market and finance through foreign partners. Second, all four companies are being faced with the need to become network organizers. Vidoeton and Vistula have made some progress in this respect but the two Romanian companies have not yet reached the stage of network organizer. National networks in the Romanian firms are restricted to R&D while in the other two cases they are present in production. Local networks are very weak. Government and the EU have played various roles in the growth of companies and in network alignment, which have ranged from being irrelevant to being highly instrumental in the case of R&D

networks. Third, all four companies have made significant sectoral impact in terms of upgrading and competition effects which may be expected given that these are 'blue chip' companies in their respective sectors. Fourth, all four domestically con-trolled companies have from a traditional corporate governance perspective an unfavourable ownership structure. They are all either under dispersed ownership or are owned by employees and management.[3] In all four companies there is notable continuity of management and a past good track record in terms of business performance and technological capability. This suggests that the company resources (management and organization), rather than corporate governance factors, better explain their current performance.

Determinants of network alignment

In this section, we summarize the main conclusions based on the ten case studies. Our first conclusion is that the strategy and structure of firms dominate the scope and scale of network alignment. If we order the elements of network alignment according to their importance then the strategy and structure of the company is the strongest influence shaping the nature of networking. This, together with contextual factors, explains the differences in network alignment across cases. Second, networks that are being created in CEE are for the time being dyadic and confined to pro-duction. Third, linkage capabilities are crucial to the network-based strategy of all three types of firms, that is, for their role as network organizers. Fourth, among con-textual factors national and local networks are weak factors in network alignment while EU and government policies can often have an indirect effect on network alignment. Fifth, networks are predominantly production networks and, to a very limited extent, technology (knowledge) networks. Sixth, EU and national govern-ments do not play any direct, be it positive or negative, role in network alignment.

First, the strategy and structure of firms determine the scale and scope of network alignment. This is not to deny that other elements of network alignment do not play an import-ant role but very often they can be considered to be secondary. The structure and strategy of MNCs strongly shape the depth and the extent of industrial networks. Soufflet and Sokołow are oriented towards building their supplier base by offering technical assistance to farmers. This orientation arises naturally from the pre-dominantly market-seeking orientation of their foreign direct investment (FDI). ABB has been very quick and successful in integrating its local subsidiaries into a global company network. Tesco has applied its business processes and practices to its CEE operations. EBS is developing links with local upstream suppliers. Elektrim's foreign strategic investors and their controlling interests have strongly shaped com-pany strategy. In all cases where foreign investors are present as full owners or as strategic investors their strategies have been decisive in determining the extent and nature of network alignment and local sourcing that has taken place. When faced with negative externalities in the business environment such as poor supplier networks or weak support from government for agriculture these strategies tend to become more conservative or less ambitious in terms of network building. Equally, strategy is a self-discovery process and in a few instances investor strategies have been re-shaped by the prospects for growth or by the difficulties, which initially were not foreseen. Examples are R&D and the technology links of ABB with local universities or moves to assist farmers made by food MNCs.

Domestically controlled firms have the strongest need for network-based growth as a way to overcome the resource constraints that they are faced with. Access to technology, to finance and to export markets can be more easily achieved through a network-based strategy than through generic expansion. Videoton and Vistula are good examples of the firms that have advanced in building network relationships and which in relation to domestic firms started to operate as network organizers. Dobrogea and Braiconf are examples of the firms that do not yet operate as network organizers but which have grown largely due to networking or linkage capabilities.

Second, for the time being industrial networks in CEE are most often vertical and dyadic and confined to production, that is, involving parent company and local subsidiary (ABB, EBS, Tesco) or local firm and foreign strategic investors (Elektrim, Sokołow). Domestically controlled firms grew through a combination of generic expansion and networking or reliance on foreign buyers (Braiconf, Vistula, Videoton) or technology suppliers (Dobrogea) or on foreign strategic partners (Elektrim, Sokołow). Domestically controlled firms with good organizational capabilities in sectors that require local subcontracting and contacts with multiple foreign buyers are the only ones involved in multiple networks (Vistula, Videoton). In this respect, they seem to be the best potential agents of network alignment or growth in these economies. In many CEECs, FDI is very important in terms of sales, employment and even more in terms of profit generation and investment. However, from a long-term and structuralist perspective domestic firms which are capable of becoming network organizers seem to be equally, if not more important for building externalities and synergies.

Three foreign investors (EBS, Tesco and ABB) have fully integrated their CEE subsidiaries into their global operations and have upgraded them in terms of organization and productivity. Their market-seeking motives (Tesco, EBS) or combination of market/efficiency/knowledge seeking motives (ABB) together with the absence of hindering factors in the business environment, including government and EU, explain why integration has been so successful in all three cases. However, also in all three cases, the close relationship between the parent firm and the local subsidiary is contrasted with still weak but developing relationships with local suppliers (EBS, Tesco, ABB) or R&D organizations (ABB). The Polish business group Elektrim is a good example of restricted network alignment, which is caused by problems of corporate governance and strategic orientation in the presence of oligopolistic competition from foreign strategic investors.

Third, our cases suggest that the issue of control is important in terms of the strategic orientation of companies but equally the linkage capabilities or ability to grow based on networking with foreign partners seem to be even more important. All three groups of firms are evidence of the importance of 'linkage capabilities' for company growth, whether domestic firms or foreign MNC subsidiaries. The importance of this capability and, related to it, a network-based strategy, stems from one of the crucial inherited weaknesses of ex-socialist firms, that is, weak system integration at product level and process integration at network level (see Radosevic 1999b). This inherited intra-firm deficiency operates jointly with weak systemic phenomena in CEECs, such as externalities, networking, complementarities and synergies.

A Romanian food company (Dobrogea) and a clothing company (Braiconf) are examples of strong intra-firm capabilities but still weak 'linkage capabilities', which are essential for network alignment to take place. In the case of Dobrogea, networking in R&D is important for product development and differentiation but its production network is limited. When compared to Vistula and Videoton these two firms operate as 'laggards' with possibly similar potential to become network organizers in the future. This lag can be explained by a combination of weaker intra-firm organizational capabilities when compared to two very successful CEE cases, that is, Videoton and Vistula, and by the less favourable impact of other factors, that is, national and local networks, EU and government.

Fourth, the biggest weakness of network alignment in CEECs is weak national and local networks. The domestically controlled electronics group (Videoton) and the domestic clothing company (Vistula) have managed to establish domestic subcontracting networks and become their network organizers. Foreign-owned companies are embarking on this process but not so quickly and to a smaller extent, except in cases of the malting (Soufflet) and meat (Sokołow) industries where the local supply base is the key to increased market share. Weak local and national networks, for whose development substantial investment is needed, illustrate and support econometric evidence on absent or negative spillovers of FDI in CEE (Konings 2000). Our sample suggests that the operations of foreign investment enterprises are in no way by themselves a guarantee that weak network relationships can be resolved or improved. Our evidence suggests that there is no straightforward relationship between foreign presence and the degree of network alignment.

Fifth, industrial networks are predominantly production networks and to a very limited extent technology (knowledge) networks. Knowledge transfer is an inevitable part of any production linkage as in the case of subcontracting in clothing or electronics. However, explicit knowledge or technology networking is rare in the cases analysed. When there is intensive knowledge transfer it is confined to production links, for example, support to farmers (Soufflet, Sokołow). In the case of Dobrogea, R&D networks have been important for product development. In the case of Videoton, the company has been involved in a few small design projects. Based on their own efforts the clothing companies (Vistula, Braiconf) have developed design capabilities. In all these cases, technology development involved a conscious strategic effort. Our case studies suggest that there is no automatic conversion from production to technology networking. The requirements for further technological networking are emerging as the next structural barrier to growth for CEE enterprises.

The increasing importance of intangible activities in business, including complex projects, customized solutions and software-based services, will be the test of how much CEECs can improve their national systems of innovation, which could complement the needs of such companies. There are increasing signs that in some sectors CEECs, for example Hungary, are becoming, in European terms, very important production locations. However, as profit margins and power in value chains are moving towards non-production activities the real test for long-term growth of CEE is the extent to which the region will be able to integrate itself into global technology networks. This will have important implications for the long-term nature of European industrial integration.

Sixth, for domestic firms the EU operates as a favourable factor through its proximity and demand (Videoton, Braiconf, Vistula), as a source of competition from the EU companies (Elektrim, Dobrogea) or as a source of know-how (Sokołow). EU accession has further reinforced these advantages and in the case of agriculture it is likely to offer new market opportunities. For foreign investors CEECs are new markets (Tesco) or markets and production locations (ABB, EBS, Soufflet). For EBS, the opening of CEE was an essential strategic opportunity. For ABB, expansion to the east was logical given the global nature of its activities. Tesco has successfully pioneered expansion to CEE in the retail business where such expansions are fraught with numerous risks. For them, EU accession does not seem to alter much in terms of strategic orientation and perceived benefits from their CEE presence. For Soufflet, accession may open up the opportunity to export to the EU. However, despite the seemingly secondary importance of EU and EU accession in network alignment in all cases they give a clear focus and long-term orientation to company strategies and coherence to network alignment. This conclusion as to the secondary but nonetheless strategic importance of EU accession in building industrial networks may be due to bias in our case studies which do not involve industries (with the partial exception of Elektrim) where regulatory aspects are prominent.

National governments are neither the source of problems nor are they facilitators of network alignment. Similar to the countries of the EU, this factor operates as secondary due to the passive role of government in privatization. In a few cases, governments have provided rents to local investors (Elektrim, Videoton), which have been used productively. The assessment of the government's role in network alignment via competition policy (telecom liberalization and the position of Elektrim), subsidies (support to local suppliers in agriculture in case of Soufflet, EBS and Dobrogea) or R&D support (Dobrogea) is much more complicated and our cases do not give a basis for its full assessment.

Resume

Network alignment is driven by *complementarities* between the actions of different actors. The strongest network alignment occurs among domestically controlled companies, in particular, Vistula and Videoton. A good organizational coherence and developed organizational capabilities, which match well with the interests of foreign buyers, have transformed these organizations into organizers of local supply/subcontracting networks. This has been reinforced by factors such as EU proximity (Videoton) and its competitive pressure (Vistula), by supportive local networks and initial government rents acquired through privatization (Videoton). Soufflet, the French MNC, which is active in the malting industry in CEE, has also become a network organizer by assisting the restructuring of hitherto weak supplier networks of farmers. Also, Sokołow, a domestic company with a foreign strategic investor, is active in developing links with farmers. In these two cases there are also the strong complementary interests of local farmers and strong domestic demand. However, the EU still operates only as a potential attractor while government's role is either irrelevant or is considered as not supportive.

MNCs have resolved ownership/control problems, have much larger resources at their disposal than local firms and have fully integrated their CEE subsidiaries into company networks. Domestic companies with foreign strategic owners are sharing control and are trading access to local markets for foreign technology (know-how) and finance, which is provided by foreign strategic investors. Domestically controlled companies do not have ownership/control problems despite unfavourable corporate governance structures, but face much greater deficiencies in resources (technology, marketing, finance). Although formally independent companies their growth is based on strong links with foreign partners in supplier (Videoton) or buyer (Braiconf, Vistula) driven supply chains. These differences in governance and resource dimensions strongly affect the scale and scope of network alignment.

The entry of MNCs as well as non-equity links of domestic firms with foreign buyers have significant effects on industrial restructuring and on the nature of competition in the sectors. In all cases, the entry of MNCs has changed the nature of competition in individual sectors (EBS, Soufflet, Tesco, ABB). In cases where the presence of foreign investment is indirect via strategic investors (Elektrim, Sokołow), as major buyers (Vistula, Videoton, Braiconf) or as competitors (Dobrogea), the sectoral effect is equally strong.

Our case studies suggest that the companies surveyed have been integrated at the level of production with technological integration being still exceptional. They all grew based on networking or networking combined with generic expansion. Firms have not yet overcome weaknesses in system integration at the product level and process integration at firm level, but those that have improved are the ones that have developed linkage capabilities. CEE firms operate in a context in which their growth is constrained by weak external networks, be they national or local networks, or by weak supporting infrastructures or anti-competitive regulations. Their competitive strength is improved productivity, acquired production know-how and improved linkage capabilities. The comparative strength of the firms analysed lies in production know-how, though several cases (Vistula, Braiconf) show functional upgrading towards non-production activities, but only for the domestic market. Key bottlenecks to developing complementarities are weak local and national networks.

Notes

1 All case studies are available at <http:///www.ssees.ac.uk/esrcwork.htm>
2 Original Design Manufacturing (ODM) is the design and manufacturing by domestic firms with little or no assistance from the foreign customer, of goods to be sold under the brand of the foreign customer firm.
3 Sixty-five per cent of Vistula's shares are in public offering, 15 per cent are owned by management and 20 per cent by employees. Dobrogea is 98 per cent owned by employees and management with 2 per cent held by members of the public. Braiconf SA has 40 per cent share ownership by employees through the Association of Employees with 60 per cent offered on the stock market of which 27 per cent were bought by Romanian interests from third countries. Videoton management undertook its own leveraged buy-out and owns 85 per cent of the shares.

References

Konings, J. (2000) 'The effects of direct foreign investment on domestic firms: evidence from firm level panel data in emerging economies', *Centre for Economic Policy Research*, Discussion Paper Series No. 2586, October.

Lall, S. (1992) 'Technological capabilities and industrialization', *World Development*, 20(2): 165–86.

Milgrom, P. and Roberts, J. (1995) 'Complementarities and fit: strategy, structure and organizational change in manufacturing', *Journal of Accounting and Economics*, 19: 179–208.

Peng, W.M. (2000) *Business Strategies in Transition Economies*, London: Sage IBS Series.

Peng, W.M. and Heath, P.S. (1996) 'The growth of the firm in planned economies in transition: institutions, organizations, and strategic choice', *Academy of Management Review*, 21(2): 492–528.

Radosevic, S. (1999a) *International Technology Transfer and 'Catch Up' in Economic Development*, Cheltenham: Edward Elgar.

Radosevic, S. (1999b) 'Alliances and the emerging patterns of technological integration and marginalization of central and eastern Europe in the global economy', in D. Dyker (ed.), *Foreign Direct Investment and Technology Transfer in the Former Soviet Union*, Cheltenham: Edward Elgar, pp. 27–51.

Radosevic, S. (2002) 'European integration and complementarities driven network alignment: the case of ABB in central and eastern Europe', Project Working Paper No. 11, February, UCL – SSEES, London.

Radosevic, S. and Yoruk, D.E. (2001) 'Videoton: the growth of enterprise through entrepreneurship and network alignment', Project Working Paper No. 3, June, UCL – SSEES, London.

Radosevic, S., Dornisch, D. and Yoruk, D.E. (2001) 'The issues of enterprise growth in transition and post-transition period: the case of Polish Elektrim', No. 1, April, UCL – SSEES, London.

Yoruk, D.E. (2002a) 'Industrial integration and growth of firms in transition economies: the case of a French Multinational Company', Project Working Paper No. 20, March, UCL – SSEES, London.

Yoruk, D.E. (2002b) 'Growth of a Polish meat company: mergers and acquisitions and the role of strategic investors', Project Working Paper No. 18, March, UCL – SSEES, London.

Yoruk, D.E. (2002c) 'Role of network development in the growth of firm: the case of a Romanian bakery company', Project Working Paper No. 27, July, UCL – SSEES, London.

Yoruk, D.E. (2002d) 'Global production networks, upgrading at the firm level, and the role of network organiser: the case of Polish Vistula', Project Working Paper No. 28, July, UCL – SSEES, London.

Yoruk, D.E. (2002e) 'Effective integration to global production networks: knowledge acquisition and accumulation: the case of Braiconf SA in Romania', Project Working Paper No. 26, July, UCL – SSEES, London.

Yoruk D.E. and Radosevic, S. (2000) 'International expansion and buyer-driven commodity chain: the case of TESCO', Project Working Paper No. 4, November, UCL – SSEES, London.

Yoruk, D.E. and von Tunzelmann, N. (2001) 'Role of multinationals and network alignment in East Europe: the case of a agribusiness company', Project Working Paper No. 6, January, UCL – SSEES, London.

6 Network realignment in the CEE food-processing industry

Nick von Tunzelmann and Deniz Eylem Yoruk

Introduction

This chapter is concerned with the contributions to network formation of both domestic and foreign agents operating in the food-processing industry of some countries of Central and East Europe (CEE). Its primary focus is on what foreign multinational companies (MNCs) are or are not doing in reorganizing and upgrading the CEE industry. These companies are among the most active agents involved in 'realigning' the networks that offer the potential for upgrading, but we find that their contribution is incomplete in the sense of not (yet) forging a new coherent alignment. At the same time, they are themselves engaging more intensely in global competition, into which their activities in the CEE countries are being drawn. Moreover, other factors such as the response of domestic firms to these developments in their home market are also significant.

The network alignment framework developed in Chapter 3 is employed and extended here to analyse the CEE food-processing industry. The sector exemplifies the shift in network alignment from state-orientation to MNC-orientation. To present this shift, the chapter will look briefly at the pre-transition situation of food-processing in the CEE countries, that is, dominated by political hierarchies. We see this as a context characterized by widespread 'network failure' of the second type instanced in Chapter 3 (where networks are present but anti-developmental). With transition, the targets and associated strategies have shifted, more in line with western values and perceptions, and these shifts have radically altered business practices. Nevertheless, these changes have not been sufficient to bring about convergence of different networks, and this is leading to the third type of network failure (where resource flows are mutually inconsistent).

The chapter examines the resources and capabilities attained by domestic firms and those being increasingly attained by foreign firms operating in the region – new patterns of ownership, new market and knowledge opportunities. We find the foreign agents have strengthened the networks that were previously weak but perhaps at some cost to the networks that were previously strong. We draw the conclusion that there is a connection between the global context in which large players are engaged and the continuing problems of network alignment in the CEE countries.

The CEE heritage: network failure

In the Soviet era, with the collectivization of agriculture in most socialist countries (though Poland was something of an exception), agriculture ceased to be competitively organized. Agricultural collectivization had substantial effects on the organization of food-processing. The 'upstream' branch of food manufacturing tended to remain under the thumb of agriculture and was essentially an appendage to agricultural production. In the state-monopolized 'downstream' branch, distribution tended to take precedence over innovation. In processing, the state-owned enterprises (SOEs) which were characterized by an over-concentration of monopolistic structures, little competition, a limited role for prices and costs, actual disincentives for innovation, under-investment, administrative interference, etc. (Duponcel 1998), dominated the industry in this era.[1] The direct or indirect influence of the centralized state protected the power of the processors, not necessarily in the best interests of consumers.

Neither upstream nor downstream branch managed to establish itself as a nucleus for innovation in the socialist system of production, which featured a politically imposed division of labour between production on the one side and technology on the other. Such segmentation was symptomatic of a deeply divided overall production system, in which supply was supposed to dictate demand but remained largely unresponsive to it. Figure 6.1, panel A, depicts the Soviet pattern of top-down dominance of agriculture, organized into various kinds of collectives, which took responsibility for downstream processing. The resulting products, often of low quality, were fobbed off on customers through a captive distribution system.

Transition in the western food industry: from supply-dominated to demand-driven

A stagnating, supply-driven industry in CEE countries was left to be revitalized primarily by the inflow of foreign technology following transition. Although the food-processing industry is widely ignored for development purposes as rather traditional and backward-looking, closer assessment of historical experience would show that it has been central to the industrialization of a number of now advanced countries (e.g. Switzerland, Denmark). The western food-processing industry has proven to be significant in terms of its contribution to total manufacturing output, employment and profitability, and its considerable 'comparative advantage' in terms of global competition, unlike the much studied high-tech industries (Davies and Lyons 1996).

Despite the fact that relatively little by way of 'in-house' R&D takes place within many firms in the industry, it is moving away from its old characteristic of being in the terminology of Pavitt (1984) 'supplier-dominated' by mechanical engineering firms supplying it with machinery − though it continues to be somewhat supplier-dominated as the new suppliers include dedicated biotechnology and pharmaceutical firms, providers of smart materials (e.g. for packaging) and

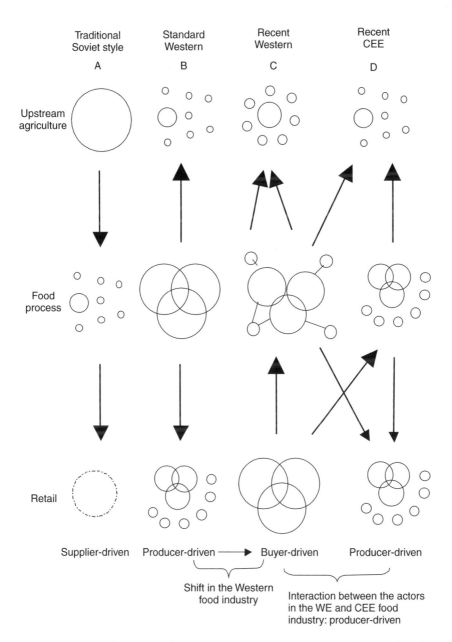

Figure 6.1 Historical transition of western and eastern European food industry in the value chain.

Source: Authors.

advanced instrumentation, etc. It is becoming very much a 'multi-tech' industry (Granstrand *et al.* 1997), with an increasing bias towards adopting advanced areas of technology.

Changes in technology are having complex impacts on changes in organization and governance in the industry. As shown in Figure 6.1, panel B, farmers in western countries typically used to be small producers in competitive conditions and produced commodities which would be graded for quality by independent assessments or by the purchasers themselves. Food processors were often large producers in oligopolistic or even monopolistic market conditions and aimed to produce branded products, in which the brand name was intended to act as a way of differentiating the product in the eyes of final consumers, and providing the basic mechanism for leveraging profits. In the 'visible hand' structure of this standard western structure, power emanated from the middle, that is, the corporations which made up the oligopolistic nerve centre of the industry. Upstream, the farms were fragmented; downstream, the retailers were divided into some of moderate power and a huge penumbra of small grocers.

In a number of western countries, the balance of power has nowadays shifted well downstream to the retailers. In countries like the UK, the oligopolistic supermarket chains now effectively dominate the whole food supply chain, to the point where they have supplanted the processors in directly controlling even the growing phase in agriculture (Galizzi and Venturini 1996: chs 3, 5). Panel C of Figure 6.1 provides a representation of this emerging pattern, with substantial consolidation among the retailers, some steps towards consolidation upstream through the development of agri-business, and the ongoing transformation of the oligopolies into becoming systems integrators embedded in more complex networks.

Changes in processes have shifted away from being mainly supply-driven (faster speeds, reduced costs, etc.), derived from mechanization and process automation, to being more consumer-driven.[2] In those respects, the process changes have aligned with product innovations as responses to shifting consumer demands. The changing needs of consumers in turn reflect changes in their capabilities, driven by demand-side factors (Christensen *et al.* 1996).[3] Such changes are beginning to make some headway in CEE countries, but still with a long way to catch up.

The overall structure of the CEE food-processing industry exhibits a producer-driven structure, similar to the former Western model (Figure 6.1, panel D). The arrows that go from panel C to panel D represent foreign penetration in the processing and retailing sectors of the industry, as the CEE food industry has become highly exposed to recent changes in the west European food industry, shifting from a supplier- to a demand-driven focus. These changes reinforce the willingness of domestic firms to establish more networks especially with foreign firms, yet there is little sign that such interest is being adequately reciprocated by the foreign firms operating in the host countries.

The transition of the CEE food-processing industry in firms

The domestic producers in the CEE countries, and subsequently their foreign counterparts, confronted a fragmented agricultural sector in the aftermath of the abandonment of collectivization. It rapidly became apparent that little headway could be made, least of all in expanding exports, without a rapid upgrading of the industry built around network formation and the imposition of higher standards.

The analysis in this section is based on our interviews with thirty-eight foreign and domestically owned firms (including domestic firms with foreign strategic investors) in Poland and Romania (nineteen in each country) during 2001–02. The results are discussed through comparisons of the four types of firm: Polish domestic, Polish foreign, Romanian domestic and Romanian foreign.

New forms of organization

Privatization of the food industry has proceeded more slowly than first anticipated, even in relatively better-off countries like Poland and Slovenia, and a huge amount of consequent restructuring still needs to be carried out, especially in the more upstream branches.[4] Simple market-focused strategies have given some potential for control to domestic ownership, but without the attendant capabilities in marketing and technologies these have had limited economic impacts. In order to promote such capabilities (and others, e.g. financial), firms have oriented themselves to networks and inter-firm alliances to supply the missing requisites.

The network organizers in the CEE can be 'any actors with the necessary capability and resources: a user or supplier firm, a bank, a holding company or a financial-industrial group, a foreign-trade organization, a design institute, a foreign firm or, in some cases, even the state' (Radosevic 1999, p. 309). This is because different modes of governance may be called upon for the production of both resources and products, and the choice of governance mode may have a substantial impact on the capabilities of different units.

Given the management, finance and technology gaps that typify CEE activities, foreign firms appear as the most active network organizers. We argue that their contribution is largely focused on production networks, and is insufficient to direct multiple networks towards one another. The latter reflects the enduring network failures traced by the CEE heritage.

Figure 6.2 shows a marked difference in equity-based activities as between foreign and domestic firms. The foreign firms in both countries have undertaken a considerable number of greenfield investments (especially in Poland) and a still larger number of brownfield investments. Most of the domestic firms in Romania have had no equity-based activities, though in Poland four firms have made brownfield investments and three have been involved in mergers.

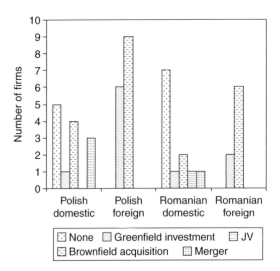

Figure 6.2 Equity activities of domestic and foreign firms in Poland and Romania.
Source: Survey by authors.

In Poland, production-oriented strategic alliances within the industry are predominant (Figure 6.3(a)), whereas in Romania there are a greater number of consultancy relationships for managerial and organizational improvements, including foreign consultancies (Figure 6.3(b)). This points to a continuing division of labour between different functions of firms of the kind outlined in Chapter 3, although there has been more internalization inside Polish domestic firms than their Romanian counterparts.

New markets

The initial stages of transition imposed powerful and often negative shocks on the socialist-based system in the CEE countries. The first few years of transition in the early 1990s were marked by a decline, often quite sharp, in consumer demand because of falling incomes, increased competition including that from imports (mainly of higher quality goods), and the loss of those former export markets (especially other Council of Mutual Economic Assistance (CMEA) markets, above all the Former Soviet Union). There was an offset in terms of an increased ability to export to the West, but this was only partial, and based on accepting low prices rather than through undertaking new trade agreements. Though much was expected of the industry in view of its comparatively large extent, in practice food-processing was among the worst performing industries in early transition, because of lack of resources and obsolete physical assets and processes.

The situation was met by the subsequent inflow of foreign direct investment (FDI). The relations with foreign headquarters turn out to be mainly of the

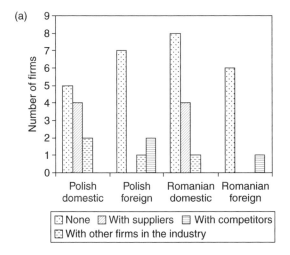

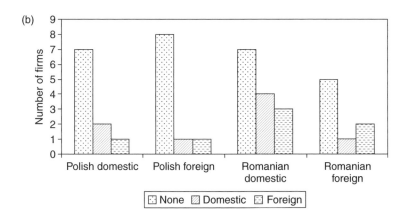

Figure 6.3 (a) Strategic alliances and (b) consultancy relationships of domestic and foreign firms in Poland and Romania.

Source: Survey by authors.

'mother' kind, with a smaller number that might be thought of as 'sisters', especially for Romania (Figure 6.4).

While penetrating these emerging markets, the foreign producers aimed to satisfy growing domestic demand for high value-added foodstuffs, such as confectionery, ice cream and beverages. The FDI began by targeting the largest, most stable and comparatively well-off markets for food products, in particular Poland. The desired shift of FDI to other countries has had to await the extension of those conditions of a stable and growing domestic market to their situations.

While there is some evidence that efficiency-seeking has been one of the determining factors behind the relocation eastwards, there is also every indication that

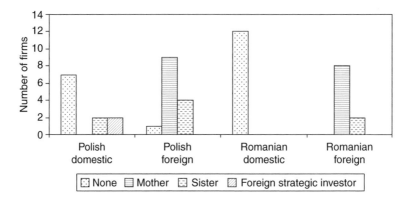

Figure 6.4 Hierarchical dyadic relationships of foreign firms in Poland and Romania.
Source: Survey by authors.

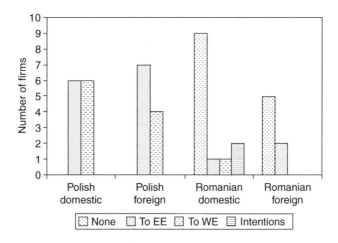

Figure 6.5 Destination of exports by domestic and foreign firms in Poland and Romania.
Source: Survey by authors.

it was not the major factor in this industry. This is suggested by the pattern of export activities in Figure 6.5. Romanian firms have few exports to either eastern or western Europe, though Polish firms – and especially the domestic firms – score highly on this measure. Nor are there many indications of any subsequent reinforcement of efficiency promotion, for example, through workforce redundancies, except in ways that reflect global rather than local trends. The great bulk of evidence instead supports the view that the main motivation for FDI was expanding market share (see also Duponcel 1998, p. 15). In the first instance, this was to gain toeholds in markets whose real promise might look to be some way off in the future. In some cases, this was fostered by a sense of stagnation in many western markets for food products. In more recent times, a significant degree of reconcentration, in areas where appropriability (e.g. through brand-naming) is high, has been fostered by foreign merger and acquisition activity.[5] Therefore, they seek assured domestic markets, often supported by import protection.

As it is the brand name which constitutes the main source of leverage in markets for the large firms, it is therefore often the means of competition between domestic and foreign firms. In many of these cases, local brands continued to have a majority of market share even in such brand-dominated segments as carbonated drinks (colas) and chocolate. The issue of whether to maintain the locally recognized brand name or merge it into the globally recognized one depended on the circumstances; for instance, upon the failure of greenfield investment in Poland, Cadbury Schweppes acquired the renowned Polish brand Wedel and was forced to keep the Cadbury brand separate. The necessity to allow for local tastes did, however, compel the foreign investors to be attentive to their local supply chains for raw materials and ingredients in the host CEE countries.

The western retailers supply technologies as well as demanding products when they move into the CEE countries. Such technological opportunity is, however, matched by due regard to appropriability. Based on its success in providing cheap but reliable 'own-label' products in its home-country stores, the British retailer Tesco has aimed to diffuse own-label products in the CEE stores as well. This diffusion has, however, been relatively gradual, because of having to change customer habits towards appreciating own-label products as 'value for money' on the demand side (e.g. through promulgating suburban-located hypermarkets), and having to induce farmers and other suppliers to observe contractual terms for quality, quantity and hygiene on the supply side (Yoruk and Radosevic 2000). However, retailers have another possibility for putting pressure on the supply system, which is to squeeze the local processors as well as, or instead of, the local farmers. Controversy rages as to whether such pressure is fair expression of market forces or unfair expression of power relations (*Business Central Europe Magazine*, May 2000). Tesco sees these relations as the pathway to long-term relations with suppliers. However, those relations we observed had the appearance of being market rather than network relations, that is, denominated by monetary exchanges rather than exchanges in kind, and hence liable to the vagaries of shorter-term financial exigencies.

New sources of knowledge

The movement of capital eastwards has been widely envisaged as embodying new technologies (at least to the host country) and necessitating training for new skills while also bringing in managerial and technological skills for the restructuring and modernization of the industries in transition countries. The achievements here have been perhaps less impressive. To develop a suitable supplier environment for themselves, most of the foreign investors cooperate with their human resource and

R&D units in their mother country (indicated by the nature of dyadic relations portrayed in Figure 6.4). This implies strong dependence on the home country of the foreign investors for knowledge accumulation. Few foreign investors have any extensive research facilities in their affiliates in these host countries, but they become application areas for the research conducted in the home country.

In our investigation, the new sources of knowledge, especially in technology, were explored in greater detail. The legacy of the communist era bequeathed a fixation on agricultural machinery as the technological solution, but much of this is unsuited to the fragmentation of farm sizes after communism. The kinds of machinery that are really wanted are often widely lacking, like milking machinery in Romania. In addition the communist system bequeathed a lack of concern for environmental and ecological aspects of farming, where there have been only limited changes, for example, by reduced taxes on environmentally friendly produce.

Health and safety standards are arguably more important for advancing the industry than mechanization. Most of the Polish firms we contacted have ISO certificates and are aware of the importance of hygiene and quality in the food-processing industry. The impact of the regular inspections by the Polish Veterinary Inspectorate required by ISO certification pushes the need for hygiene and quality back up to their suppliers, which thus forces the farms to improve their own standards.[6] Romanian firms perceive ISO certification as the only way to export to the EU; nevertheless, their attitude is the opposite of Polish firms (Figure 6.6). Their awareness of ISO certification is high but their adoption of it low. The significance of attaining accreditation is shown by the example of Bulgaria, which still faces barriers to trade in trying to export meat and dairy products to the EU (*AgraFood East Europe*, March 2001).

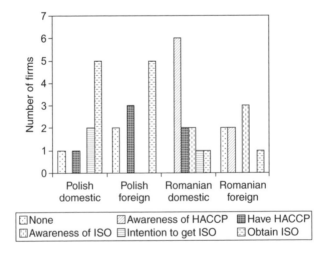

Figure 6.6 Attitudes towards quality management by domestic and foreign firms in Poland and Romania.

Source: Survey by authors.

When they entered CEE markets, foreign investors gave little thought to the quality of agricultural produce. With the lure of markets that had the potential for expansion, sometimes when western markets were stagnating, the question of the supply side was confined to issues such as which site or plant to acquire. In a number of cases, the agricultural materials were imported in order to avoid any problem of making use of domestic supplies. Although this was probably envisaged in most cases as an interim arrangement, in a number of cases it still persists, particularly in Romania. Investors have also imported animal breeds and seed and plant varieties to revive domestic agriculture. According to our interviews, the foreign investors consider that there has been a lack of commitment by local and national governments within the CEE countries to improve agricultural technology.[7]

In effect the foreign investors, despite imposing 'mother–daughter' relations on their CEE subsidiaries, have thus been sucked into trying to revive the upstream end of the industry, by having to teach the farmers how to obtain the quantity and quality of output which they need for downstream processing, and have been compelled to act as 'network organizers'. A possible solution is to organize local cooperatives as a network form of organization; while this has been partially successful, for example, for cooperative purchasing of milking machines in Poland, cooperation is distrusted in many of these countries as being too like collectivization. A second option is to consolidate local smallholdings into large farms, and this has been apparent under the shelter of foreign companies in the Polish meat producers.[8] The foreign producers are thus drawn into acting as hubs for local supply chains, with major roles in providing know-how (including biological as well as mechanical technologies) and distribution outlets. They have utilized agronomists who supervise the farmers during the harvest period regarding when and how to use the machinery, sow the seeds, etc. and show them what is good and bad practice directly on their own farms. At other times of the year, they might choose to pre-finance the farmers by supplying capital in the form of seed, fertilizer, animal feed or machinery, depending on the particular segment of the industry. Often such capital in one form or another is supplied at the beginning of the production season, in return for the output they will eventually receive from the farmer, in a similar fashion to domestic firms. In this way, they control the quality of the seed, fertilizers and animal feed the farmers use, and guarantee the quality and timing of the harvest through the use of machinery.

Improvements in distribution (e.g. of milk) and feed were given particular emphasis by foreign investors from the beginning of their involvement. Typically, the foreign companies look out for younger and more enterprising farmers, and select them assiduously. One problem they encounter is that many in younger age groups are quitting farming, leaving them with an 'adverse selection' of less entrepreneurially inclined farmers to select from. An alternative strategy sometimes resorted to is to import western farmers, like the German farmers who have settled in western Poland, occupying land close to the foreign investors' factories and working with them, such as the Dutch potato processor Farm Frites-Aviko. These have the advantage of needing less start-up capital and practically no training.

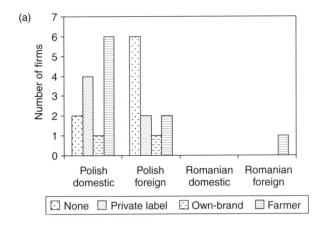

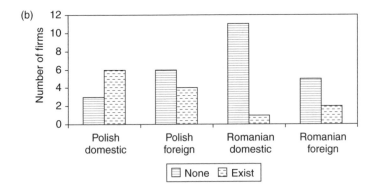

Figure 6.7 (a) Subcontracting relations and (b) employment of agronomists in domestic and
foreign firms in Poland and Romania.

Source: Survey by authors.

Note
One-third of Polish domestic firms have a foreign strategic investor.

Domestic manufacturing and processing firms develop production-based linkages, like subcontracting of private labels downstream (see Figure 6.7). Upstream,
linkages with farmers help both domestic and foreign firms overcome systemic
quality and quantity problems in agriculture by closely working with farmers and
by employing agronomists within the firm. The foreign firms and domestic firms
with foreign investors in Poland are more active and influential in training of farmers via subcontracting, since their agronomists are trained abroad and apply the latest agricultural techniques, compared to domestic firms whose relationships with
farmers are based on controlling the health and safety regulations during cultiva-
tion and collection. In Romania, there is very little exercise of subcontracting
relations and a much reduced level of employment of agronomists.

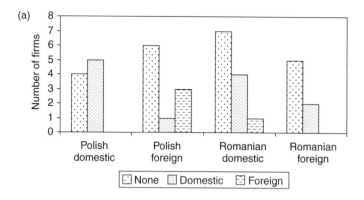

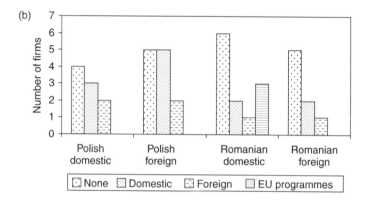

Figure 6.8 Cooperation of domestic and foreign firms in Poland and Romania with (a) foreign and/or domestic universities and (b) research institutions.

Source: Survey by authors.

Note

Most of the relationships between domestic research institutions and foreign firms in Poland are compulsory for specific tests that the latter are obliged to meet.

Domestic companies try to work with government laboratories and local universities, inherently based on informal personal links, but foreign companies largely or entirely ignore them (Figure 6.8). The kind of cooperation on a few occasions extends to innovation projects but mostly is constrained to technical advice and problem-solving activities. The transition has so far done little to overcome the divorce between production and technology identified in communist times earlier (see Jasinski 1997; Chataway 1999, for the Polish case). In some key ways it has worsened the situation, through the collapse of business R&D. Little was done to reorient the Academy-led systems to practical business needs, and academic research remained theory oriented, not uncommonly generating brain drains of many of the best talents to the west and especially the USA. With technology transfer from the west becoming the predominant vehicle for technological catching-up in industries like food-processing (Hirschhausen and Bitzer 2000), indigenous sources of knowledge bases have been substantially bypassed, to the extent that it has been claimed that there has been if anything a devaluation of human capital with the transition process.

Overview of the firms

While domestic companies like Dobrogea (a bakery producer) in Romania (Yoruk 2002b) are sometimes able to take advantage of new market opportunities that are partly the consequence of opening up (e.g. tourism), the market opportunity factor is what especially underlies the timing and extent of FDI. The geographical pattern of FDI has been one of moving first to larger and relatively wealthier markets. On the supply side, there is an observable impact of new technological paradigms like information technology, but this appears more muted than the demand-side opportunities, as reflected in market-seeking rather than efficiency-seeking strategies.

Domestic companies are tempted to diversify in a context of foreign competition and new market opportunities. For the foreign companies, although the CEE acquisitions were often an instrument of their diversification strategies, they did not go much beyond what was being done in their home country in this respect (Yoruk 2002c). Their main aim was consolidation and reinforcement of their existing fields ('relatedness'), in which they could reasonably be assured of comparative advantage.

Domestic companies fare better if they undertake in-house R&D activity, which attracts foreign interest and allows participation in EU projects (e.g. Dobrogea in Romania). Foreign investors draw on their networks at home for the benefit of the domestic firms in the host country. Although MNCs' intentions were to 'play at home' in their CEE activities, they were somewhat unwittingly driven into greater development of upstream technological capabilities in their host countries than they had probably envisaged at first. This was because the agricultural capabilities they encountered, following communist-era collectivization and subsequent fragmentation, proved to be so backward in terms of both quantity and quality. In regard to the more downstream branches of the industry, they are adopting mainly private means of upgrading, for example, through their own training schemes or standards implementation (ISO or their own), rather than feeding into local or national systems in the host countries. Skill development in various dimensions remains a key issue.

The extent to which foreign investors following transition can leverage their new ownership has major impacts on the areas in which acquisitions take place and their nature. The particular branches of the food industry that have received most attention reflect the relative ability to benefit from marketing (brand names) and from newer technologies, as Sutton (1991) indeed predicted for this industry. Both entry modes and subsequent developments stress high control. Particularly noteworthy in the second half of the 1990s was an enhancement of foreign control by some of the more aggressive foreign investors, seeking to tighten control of the CEE markets for their particular product through expanding market share. In secondary rounds of takeover they acquired more domestic small and medium size enterprises (SMEs) and also the previous acquisitions of some of their weaker western rivals. Downstream relations tend to remain vertically disintegrated for producer-driven chains, though the reverse impact of buyer-driven chains will no doubt change this.

Conclusions: network realignment?

A previous study concluded that unless 'network failures' originating in socialist production and still endemic in the post-socialist system of production in the food-processing industry were resolved, there was no prospect for the CEE food-processing industry to catch up with the West that was shifting even further towards a demand-driven system (von Tunzelmann and Charpiot-Michaud 2000). Some new twists have been added to that story, although it remains the core of our perspective.

The network failures have become more apparent at the 'national' level in CEE countries, while a more optimistic picture may be emerging in respect of local and global networking, albeit guardedly. The national failure consists of getting market-based systems to work alongside other modes of governance – corporate hierarchies, political hierarchies and networks. In terms of resources, the failings appear to lie principally in intangible capital (technology) in ways that go beyond simple embodiment in physical capital (machinery and equipment), and even more in human capital linked to various types of skills, mostly of a 'cognitive' kind (knowledge-based). The foreign MNCs bring some relief and upgrading but mesh least adequately with domestic capabilities and resources at this national level, where much of the catching up still needs to be taken on. They are involved in their own wider engagement with 'global capitalism', and bring such issues into the domestic scene in CEE countries.

The FDI has greatly enhanced the role of global networks emanating from western markets. This has fed through to the domestic acquisitions in terms of higher quality standards, and to some degree rubbed off on the surviving domestic companies. Improved management has allowed them to raise the profiles of local networks. The governments of the CEE countries have put most of their efforts into privatization, that is, simply changes in ownership, thus creating one base for strengthening local networks, though without the management and other input from the firms themselves this contribution would be rather 'shallow'. Less was done to reorient resources towards building national networks, for example, through enhanced human resources in R&D. With little interest shown by the foreign companies in developing host-country national networks, these have atrophied.

In the food-processing industry, the target of competition is a moving one. The western industry in this formerly 'low-tech' sector is shifting rapidly towards high-tech methods and products. This leaves the industry in the east either retreating into the remaining 'low-tech' niches, or instead trying to imitate the up-market shift of the western industry. In the longer term, we see little effective alternative to adapting the food-processing sector in the east towards high-tech operations. At present, we therefore see a severe breakdown, even a schism, between the scientific 'potential' generated by education and the new scientific needs for applications.

This schism can be described as 'network failure'. The ways in which such 'network failure' is apparent vary from one country to another, depending on the surrounding conditions. In Romania, the main problem seems to lie on the supply side in agriculture, whereas in Poland it is on the demand side in marketing. National specificities have to be allowed for, but the national systems and networks have largely imploded. The need is now overwhelming to integrate production with technological development, which will mean not reverting to the old S&T systems and their vertical division of labour, but a new demand-driven system.

Notes

1 In the late 1980s, some 75 per cent of Hungarian processed food production came from 138 large SOEs; in Poland around the same time about 80 per cent came from 196 of them (Duponcel 1998: 21).

2 For example in packaging, the new processes are designed to meet consumer demands for (i) ease of use (e.g. ring-pull cans and tear-strip openings), (ii) new eating habits (as for ready meals), (iii) food safety (e.g. avoiding the 'migration' of packaging materials into the product), (iv) environmental friendliness (e.g. avoiding non-biodegradable and wasteful packaging).

3 Among these demand factors are rising incomes, globalization of tastes, smaller families, increased female employment, greater concern for health and safety and for environmental sustainability, and so forth.

4 The delay in Poland is mostly due to disputes in the sugar industry.

5 By 1995, four MNCs accounted for nearly 80 per cent of sales of biscuits in Hungary (Duponcel 1998). Particularly, the brewing branch has experienced concentration in foreign ownership and in markets in the Czech Republic, Poland, Russia and Romania (Goodale 2002; Gorzynski 2002; Tolkacheva 2002; and SAB web page). Foreign strategic investors in the Polish meat industry have induced mergers, leading to oligopolies (see Yoruk 2002a).

6 The positive contribution that the enforcement of these standards makes is to open up the possibility of export licences to the EU, which twenty-five out of eighty working dairies had received by early 2001, a considerable recovery from the 1997 ban referred to earlier.

7 National governments have taken short-term measures to try to boost conditions, for example, by subsidizing fertilizer imports (Bulgaria) or emergency grants for cereals (Romania), but these are evidently stopgap in nature.

8 In mid-2001, it was reported that only 28 per cent of Polish farmers had adjusted the size of their farms to changing market conditions (*AgraFood East Europe*, July 2001). Bulgaria has a policy of government support for consolidation, but it is voluntary (ibid., Jan 2001).

References

AgraFood East Europe, various issues.

Business Central Europe Magazine, May 2000.

Chataway, J. (1999) 'Technology transfer and the restructuring of science and technology in central and eastern Europe', *Technovation* 19: 355–64.

Christensen, J.L., Rama, R. and von Tunzelmann, N. (1996) *The European Food and Beverages Industry*, European Information Monitoring System (EU), Luxembourg.

Davies, S. and Lyons, B. (1996) *Industrial Organization in the European Union*, Oxford: Clarendon Press.

Duponcel, M. (1998) 'Restructuring of food industries in the five Central and Eastern European front-runners towards EU membership (CEEC-5)', Centre for Economic Reform and Transformation (CERT) Discussion Paper, 98/6, Edinburgh: Heriot-Watt University.

Galizzi, G. and Venturini, L. (1996) *Economics of Innovation: The Case of Food Industry*, Heidelberg: Physica-Verlag.

Goodale, G. (2002) 'U.S. beverage distributor upping market share', *Warsaw Business Journal*, 18 Feb 2002.

Gorzynski, M. (2002) 'Consolidation of ownership and market consolidation: the role of relational investors on the Polish beer market, 1990–99', mimeo, CASE.

Granstrand, O., Patel, P. and Pavitt, K. (1997) 'Multi-technology corporations: why they have "distributed" rather than "distinctive core" competencies', *California Management Review*, 39: 8–25.

Hirschhausen, C. von and Bitzer, J. (eds) (2000) *The Globalization of Industry and Innovation in Eastern Europe*, Cheltenham: Edward Elgar.

Jasinski, A. (1997) 'Academy–Industry Relations for Innovation in Poland', STEEP Discussion Paper No. 41, www.sussex.ac.uk/spru

Pavitt, K. (1984) 'Sectoral patterns of technical change: towards a taxonomy and a theory', *Research Policy*, 13: 353–69.

Radosevic, S. (1999) 'Transformation of science and technology systems into systems of innovation in central and eastern Europe: the emerging patterns and determinants', *Structural Change and Economic Dynamics*, 10: 277–320.

Sutton, J. (1991) *Sunk Costs and Market Structure*, Cambridge, MA: MIT Press.

Tolkacheva, J. (2002) 'Food industry is feeding Russian economic growth', Reuters, Jan 13, Moscow.

von Tunzelmann, N. and Charpiot-Michaud, F. (2000) 'Food processing in western and eastern Europe: from supply-driven towards demand-driven progress', in C. von Hirschhausen and J. Bitzer (eds), *The Globalization of Industry and Innovation in Eastern Europe*, Cheltenham: Edward Elgar, pp. 161–84.

Yoruk, D.E. (2002a) 'Growth of a Polish Meat Company: Mergers and Acquisitions and The Role of Strategic Investors', Working Paper No. 18, ESRC project, SSEES, UCL, www.ssees.ac.uk/esrcwork.htm

Yoruk, D.E. (2002b) 'Role of Network Development in The Growth of Firm: The Case of a Romanian Bakery Company', Working Paper No. 27, ESRC project, SSEES, UCL, www.ssees.ac.uk/esrcwork.htm

Yoruk, D.E. (2002c) 'Industrial Integration and Growth of Firm in Transition Economies: The case of a French Multinational Company', Working Paper series in Economics and

Business, No. 20, Centre for the Study of Economic and Social Change in Europe, SSEES, University College London, www.ssees.ac.uk/esrcwork.htm

Yoruk, D.E. and Radosevic, S. (2000) 'International Expansion and Buyer-driven Commodity Chain: The Case of Tesco', Working Paper No. 4, ESRC project, SSEES, UCL, www.ssees.ac.uk/esrcwork.htm

7 Patterns of industrial upgrading in the clothing industry in Poland and Romania

Deniz Eylem Yoruk

Introduction

The intensity of international competition today forces firms to cope with continual new challenges, find market niches and develop cultures of innovation with a rapidity that is unprecedented. The literature on capabilities of firms tends to emphasize internal over external determinants in fostering capabilities within the firm and generating the growth of the firm. Here we argue that internal factors must be complemented by external factors, allowing for the acquisition and absorption of external knowledge by the firm.

The main external factor emphasized in this chapter is the firm's *industrial networks* with other domestic and/or foreign organizations. These networks allow actors to access the resources of others (Hakansson 1987) and to triangulate with the state and market as discussed in Chapter 3 of this volume. Organizations that participate in networks can be in the value chain (suppliers, buyers), in the market (consumers), or in other relationships with firms such as universities, state organizations, research institutes, market research and consulting firms, etc. The extent to which firms can establish and utilize these international and national linkages is a significant indicator of both the capability to upgrade and the scope of upgrading.

Industrial upgrading is the outcome of gradual acquisition of new or enhancement of deficient intangible assets by enterprises, which enable them to shift from lower to higher value-added products, processes and activities (Yoruk 2003), and further integrate into advanced networks. Following Kaplinsky and Readman (2001), we identify four categories of upgrading: product, process, functional and managerial[1] (see Table 7.1). They describe industrial upgrading as a linear sequence from process, to product, to functional, and to chain upgrading. However, in practice the order of stages is often not clear nor is whether some stages occur simultaneously. Based on empirical evidence, we identify the patterns of industrial upgrading in the clothing industry in Poland and Romania over the last decade. We show how involvement in buyer-driven supply chains (i.e. predominantly production networks) affects the upgrading process and the role of networking in the course of upgrading.

Micro-level studies in transition economies usually deal with ownership transformations and restructuring of enterprises. This chapter uses the network alignment

Table 7.1 Definitions of types of industrial upgrading

Type of upgrading	Definition
Managerial	Improving the efficiency and effectiveness of production and non-production activities by acquiring new forms of organizational and managerial methods (such as teamwork, training, quality management, changes in perception of business relationships with suppliers, customers, etc.), or by re-organizing the existing managerial activities to facilitate internal and external learning.
Process	Increasing the efficiency of existing technological processes within the firm by means of minor and major change capabilities, by re-organizing the production system or introducing superior technology.
Product	Introducing new products either through creative adaptations of competitors'/customers' products or improving existing firms' products by minor and major change capabilities, or moving into more sophisticated product lines.
Functional	Increasing value-added by adding new, or withdrawing old, activities conducted within the firm, or moving the major locus of activities to different functions (e.g., from manufacturing to design).

Source: Managerial upgrading definition: Yoruk (2003); Process and product upgrading definitions: Author; and Functional upgrading definition: Kaplinsky and Readman (2001).

framework to understand the impact of industrial networks, both foreign and domestic, on the industrial upgrading of clothing companies in Poland and Romania over the past decade. Using this approach we assess the process of enterprise restructuring over the medium term, that is, over the last ten years.[2]

The research presented here was carried out in ten relatively large clothing companies in Poland and Romania. The companies interviewed were selected on the basis of the results of a questionnaire sent to 62 (29 Polish and 33 Romanian) clothing companies with more than 500 employees. The aim of this two-page questionnaire was to determine the nature of their equity and non-equity relationships[3] with other foreign and domestic organizations in terms of quantity and content of activity. The companies selected are scattered over different regions in each country, and differ in terms of the extent of their partnerships with foreign and domestic partners.

We distinguish between the five companies in each country by ranking their success in upgrading, networking and growth on a scale of 1–5, where 1 is the most advanced and 5 is the least advanced. In both countries, the first two companies (1 and 2) have significantly better competitive advantages in both international and national linkages than the last two (4 and 5). The mid-range companies (3) differ: the Romanian one, a rubber producer, only went into garment production after 1990 and the Polish company, a lingerie producer, has abandoned original equipment manufacturing (OEM)[4] and managed to survive without it (see Annex Table 7A.1).

These companies are still undergoing organizational or technological restructuring and are developing their corporate strategies. We focus on the extent to which their upgrading takes place through networking activity and formulate tentative conclusions about how this process differs between Poland and Romania.

After a brief overview of the theoretical and conceptual context to our case studies we outline a framework within which to analyse the patterns of technological upgrading in transition economies, particularly in the clothing industry. We go on to consider the empirical evidence on upgrading and the role of networks in the clothing industries in Poland and Romania.

Industrial upgrading in the CEE clothing industry

Figure 7.1 presents a schema of upgrading for the clothing industry, which is shown as a process of steps related to capital accumulation and learning. It starts with simple assembly, usually under the outward processing traffic (OPT) regime in Europe. OPT is a relationship in which the buyer supplies the producer with fabrics that are assembled according to the design prepared by the buyer and subsequently re-imported.[5]

An OEM relationship comprises different steps which involve the producer undertaking more tasks within the production process. These include cutting-out according to patterns supplied by the buyer (cut and make (CM)), preparing and grading the patterns (using computer aided design (CAD)) according to the prototype supplied by the buyer and carrying out all the preparations for the manufacture of the finished product, purchasing the materials required for production. This involves development of networking skills and thus familiarization with the upstream of the industry (cut, make and trim (CMT)), dispensing with the necessity for an '*intermediary*' between the central and eastern European (CEE) firm and the global brand-manufacturer, retailer or brand marketer and exporting from the own collections of the CEE firm (direct exporting, see Figure 7.2). Figure 7.2 depicts that direct exporting indicates leapfrogging in the supplier chain of the brand-manufacturer, from the second to the first tier. Although local companies have the potential to become direct exporters, they lack both competitive power and global marketing abilities. OEM gradually enhances the domestic firm's production and technological capabilities.

In addition, the trend towards own-label supply chains enables OEM producers to have direct links with retailers. Own-label supply chains are interested in providing garments to consumers at the lowest possible prices and are willing to purchase collections from local companies under their own brand rather than dealing with the technical specifications.[6]

Direct exporting is usually preceded by the domestic own-brand manufacturing (OBM-domestic) stage (see Figure 7.1). The foreign OBM stage in the European market is preceded by own-design manufacture (ODM) (Gereffi 1999): the firm has the capability to produce original designs rather than imitating world trends and has become a recognized brand-manufacturer.

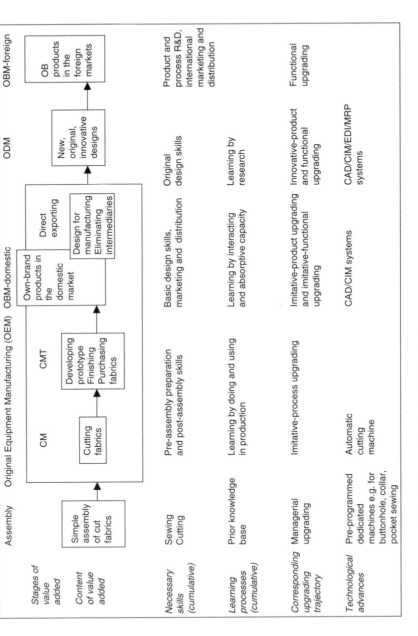

Stages of value added	Assembly	Original Equipment Manufacturing (OEM)		OBM-domestic		ODM	OBM-foreign
		CM	CMT	Own-brand products in the domestic market	Direct exporting	New, original, innovative designs	OB products in the foreign markets
Content of value added	Simple assembly of cut fabrics	Cutting fabrics	Developing prototype Finishing Purchasing fabrics		Design for manufacturing Eliminating intermediaries		Product and process R&D, international marketing and distribution
Necessary skills (cumulative)	Sewing Cutting	Pre-assembly preparation and post-assembly skills		Basic design skills, marketing and distribution		Original design skills	
Learning processes (cumulative)	Prior knowledge base	Learning by doing and using in production		Learning by interacting and absorptive capacity		Learning by research	
Corresponding upgrading trajectory	Managerial upgrading	Imitative-process upgrading		Imitative-product upgrading and imitative-functional upgrading		Innovative-product and functional upgrading	Functional upgrading
Technological advances	Pre-programmed dedicated machines e.g. for buttonhole, collar, pocket sewing	Automatic cutting machine		CAD/CIM systems		CAD/CIM/EDI/MRP systems	

Figure 7.1 A stylized pattern of industrial upgrading in the clothing industry.

Source: Author's compilation based on Duruiz and Yenturk Coban 1988; Gereffi 1999; Hobday 1995; and interview outcomes.

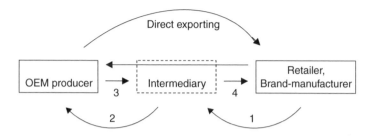

Figure 7.2 Elimination of intermediaries and the direct exporting stage.

Source: Author.

Industrial upgrading and networks in Polish and Romanian clothing companies

This section examines how much CEE clothing companies benefit from networks. The industrial upgrading is assessed using four indicators: the extent of OEM relations; the extent of own-brand production; the extent of industrial networks with domestic companies; and the extent of relationships with universities, research institutes and market research and consulting firms.

Table 7.2 summarizes Polish and Romanian clothing firms' upgrading patterns. The first two columns compare the number of Polish and Romanian firms with respect to each indicator within our sample while the third and fourth columns present generalizations.

Extent of OEM relations between CEE clothing companies and foreign buyers

Before transition, the CEE firms had ongoing OPT with foreign companies via foreign trade organizations (FTOs), though the extent of this type of production was limited compared to production for the domestic market and exports to the Council for Mutual Assistance (CMEA) market. Local firms were extremely passive in these relationships, since the FTOs handled commercial contacts between buyer and supplier, leaving the domestic firms with the responsibility only of developing production capabilities.

There were several reasons why, after transition, CEE clothing firms increased CMT with foreign buyers rather than focusing on their own-brand names. First, they had inherited huge production capacities, which they needed to continue to employ after the demise of the CMEA market. Second, local demand was negligible. Third, they were uncompetitive in foreign markets, having in the past produced only for the Soviet market, which was not demanding in terms of quality. Finally, and most importantly, they lacked the finance needed to strengthen their brand names.

Table 7.2 Summary of comparison between Polish and Romanian clothing firms

Indicators	PL	RO	Poland (PL)	Romania (RO)
OEM	4	5	Source of finance Focus on diminishing its share in total production	Learning by doing and using Introduction of technological advances to the firm Knowledge transfer from technicians of the buyers to the firm Focus on proliferating and deepening OEM
OBM-domestic	5	2	Early development of and intensive effort to strengthen own-brands in domestic markets Target is to be OBM in foreign markets	Laggard in own-brand production (only a handful make effort to strengthen their brands in the domestic market)
Production networks with domestic firms	4	0	Organized web of networks via a network organizer, others being a part of it in a hierarchical structure (large firms are licensees, whereas small laggards are subcontractors)	None
Relationships with universities, research institutes	0	4	None	Extensive, for consultancy on machinery and organization of production process
Relationships with market research	4	2	Extensive due to significance given to market position and customer demand	Emerging perception of customer recognition
Relationships with consultancy agencies	2	1	Limited, during the mid-1990s	Present with independent consultants

Source: Author.

Given the contraction of the domestic markets and the disappearance of the CMEA market, it would have been difficult for many clothing companies to survive in the early transition period without OPT. Even today local demand, especially in Romania, is not sufficient to generate profits. Companies are well aware that they cannot develop businesses by relying solely on OEM. In the late

1990s/early 2000s, labour costs in Poland increased *vis-à-vis* Romania. This decreased the share of OEM production in the total production of Polish firms compared to Romanian firms, though it still remains considerable. However, Polish firms are in a better situation regarding the domestic market, which is able to absorb their collections.

Extent of own-brand production in the domestic market

Large CEE clothing firms do not have their origins in OPT relationships with foreign buyers. They all have long histories, their own-brand names and experience of exporting largely to the CMEA markets. After some time, the more advanced companies started to rejuvenate their brand names in order to grasp future export opportunities. As OEM production is significantly less profitable than OBM-domestic, they recognized that their long-term future lay in OBM-foreign.

Some Polish firms followed the advice of consulting firms to pursue opportunities for market segmentation; some developed their own OBM strategies. They have successively added new brands with different competitive power, control and reputation to their traditional brand names, and have succeeded in generating value from these investments. For example, P.1 divided its consumer segments according to income and complementary products and P.2 introduced a novelty into the domestic market by advertising its '100-way suits' for different occasions.

In Romania, firms R.1 and R.2 have added an entirely new brand to their traditional range. The old brand names were weak in the face of competition from cheap imports from other low-cost garment producing countries. The formation of different lines within new brands has been driven either by the changing CMT orders from foreign buyers (imitative) or by the firms' own designers (innovative). These improvements have been realized in a period of transition by utilizing the knowledge gained from OPT partnerships. However, only a handful of firms has managed to achieve this.

Extent of industrial networks with domestic companies

Industrial upgrading in national production networks involves vertical links between large and small firms and horizontal links between more advanced and less advanced large firms. When large companies establish OEM with a foreign buyer, they shift the production of these orders to small subsidiaries under their own management, but owned and controlled by the parent firm. This structure is exemplified by large Polish companies. Small firm partners frequently were integrated with large ones to form the giant state companies of the communist era, and then had been hived off during the transition period. Moreover, most of the linkages take place within the national market; from our sample firms, only P.1 is considering shifting part of its OBM-domestic production to low labour cost countries.[7] Within Romania larger companies have developed networks of subcontractors, which are independent firms, unlike the equity-linked subsidiaries in Poland. This enables them to meet the requirements of foreign buyers in terms of both capacity and costs, while differentiating their own high-quality, high-priced products. They still do not have such networks, though R.2 has plans to create one.

Horizontal networks have followed a somewhat different format. After launching a new brand in 1998, the vice-president of P.1 developed the idea of complementing the company's own products within this new brand with the products of other large Polish clothing firms. P.1 subcontracts to less advanced companies, to which it gives the designs and the materials, and cooperates with more advanced firms, to which it offers only suggestions concerning designs. All the companies producing for this brand have become licensees of P.1 for this particular brand (see Figure 7.3).

In Poland, similar network-building attempts by companies that have tried to diversify (e.g. P.4) rather than specialize (e.g. P.1) have failed.[8] Apart from the marketing cooperation of R.1, a shirt producer, with a tie producer no similar network formation has been observed in Romania. However, the shirt and tie producers are

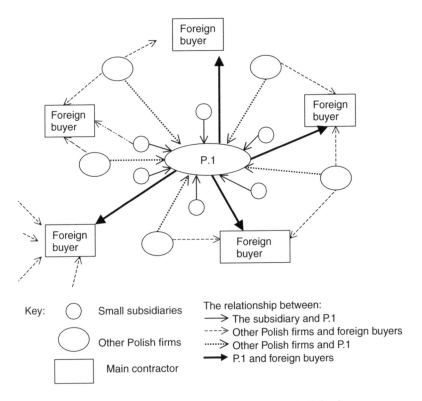

Figure 7.3 An illustration of production networks among agents in Poland.

Source: Author.

considering opening jointly owned shops for the distribution of their products, just as men's shirt and suit producers in Poland did in the mid-1990s.

Extent of relationships with universities, research institutes and market research and consulting firms

The relationships between clothing companies and organizations other than firms are determined by needs. According to our sample the pattern of relationships differs between the two countries. There appear to be more university and public research institute links in Romania than in Poland. New technology can only be accessed externally, under package purchases that include installation and training in the use of the machinery. If firms encounter serious problems they generally contact equipment suppliers. In Romania, once the warranty has expired, the textile-engineering faculty of the University of Iasi might be consulted or a textile industry R&D institute that has been reinstated since transition. Investments in new machinery are also discussed with these organizations, which provide information on the state of the art and where to find it, and also advise about where in the factory the new technology should be employed in order to get the maximum benefit, or indeed whether it is needed at all. While there is a specialist faculty for textiles and clothing in Łódź in Poland, none of the companies interviewed mentioned any kind of relationships with its members apart from recruiting graduates as production managers, technologists or designers. The academics at the University of Łódź lamented firms' lack of trust and interest in the scientific activities of the university, especially since the Central Textile and Clothing Research Institute in Poland closed down in the 1990s.

Romanian embassies in west European countries and state organizations in Bucharest play a bigger role by arranging events that allow Romanian firms the opportunity to meet potential foreign buyers. Local chambers of commerce also organize these kinds of meetings. There do not appear to be similar activities organized for Polish clothing firms.

Regular participation in international and national textile and clothing fairs facilitates the exchange of knowledge and acquisition of information about the latest machinery, fabrics and designs. Polish firms show their collections at the Poznan international fair twice a year where they get orders from retailers and meet new customers. Moreover, Polish companies are very concerned about their market share since they are in competition with one another, and work very closely with market research agencies. In the mid-1990s, the more advanced companies benefited from cooperation with consulting firms, but this cooperation has been discontinued.

The effects of network alignment in the Polish and Romanian textile sectors

In the early 1990s, the Romanian companies continued their OPT production, whereas the Polish companies advanced to the first stages of OEM. Then, in the mid- to late-1990s, the Poles became domestic-OBM producers, with their own 'designs for manufacturing'; produced by well-known and very professional Polish designers. The more advanced Romanian firms are just entering the domestic-OBM stage and still endeavouring to develop design skills and marketing and distribution systems, whereas the less advanced firms are a step behind (see Figure 7.4).

Technological advances, as one way of adapting to changes in network structures, have influenced process upgrading in Polish and Romanian firms. The more advanced Polish companies followed technological changes in the industry more closely in the late 1980s than their Romanian counterparts. The leading Polish companies have had their own CAD systems for 6–12 years; whereas even the

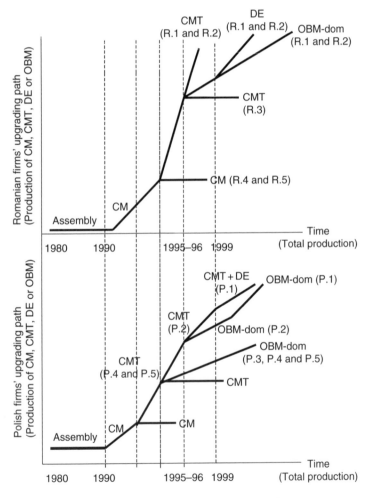

Figure 7.4 Upgrading path of Romanian and Polish clothing firms over time.

Source: Based on Garnsey (1998), and interview material.

more advanced Romanian companies have had these systems for only 2–3 years. However, even in the more advanced Polish firms, automatic cutting machines were introduced only 2–3 years ago. While at first sight Polish companies appear to be more competitive than Romanian ones, some qualification is needed. In the late 1980s Poland was much more open to links with the west than Romania. However, despite the late introduction of CAD systems in Romania, the distance between Romanian and Polish firms has narrowed.

In the early stages of process upgrading, companies focused on 'inter-organizational learning' with foreign customers, which has enabled them to upgrade rapidly from relatively simple to increasingly complex forms of international OEM arrangements. The first two stages of OEM relationships operate as 'on-the-job training' in terms of technological learning. Firms learn what machinery, sewing techniques and fabrics are needed for quality production.[9] Also, the foreign buyer is involved in the training of engineers and technicians and gives advice on the purchase of machinery, production, management and financing. A technician from the buyer, who visits for several months during the production of the ordered pieces to monitor quality, teaches employees how to do a particular task or how to use a particular machine[10] and participates in the problem-solving activities of the firm.[11]

This type of learning is apparent both in use of the machinery and in management. In terms of machinery, the dominant type of learning is 'learning by using' (Malerba 1992), through use of technology or learning on-the-job. Advisers from foreign buyers help to reorganize production lines and thereby increase efficiency and productivity, usually working directly with CAD unit personnel. Arguably, however, it is in the area of business skills that the CEE companies need to learn most and where they derive the greatest benefits from their relationships with buyers. They learn how to negotiate and execute contracts, organize divisions in the company, market and distribute products, etc. Therefore, the duration of and progress in learning is strongly related to management's abilities to develop close relationships with other parties, such as business partners, universities, consultants, etc. – that is, to develop linkage abilities.

In a number of respects Romanian companies appear to be making less progress than their Polish counterparts. This may be due to organizational differences. In Poland, the privatization process has modified the previous sectoral structure in such a way as to create new forms of multi-location domestic companies. Before transition there were big clothing enterprises throughout Poland with their own small satellites in the vicinity, whereas in Romania there was one central state enterprise, which hierarchically controlled all the clothing factories in Romania. Thus, Chandlerian multi-divisional organizational structures in Poland have enabled firms to cope with complexity. However, the hierarchical structure that was originated by the Romanian state was dismantled and stand-alone big companies have been created and left to cope with organizational problems with which they have no experience.

In contrast to Poland, the late integration of Romania into international production networks (IPNs) can partly be explained by delays and failures in privatization in Romania. The different sectoral structures in Poland and Romania during the communist regime are another factor. Finally, because of their poorer financial condition, the Romanian companies have fewer opportunities than their Polish counterparts.

More generally, it is clear that Romania suffered more during the communist era in terms of bureaucracy in management and outdated technology. Thus, Romanian firms show a greater propensity to follow a stylized pattern of upgrading, first opening up and then catching up with the rest of the world. Ongoing difficulties both in the financial sector and in markets do not help Romanian firms to focus on their own-brand production. Thus, they are, and will continue to be, locked into OEM relations for the next few years. It should be noted that some large Polish firms are in a similar situation as a result of the mis-management of companies by National Investment Funds, the appreciation of the zloty, the invasion of cheap clothing from the Far East and the increasing labour costs in Poland.

We can see a number of respects in which Romanian firms lag behind Polish firms. The more advanced Romanian firms are predominantly CMT producers and have only recently started to export their products directly. However, the more advanced Polish firms have been CMT producers as well as direct exporters for longer than their Romanian counterparts. Moreover, unlike Romanian firms, Polish firms have the skills necessary to make them eligible to hold licences from west European firms, such as Pierre Cardin, in the domestic market. Moreover, almost all companies have held the Woolmark licence for many years, as Polish customers consider it a guarantee of quality.

Paralleling Ernst's (1998) comparison of the Korean and Taiwanese electronics industries, Polish companies have focused more on the development of *own-brand* products and on a *European brand image* as a long-term goal, while Romanian firms have focused primarily on the continuous upgrading of their position as OEM suppliers. However, despite this emphasis by Polish companies on domestic-OBM, only 3 of the 5 companies studied have managed to increase its proportion relative to OEM. However, continuing competitive weaknesses *vis-à-vis* foreign producers – even in their domestic markets – compel them to continue OEM. For most Polish companies, therefore, this focus remains a major long-term target rather than an accomplished fact.

Ultimately, all clothing producers want to move from production to fashion design (i.e. functional upgrading). The more advanced Polish firms are making positive efforts towards this, while even the more advanced Romanian firms have not got beyond perceiving the need for effort.

The comparison depicted in Figure 7.4 shows the process of upgrading over time by coupling the firms with associated upgrading stages. The graph shows whether the firm stays in a steady state or moves on: passing into CMT from CM or staying in CM, passing into domestic-OBM while simultaneously continuing CMT (+ Direct Exporting (DE)) or staying in CMT.

The slopes are also important. They show the speed of changes in relative shares of the upgrading stages in the total production of the company.[12] At the top of the Romanian figure, for example, the steeper slope of CMT compared to OBM means that the share of CMT still surpasses the share of OBM-domestic in total production. The Polish figure tells us that the volume of OBM-domestic is increasing, whereas that of CMT is decreasing in more advanced firms only. Figure 7.4 shows the positioning of every firm in our sample. For instance, P.3 has nothing but OBM-domestic and DE and manages to survive due to its niche in a distinct segment, that is, lingerie.

Conclusions

This chapter shows the differences in the structural influences of buyer-driven global networks on the industrial upgrading of Polish and Romanian clothing firms. Both Polish and Romanian clothing firms see these global buyers as exemplars and experience more or less the same network relationships with them. The differences in their upgrading patterns are due primarily to the differences in their networks with other domestic organizations and in their capability development. As the level of accumulation of knowledge and skills differs among the firms, the pace and level of upgrading also differs. The upgrading pattern described in this chapter should not be taken as inevitable; some firms might skip some sequences. This means that some might move between or simultaneously engage in OEM and domestic-OBM, while others might focus only on OEM or on domestic-OBM. Consequently, it is not really a question of the positioning of countries on a single upgrading ladder; but rather that different upgrading ladders have been climbed in each country. There is no single pattern.

Overall it appears that Polish firms have been able to upgrade more effectively than their Romanian counterparts. Polish firms are stable at the second stage of OEM and show no tendency to form closer links with foreign buyers. Instead, they are gradually trying to loosen their ties and nurture their own brands. In contrast, Romanian firms are trying to deepen their relationships with foreign buyers and increase their customer base as much as possible.

It is interesting that the firms in the two countries exhibit rather different strategies. With respect to their domestic networks, Polish firms have a largely production-oriented approach, whereas Romanian firms exhibit a knowledge-seeking approach. Therefore, Polish firms develop close relationships only with other firms, whereas Romanian firms are in need of consultancy on both technical and in organizational issues and rely on universities and public research institutes. Indeed, while being stuck in OEM might lead some firms to be labelled as laggards, as the Romanian upgrading path shows, this does not necessarily mean that these firms lack the capabilities to upgrade. Other factors coming into play include the transfer of knowledge and technology within OEM partnerships and the use of domestic networks. Patterns here differ from firm to firm.

Annex

Table 7A.1 Information about the companies in the research sample

Company code	Year and method of privatization	No. of employees	Percentage of exports	Products
R.1	1996 – MEBO	Over 1,500	90	Men's shirts, ladies' blouses
R.2	1994 – MEBO	1,000–1,500	95	Women's outerwear
R.3	1995 – MBO	750–1,000	75–80	Men's/women's outerwear
R.4	1994 – direct privatization	900	92	Knitwear
R.5	1995 – direct privatization	1,000–1,250	96	Men's wear
P.1	1993 capital privatization	Over 1,500	11–25	Men's suits
P.2	1993 joined to NIF	750–1,000	60	Men's suits
P.3	1995 capital privatization	500–750	26–50	Lingerie
P.4	1992 joined to NIF	1,000–1,500	75	Women's outerwear
P.5	1991 (commercialization), then joined to NIF	1,000–1,500	73	Knitwear

Source: Questionnaires sent to the Polish and Romanian firms in November–December 2000.

Notes

1 Our fourth category differs from theirs: here managerial, as opposed to chain upgrading in Kaplinsky and Readman.
2 While the prolonged and sluggish privatization programmes have extended restructuring, ten years is still a short period for its completion. Moreover, in East Asian economies, upgrading has often gone on for 30–40 years.
3 Equity relationships consist of joint venture and minority or majority acquisitions; non-equity types of relationships consist of subcontracting, OEM, licensing, research consortia, strategic alliances and cooperation with competitors.
4 For abbreviations, please see the acronyms at the beginning of the book.
5 This mode of production was driven by EU regulations protecting the European textile industry (Cleanclothes 1999). OPT originated as a preferential trade regime granted by the EU during the 1970s for developing countries (Pellegrin 2000). It is through the extension of these regulations today that buyer companies in CMT relationships still do not leave the OEM producer firms total control over the choice of fabrics. Yet, most large CEE companies still use European fabrics, even in their own brandname production, to maintain high quality.
6 There are two basic shortcomings to this kind of relationship: possible exploitation of the renowned brand name of the local producer by the foreign retailer in the domestic market, and the push by the retailer to get same-quality garments with the brand of the OEM producer at a low cost.
7 Another example of this strategy is a Gdansk-based OBM, which has established its vertical networks in countries in the far east and distributes its designs in its own shops in Poland and other CEE countries (Stec 2003).
8 P.4, one of the well-known women's wear producers, decided to diversify into men's wear. It organized a network with other Polish men's wear producers. However,

it could not compete with established brand names and was forced to re-focus on women's wear.

9 For instance, the Polish companies in shirt production have licences from global brand-manufacturers to use the techniques required to maintain standards: they cover the seams with high-density overcast stitching, sew buttons with cross-stitches for long-fast guarantee, use HAI collars tailored and stiffened with a high stand and replaceable fins, and stitch collars and cuffs with 0.6 cm wide quilting (*Poznan Fair Magazine* 2001).

10 Sometimes the buyer provides specialized machines for the production of a particular seam, button, collar, etc., and rents it to the OEM producer for the duration of the production of the ordered pieces. Unless the OEM producer purchases the machine for its own-brand production, the buyer firm takes the machine back when the particular production ends.

11 As both sides develop good relations, when these technicians leave their company, they might bring the OEM producer as a supplier to their new company (interview with R.2).

12 The slope of each line can be defined as follows:

$$\frac{\text{change in production of upgrading stage}}{\text{change in total production}}$$

where the upgrading stage is CM, CMT, DE or OBM-domestic. Please refer to the titles of axes in the parenthesis where the slopes are the concern.

References

Cleanclothes Campaign (1999) *Romania-Factory visits*, cited February 2001, Available HTTP: <www.cleanclothes.org/publications/easteuroma.htm> (accessed 29.09.03).

Duruiz, L. and Yenturk Coban, N. (1988) *Technological and Structural Change in the Turkish Clothing Industry*, Istanbul: Turkish Social Science Association.

Ernst, D. (1998) 'Catching-up, crisis and truncated upgrading, evolutionary aspects of technological learning in East Asia's electronic industry', *DRUID Working Paper* No. 98-16.

Garnsey, E. (1998) 'A theory of early growth of the firm', *Industrial and Corporate Change*, 7: 523–56.

Gereffi, G. (1999) 'Industrial upgrading in the apparel commodity chain: what can Mexico learn from East Asia?' Paper presented at the International Conference on Business Transformation and Social Change in East Asia, Taichung, Taiwan: Tunghai University of East Asian Societies and Economies, June 10–11.

Hakansson, H. (1987) 'Introduction', in H. Hakansson (ed.) *Industrial Technology Development, a Network Approach*, London: Croom Helm.

Hobday, M. (1995) 'East Asian latecomer firms: learning the technology of electronics', *World Development*, 23: 1171–93.

Kaplinsky, R. and Readman, J. (2001) 'How can SME producers serve global markets and sustain income growth?', *University of Sussex Institute of Development Studies Papers*, Working Paper.

Malerba, F. (1992) 'Learning by firms and incremental technical change', *Economic Journal*, 102: 845–59.

Pellegrin, J. (2000) 'German production networks in Central/Eastern Europe: competitive breakthroughs and old ghosts', in J. Lorentzen (ed.) *Globalization in Emerging Markets*, Basingstoke: Macmillan.

Poznan Fair Magazine (2001).

Stec, A. (2003) 'Tak Chinski krawiec kraje, jak w Polsce sie sprzedaje (As the Polish market sells, so the Chinese tailor cuts)', *Gazeta Wyborcza*, 10 February.

Yoruk, D.E. (2003) 'Impacts of inter-organisational networks on industrial upgrading at the firm level: evidence from the Romanian food processing industry', *New Europe College Regional Program Yearbook 2001–2002*, Bucharest: New Europe College, Institute for Advanced Study. Available HTTP: <http//library.nec.ro/papers/regional2001–2002/yearbook.htm> (accessed 29.9.03).

8 The electronics industry in central and eastern Europe

An emerging production location in the alignment of networks perspective

Slavo Radosevic

Introduction

During the socialist period, central and eastern Europe (CEE) countries were relatively backward in terms of production and especially in the diffusion of electronics technologies. However, after ten years of post-socialist transformation and integration with the European Union (EU) economies, central Europe has emerged as an important new location for this industry.[1] In 1999, the overall value of electronics production in CEE was $26 bn, of which $10.7 bn was in exports.

In this chapter, we try to explain the emergence of a new production and export location in world electronics. Our main question is what factors explain the emergence of CEE as a new production location? Our main argument, building on the work of Hobday *et al.* (2001) and Kim and von Tunzelmann (1998) (see Chapter 2 in this volume), which is based on the analysis of CEE electronics, is that we need to move beyond a simplified argument that focuses on one or two dimensions (be it states or markets). We explain the emergence of electronics in CEE through the alignment of networks framework, originally developed by Kim and von Tunzelmann (1998) in their analysis of the Taiwanese electronics industry. Within this framework, we explain the rise of CEE electronics production as the result of interaction between several factors, including multinational company (MNC) strategies and the actions of local and national governments. EU demand is the dominant pull factor, but EU accession plays only a secondary role in this process. This multi-level and multi-factor framework represents useful heuristics that can accommodate the evolutionary character of the changes taking place in this sector.

In the next section, we briefly review evidence of the emergence of CEE as a production location significant in the global electronics industry. The section explains the emergence of this new production location using a network alignment framework. The conclusions summarize the key arguments and ideas.

The emergence of CEE as a new production location: review of the evidence

The big technology gaps in CEE electronics before 1989 and the limited purchasing power of the domestic market, compounded by a lack of finance, meant that the only viable option was the opening of the CEE market to electronics imports. The sudden exposure to imports from Asia led, with only a few exceptions, to the disappearance of domestic producers. Illegal imports further aggravated an already difficult situation. For example, in Poland, domestic companies' sales in the sector almost halved in twelve months, falling from $725 mn in 1990 to $480 mn in 1991.[2] The majority of CEE electronics producers did not emerge from transition in anything like their earlier form, if at all.

However, the demise of the socialist electronics industry did not lead to the disappearance of this industry in CEE. After the mid-1990s, some CEE countries, for example, Hungary, the Czech Republic and Poland, gradually began to be accepted in the supply base of large foreign electronics companies. This was primarily due to factors such as cheap skilled labour and their proximity to the EU market and, in segments such as television, was based on local markets. The result was both local and export market-oriented production.

CEE thus emerged as the new production location for electronics. In 2000, total CEE electronics production reached $20.2 bn, which is still below the production level in Mexico ($27.9 bn), the bulk of this growth having been achieved in the late 1990s. Table 8.1 ranks selected countries according to the volume of their electronics production in 1999.

Growth in CEE has been confined to a few countries, with Hungary having 45 per cent of the share in 2000[3] (Figure 8.1). However, it seems that the process of expansion is established with other countries joining in.

The emergence of CEE as a new production location for electronics is thus a recent phenomenon, with momentum gathering pace from the mid-1990s. Moreover in a ranking of thirteen countries with double-digit growth rates in the 1996–2001 period, there are seven CEE countries.

Figure 8.2 depicts the share of electronics production in apparent consumption (production + imports − exports) for a group of countries. This is indicative of the extent to which a country has become a production location relative to its market. The higher the share of production in relation to consumption the greater the scope for development as a production location. Of the CEE countries, only Hungary has a share above 100 per cent. Hungary, which ranks very high in absolute and relative terms compared to the other CEE countries, still has great potential for expanding as an export and production location and achieving shares similar to those of Ireland or Singapore. Although Hungary's integration into the global electronics production network has been very rapid, it is by no means extraordinary in global terms. Also, the rankings of other CEE countries show that their potential for expanding into important production locations is far from exhausted.

Table 8.2 shows that CEE has relatively diversified production across most segments, except to some degree in three countries (Hungary, Czech Republic and Poland). Hungary's strength lies in electronics data processing (EDP), which accounts for almost 50 per cent of total production, or $3.3 bn. Two other segments, consumer electronics ($1.5 bn) and components ($1.2 bn), are significant but clearly do not match the production of parts for computers (hard disk drives, monitors, peripherals).

Table 8.1 Electronics production in selected countries[a,b] (mn $)

	1996	1997	1998	1999	2000	Average annual rate of growth 1999–96
Bulgaria	76	73	90	104	117	9.2
Croatia	191	198	208	205	241	1.8
Czech R	1,109	1,157	1,296	1,541	1,706	9.7
Hungary	1,780	3,415	4,988	6,833	9,178	71.0
Poland	1,975	2,342	2,697	2,692	2,743	9.1
Romania	559	503	509	800	952	10.8
Slovakia	324	380	599	726	869	31.0
Slovenia	492	488	514	483	522	−0.5
CE	6,506	8,556	10,901	13,384	16,328	26.4
Russia	1,748	1,819	2,231	2,836	3,224	15.6
Ukraine	426	395	429	551	697	7.3
	2,174	2,214	2,660	3,387	3,921	13.9
CEE	8,680	10,770	13,561	16,771	20,249	23.3
China	34,985	41,929	52,456	60,818	71,344	18.5
Malaysia	29,541	29,827	29,369	39,211	49,333	8.2
Singapore	43,652	43,426	37,851	40,985	50,875	−1.5
S. Korea	48,312	49,136	41,144	57,857	67,337	4.9
Taiwan	32,212	31,731	33,680	41,209	46,712	7.0
Mexico	15,395	16,862	23,072	25,260	27,983	16.0

Source: Reed Electronics Research, *The Yearbook of World Electronics Data 2001/2 and 1999/2000*, Vol. 4, East Europe and World Summary.

Notes
a 1996–99 are current figures at current exchange rates.
b 2000 are estimates at 1999 constant values and exchange rates.

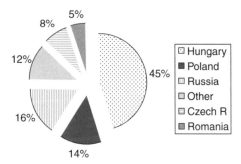

Figure 8.1 CEE electronics industry.
Source: *Reed Electronics Yearbook, 2002.*

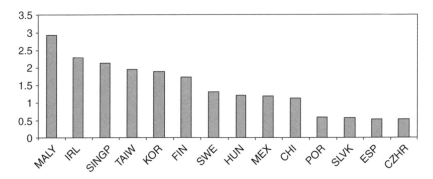

Figure 8.2 Electronics: share of production in apparent consumption, 1999.
Source: Author based on *Reed Electronics Yearbook,* 2001.

The majority of CEE exports (56 per cent) come from Hungary and are in EDP, components and consumer electronics (Table 8.3). Exports in other segments (communications and military, telecoms, medical and industrial electronics) are much smaller, reflecting a relatively low technological level of electronics in CEE. In telecommunications, no CEE is clearly specialized. This reflects poor technological capabilities in this area in the past, as well as a primarily domestic market orientation of foreign telecom equipment producers.

There are three groups of companies that constitute the electronics landscape in CEE: Original equipment manufacturing (OEM) electronics producers, contract manufacturers and local electronics firms. Chief amongst the OEM electronics producers in the region is Philips. It has built up an extensive network of factories across the region, in Hungary, the Czech Republic and Poland. Others have followed Philips's lead including Siemens, which has established subsidiaries in all CEE countries, with the main focus on telecommunications equipment. In the mid-1990s, a number of US firms including IBM and Motorola consolidated their presence in the region and by the end of the decade a number of Japanese firms had established manufacturing capabilities.

Contract manufacturers, or electronics manufacturing service companies, have emerged as important new players in world electronics. They entered early into CEE and this sector is growing at a high rate. From 1993 to 2000 the value of contract-manufacturing services in CEE rose from $0.5 bn to $4 bn, a rate similar to other European regions (see Table 8.4). However, most of this growth took place in the period from 1996 onwards.

Indigenous electronics manufacturers generally are a smaller element in the sector though there are some exceptions. Perhaps the most notable is Videoton, one of the largest firms in Hungary (Radosevic and Yoruk 2001). Before 1989, Videoton was a producer of numerous final products in the electronics area. On having its survival threatened, it was obliged to close most of its lines and following privatization continued only with the manufacture of loudspeaker systems, colour televisions and defence equipment. Videoton's major strategic shift is the

Table 8.2 Electronics production by segments, 1999, $M (%)

	EDP	Office equip.	Control and instrum.	Medical and industrial	Comms and military	Telecoms	Consumer	Components	Total
Bulgaria	4.8	7.7	9.6	4.8	4.8	10.6	32.7	25.0	100.0
Croatia	2.9	2.4	17.1	12.7	6.8	37.1	0.5	20.5	100.0
Czech R	10.4	1.9	13.0	7.1	11.2	11.0	15.6	29.7	100.0
Hungary	48.9	0.0	2.2	1.7	3.5	2.9	22.7	18.1	100.0
Poland	11.5	0.7	10.8	2.1	8.9	20.1	26.6	19.4	100.0
Romania	23.8	2.0	15.0	9.0	10.0	26.3	7.9	6.1	100.0
Slovakia	27.5	1.9	5.5	12.9	13.8	13.8	9.5	15.0	100.0
Slovenia	9.5	1.4	19.3	4.6	7.7	22.8	14.3	20.5	100.0
Russia	17.6	3.2	10.6	7.1	14.1	14.1	11.1	22.2	100.0
Ukraine	16.3	1.5	9.1	3.8	18.1	23.6	5.8	21.8	100.0
CEE	28.9	1.2	7.7	4.3	8.3	11.6	18.4	19.6	100.0

Source: Reed Electronics Research, *The Yearbook of World Electronics Data 2001/2*, Volume 4, East Europe and World Summary.

Table 8.3 Export of the CEE electronics industry, 1999

	EDP	Components	Consumer	Comms and Military	Telecoms	Medical and Industrial	Total
CEE export – total	4,006.0	2,923.0	2,441.0	466.0	301.0	114.0	10,793.0
Top exporter	Hungary	Hungary	Hungary	Russia	Poland	Czech R	Hungary
% of CEE export	82.8	33.3	60.8	40.1	19.3	41.2	56.5
Second exporter		Czech R		Hungary	Slovenia		
% of CEE exports		31.6		38.2	15.0		

Source: Reed Electronics Research, *The Yearbook of World Electronics Data 2001/2 and 1999/2000*, Volume 4, East Europe and World Summary.

Table 8.4 Electronics contract manufacturing in Europe (bn US$)

	1993	2000	2003 (est.)
CEE	0.519	3.94	12.923
UK and Ireland	1.468	5.341	6.436
Germany, Austria and Switzerland	0.907	2.515	5.21
France and Benelux	0.983	3.231	5.127
Scandinavia	0.302	3.933	4.979
Spain	0.228	0.694	1.698

Source: CzechInvest Study on Electronics based on data of Enterprise Ireland 2000.

expansion of contract-manufacturing, which today accounts for the majority of Videoton's revenues. Exports based on contract-manufacturing arrangements represent 80 per cent of total sales. Videoton's main areas of production are electronics, electrical appliances and automotive supplies.

CEE electronics: explaining the emerging production location

The emergence of central Europe as a new production location in electronics cannot be explained only by looking at available resources or factor endowments. While some factors such as labour costs and proximity carry significant weight, it is difficult to understand country differences in the penetration of foreign direct investment (FDI) by looking only at country resources.

In order to understand the dynamics of CEE electronics modernization, we need to introduce the governance or organizational aspects of the international integration of this sector. We assume that resources such as human capital, proximity or labour costs are only potential advantages which, in order to be realized, require sympathetic sectoral governance. Sectoral governance in this case is a complex set of organizational relationships between different firms (foreign and domestic), local and national governments, which must be mutually consistent with one another for the sector to grow.

We interpret the emergence of a new location as a multi-dimensional phenomenon, which requires the simultaneous existence of several factors, and complementarities among these factors. Whether complementarities will be realized depends on the governance dimension of international production integration.

This problem has been approached in the literature as a dichotomy: whether it is markets or states that are more important in generating growth through integration in international production networks (see Chapter 3 in this volume by von Tunzelmann). In the case of CEE countries, the market perspective has been dominant in transition economics, which argues that the progress in transition or convergence towards a market economy is essential for growth.

Hobday *et al.* (2001) go a step further in bringing company strategies, both local and foreign, into the state-market debate, which significantly changes our understanding of industry dynamics. Although this framework is nearer to a more realistic understanding of the drivers in the process of sectoral modernization, it still omits a variety of other factors, factors that also play quite an important role in CEE countries (see Chapter 2 in this volume). We think that the alignment of network framework as developed in Chapter 3 of this volume offers new opportunities for understanding successes or failures in industrial modernization through international production networks.

Before we analyse integration of CEE electronics using the network alignment framework two elements need to be considered. First, technological opportunities and structural change in electronics determine the prospects for network alignment in CEE. Second, network alignment takes place with given resources (physical, human, technological and organizational), which, through network alignment, are mobilized, shared and recombined. Hence, the nature and quality of resources strongly affects the prospects for network alignment. In the remainder of this chapter, we outline how the main structural changes in electronics industry have affected prospects for integration of CEE into international production networks in electronics, and discuss the major factors or endowments which operate as resources for network alignment. In the section 'Network alignment elements', we analyse the elements of network alignment and try to understand their interaction.

Structural change in electronics industry: context for network alignment in central and eastern Europe

From a location perspective the main feature of structural change in electronics is the secular trend towards a dispersed supply base or away from exclusive concentration on east Asia. Globalization, which once seemed to mean that most of the world's manufacturing jobs would move to Asia, is now forcing Asian companies to expand outside the region. This, and the spread of the contract-manufacturing model in electronics, have been strong contributory factors to the emergence of CEE as a production location, and parallels the emergence of Mexico as another important emerging location.

This location aspect of structural change in electronics is very favourable for CEE. However, the location aspect is related to several other aspects of structural change in electronics, which we highlight in this section.

First, there is a long-term trend in electronics towards moving from a highly localized to a highly globalized production pattern, involving a considerable reduction in the number of factories and the establishment of an extensive network of contract-manufacturing partners.

Second, an important feature of this new model of industrial organization is the decoupling of manufacturing from product development and their dispersion across firms and national boundaries (Ernst 2000). The rise of electronics manufacturing services is a clear indication of this trend. However, as Ernst (2000) points out geographic dispersion is heavily concentrated in a few specialized local clusters. Third, in order to resolve the paradox between increased dispersion and concentration, companies are focusing on reducing costs in the integral supply chain through outsourcing, relocation to low cost sites, reduction in the number of suppliers, common standards to improve flexibility and a global product range.

Fourth, competitive pressures are forcing electronics companies not only to move production from expensive to cheaper areas, but also to locate close to main markets in order to achieve flexibility. These drivers generate the need for flexible-manufacturing structures, which requires common standards, which, in turn, are a great incentive to transfer process technologies in order to attain these standards. Hence, CEE countries are well placed to acquire production capabilities given their skill levels.

Factor endowments and their relevance to the electronics industry

Network (mis)alignment is a problem of inter-organizational relationships or networks that cut across several networks. This governance problem does not operate in the abstract or unrelated to factor endowments or resources. Hence, the application of a network alignment framework in which to understand the emergence of the electronics industry in CEE, requires that we clearly distinguish between factors and organizational capabilities. By factors, we mean the available physical, geographical and human factors or resources, which in the international economy operate as attractors for foreign investors.

What makes the concept of network alignment distinctive is an implicit assumption that network alignment depends on the organizational capabilities of actors and networks, and on complementarities among different networks within which actors operate. We can think of factors as the resources that networks and actors can mobilize in order to generate capabilities. Only when networks are developed and complement each other may we expect that growth in the globalized economy will take place.

Any regional (national) comparative advantage or disadvantage as expressed in factors or resources is conditional upon the (non)existence of networks and network organizers. It is only they who may or may not turn this conditional advantage into a real absolute advantage. While this may be obvious in a local, regional context, the alignment of networks perspective suggests that this problem is also endemic to a globalized economy whose growth is dependent on MNCs' strategies interacting with local and national networks. Factors favourable to growth are only conditional advantages, which can operate only when network organizers and the alignment of different networks (local, national, MNCs) are in place. Advantageous determinants may be converted from conditional into real advantages only through network mobilization and the alignment of different networks.

In the case of CEE, research on FDI suggests that there are several factors that operate as points of attraction for foreign investors and that are the basis for the decisions of MNCs. The local market, proximity to the EU and low labour costs are usually the major motives revealed by surveys and econometric research for FDI (for an overview see Holland *et al.* 2000).

Table 8.5 summarizes the assessment of the quality of different factors that are relevant to electronics which we discuss briefly here.

Local market in electronics

CEE countries are small markets, in terms of both population and purchasing power. However, central European economies compare much better as production locations (Figure 8.2). In this respect, central Europe has ridden its socialist legacy remarkably well and the share of the information and communication technologies (ICT) sector in GDP in these economies has already matched the share in the southern EU countries.[4] Moreover, the share of the ICT sector in the Czech Republic and Hungary is equal to or above the EU average (Mickiewicz and Radosevic 2001). However, in terms of information technology (IT) expenditure per capita central Europe is substantially lagging behind the EU average. The per capita gap in IT is much wider than the income per capita gap.

Table 8.5 Quality of factors of relevance for electronics industry

Factor	Quality of factors
Local market	Limited and unsophisticated local demand
Labour	Large pool of skilled labour with the second level education
Education and skills	Generally favourable with varying emerging constraints in sector specific skills
R&D and engineering	Quite favourable
IT infrastructure	Varies greatly across region
Proximity to EU	Important attractor

Source: Author.

Labour cost

FDI surveys often highlight labour costs as an important motivation for locating in CEE. However, a more analytical approach would suggest that it is not nominal wages that attract investors, but efficiency wages or nominal wages in relation to labour productivity. The analysis of Rojec and Jaklič (Chapter 11 in this volume) supports this view, but also gives a more subtle understanding of wages as a determinant of FDI. Their argument is that investors are concerned with increasing the value added per labour cost. Hence, they look for locations where the labour force is able to produce the expected amount of value added per employee with given production techniques, but at lower labour cost per employee.

There is considerable evidence that firms have relocated to CEECs on the basis of labour cost. However, in some electronics segments central Europe is not able to produce at sufficiently low labour costs given the value-added level that it generates. As a result, rising costs, including unit labour cost, in some central European countries are forcing the shift of low assembly jobs to China[5] (Table 8.6). Also, some cases suggest that we may expect relocation to the east of CEE, that is, to the Ukraine and Romania. For example, Flextronics is subcontracting some of its production to the Ukraine, where labour costs are less than one-quarter of Hungary's. For contract manufacturers such as Flextronics, the search for greater efficiency will not stop at the Hungarian border and it will be only a matter of time before we see further expansion of electronic assembly to Ukraine and Romania.

R&D and design capacities

Until the mid-1990s, overall expenditure on R&D in CEE countries had been decreasing sharply. Since then expenditure has stabilized or even started to grow again (Radosevic and Auriol 1999). However, R&D intensity in the ICT sector (R&D/Value Added) in CEE is very low.

Among the big investors in the electronics industry, firms primarily interested in telecommunications have invested in central European R&D. Their activities are focused around software, which seems to be abundant in CEE. Software engineers in central Europe, in particular in Hungary, the Czech Republic and Poland, have not moved to other countries.[6] It is estimated that Hungary has around 10,000 software engineers, with only 500 having left the country. In Hungary, Nokia opened three R&D centres specializing in mobile switching and wireless software. The Hungarian R&D hub is second only to the hub at the corporate headquarters in Finland. Ericsson runs a software centre developing ATM data transmission technologies and wireless applications. So far however this pattern has not been replicated in other sectors of electronics.

ICT infrastructure

The information and telecommunication infrastructure is an important economic activity in itself as well as being an essential prerequisite for the growth of electronics.

Table 8.6 Examples of relocations in European electronics in 2000/2001

Company	From	Status	To	Year	Activity	No of lay-offs
Relocations from UK to CEE						
SMK, Japan	UK	closure	Hungary	2000	Mobile phone batteries	
Sony	Wales, UK	closure	Hungary	2000	TV sets and monitors	
Panasonic, Japan	Wales, UK	closure	Czech R	2000	TV sets	2,000
Alps Electric	England, UK	downsizing	Czech R	2001	TV sets	400
Alps Electric	Scotland, UK	closure	Czech R	2001	PCB assembly	120
Celestica	England, UK	closure	Czech R	2001	PCB assembly	570
Celestica	England, UK	closure	Czech R	2001	PCB assembly	450
					est.	4,000
Electronics: relocations from CEE						
Mannesmann	Hungary	closure	China	2000	Car audio plant	1,000
Ericsson/ Elcoteq	Hungary	discontinued	China	2000	Mobile phones	
Ericsson/ Elcoteq	Estonia	discontinued	China	2000	Mobile phones	
Flextronics	Hungary	downsizing	Ukraine	2001	Subcontracting sub-assembly work	
Lexmark	Czech R	closure		2001	Printed circuit boards	121
					est.	1,500

Source: Business press.

The gap in diffusion of IT and telecommunications between central Europe and the EU was huge in the early 1990s. As a result of privatization and liberalization in this area (both policies still being gradually implemented) and rising demand, which is also partly driven by foreign investments, this gap has decreased but is still substantial. In terms of the number of telephone mainlines per capita, central Europe is clearly at the bottom of the European ranking (Mickiewicz and Radosevic 2001). Moreover, the sophistication of the telecoms infrastructure varies greatly among the central European economies as indicated by the share of ISDN lines.

Education and skills

The structure of education in central Europe is compressed on the edges, with low shares of both least educated and people with higher education. The low share of economically active population with third level education in CEE countries (with the exception of Estonia) may represent difficulties in absorption and diffusion of new IT-based technologies in services and industry, especially in the adoption of IT. On the other hand, the large share of second-level education may guarantee sufficient capacity in use of well established IT (though the high proportion of vocational education at this level may present problems in economy-wide restructuring). The favourable structure of the general level of education in central Europe is a necessary but not sufficient condition from the point of view of the absorption and diffusion of IT. It must be accompanied by training and retraining programmes.

Proximity to EU vs flexibility as a factor in the electronics industry

The proximity of central Europe to the EU is often highlighted as an advantage for locating electronics activities. The business press suggests that producers are forced to build factories close to markets. However, proximity does not seem to be as important in electronics as, say, in automobiles. Electronics enterprises appear to adopt a more global approach and to buy on a much more international basis and for them flexibility is much more important. For example, a survey of EU contractors (EU 1997) in electronics cites one of the main reasons for subcontracting as being flexibility in terms of volume supplied. Geographical proximity figures as the least important factor in a subcontracting relationship. The emphasis on flexibility arises from the need for speed or time-to-market. This explains the rise in contract manufacturing, which can improve delivery times and reduce costs.

Network alignment elements

Although structural changes in electronics work to the advantage of CEE as an emerging location, they cannot by themselves explain either the scale or the scope of this phenomenon. Also, factors or resources operate only as potential advantages, which require network organizers, and complementary interests between global, national, supranational and local networks to be realized. In order to understand the pattern of integration of CEE countries into international electronics networks we need to introduce the governance dimension. The alignment of networks framework explicitly takes into account the governance dimension. Table 8.7 summarizes the main state of the different elements of this framework and assesses the potential for their alignment or complementarities.

Multinational companies

Structural changes in the electronics industry induced companies to respond strategically by outsourcing to achieve flexibility and faster time-to-market. In the EU market, EU companies have become increasingly exposed to Japanese competition via their subsidiaries, which forced them to shift production to CEE in order to remain competitive.

Table 8.7 Assessing the potential for network alignment in CEE electronics

Network alignment, elements	Quality of networks and actors	Complementarities for network alignment
MNCs	First movers (ex Philips, Samsung), contract manufacturers (ex Flextronics)	Low cost strategies Pressure for flexibility
Domestic enterprises: ex-socialist electronics conglomerates	With the exception of Videoton and few others very weak restructuring agents	Privatization and inherited gaps have prevented their active engagement
SMEs	No clear picture emerged	Potentially the weakest actor in generating complementarities
State administrative capability	Capability for strategic FDI or subcontracting policy varies greatly	Only Hungary and Czech Republic governments have engaged in complementary actions
Government incentives (upfront advantages)	General and specific incentives are favourable	Favourable impacts in the case of tailor-made incentive packages for strategic investors
Local governments	Entrepreneurial actor	Strong interest in maintaining employment and increasing incomes
EU demand	Important attractor	Will continue to operate as important attractor
EU accession	Secondary factor	May hinder growth of free-export zone
Overall assessment	Varies greatly across countries	Operate favourably in Hungary and the Czech Republic

Source: Author.

The EU companies Philips, Siemens, Alcatel and Ericsson, followed by the Korean firm Samsung, were the first to respond to the strategic opportunities offered by the opening of CEE. In just a few years, Philips managed to establish a network of seventeen subsidiaries in Hungary. Korean Samsung established a plant to produce televisions, while Siemens established subsidiaries in all CEE countries.

Companies' strategies that deepen linkages with the local economy are essential for network alignment. Unfortunately, case study evidence in electronics is still very poor at indicating the exact extent of local sourcing. The structure in electronics is less pyramidal than in the car industry, which limits the extent of local subcontracting. The business press suggests that networking is mainly confined to subsidiaries and parent firms, or to subsidiaries in other countries. This may not only be the result of weaknesses of the CEE supply base but also may be a feature of partial subcontracting in electronics. There is patchy evidence that local sourcing is confined to low cost components like plastic and mechanical parts.

Domestic enterprises

Local enterprises do not figure much in the complementing and opportunity exploiting strategies of MNCs, which arise from integration into EU markets. This is the most serious handicap to CEE's deeper industry integration, and largely reflects differences in historical heritage across CEE. Large ex-socialist electronics conglomerates were lagging behind in terms of technology, finance and market access. Deficiencies in resources were often compounded by protracted privatization procedures, which led to a strategic stalemate that further deepened their crisis. Indeed it is unlikely that 'local champions' in electronics or 'blue chips' will emerge for quite some time. Domestic firms, with a few exceptions, are likely to play a dependent role in global production networks. This may not be a problem since very efficient branch plants have been established in CEE. Perhaps driven by contract manufacturers (turnkey suppliers) we may see some clustering of different-sized local firms.

CEE has comparatively better developed resources (especially human capital), than organizational capabilities at firm and government level. Where they exist at the firm level, as in the case of Videoton, or at government level, as in the case of the Czech Agency for FDI, outcomes are visible. To have a strong local supply base a country must also have local network organizers, that is, companies that are capable of organizing local supply chains.

Small and medium-sized enterprises

Local sourcing in which small and medium-sized enterprises (SMEs) would play an important role usually takes time to develop. Unfortunately, we do not have systematic evidence of the extent of local sourcing in CEE electronics. Local sourcing beyond local subsidiaries is limited but has nevertheless started.

An important reason for limited local sourcing is that the quality of local SMEs has not yet reached the required level. Most SMEs were established in the last decade and are too new to have the necessary experience. The dynamic layer of SMEs is essential in order to generate a culture of electronics industry and innovation. If innovation surveys can serve as a guide, they show that the share of innovative SMEs in CEE countries is extremely small when compared to the EU.

Government policies

Although it is difficult to measure the effects of government policies the history of CEE electronics during the 1990s shows that policies do matter. In the Czech Republic and Hungary, which are leading locations for electronics, government policies have been important in understanding the patterns and timing of investments.

To understand the actions of central European governments, it is useful to classify policies into three categories: general incentives, specific incentives and strategic FDI policies.

Electronics, like other sectors, benefited from the general incentives offered to foreign investors in CEE countries. Preferential tax rates are being introduced in all CEE countries. The more that specific support polices are in place, the greater their potential to influence the decisions of investors. Two models of specific support are present in central European electronics: special economic zones (SEZ) and industrial parks.

The Hungarian government was the first to offer tax holidays and to set up free-trade zones, which meant that exporting companies paid no duties on either the components they imported or on the finished goods they shipped abroad. Many companies are set up in customs-free zones, meaning the import of supplies and equipment from any destination is tax-free. In Poland, the fifteen SEZ are the main incentives for foreign investors. SEZ are not compatible with EU competition policy and the government has modified the principles of their functioning to make them compatible with EU laws.

In addition to general and specific policies, the central European electronics sector, similar to the automotive industry, abounds with cases of individual incentive packages or arrangements with investors that are considered to be of strategic importance for national governments. Again, Hungary has, until recently, been the leading country in this respect, until 1998 when the Czech investment agency took a very active approach to FDI in electronics. In comparison to Hungary, the Czech Republic was late in introducing incentives and was perceived by potential investors as uncompetitive. With the change of government in 1996, CzechInvest, the foreign investment promotion agency, managed to increase the incentives. Moreover, the agency has established six overseas offices, with the latest one in California's Silicon Valley to attract high-tech, electronics and IT investors to the Czech Republic.[7]

Effective government policy should strike a balance between general incentives, specific incentives and strategic FDI policies. General incentives appear to be insufficient and not to be matching what individual investors expect or need. Putting the emphasis on only strategic incentive packages may not produce positive effects. For example, there is an opinion that too much UK government money has been aimed at high-profile inward investment opportunities through individualized incentive packages which, with exceptions, do little to raise the skill levels of the workforce (Deans 2002).

Some CEE governments have become aware that using incentives only as a means of attracting FDI may not be sufficient to ensure positive effects on the local economy and generate linkages with local firms. Therefore, they have embarked recently on programmes aimed at increasing local sourcing. The Hungarian government launched the 'Integrator Programme', a programme to assist small- and medium-sized companies, which supply MNCs operating within Hungary. CzechInvest has launched the Czech Supplier Development Programme, which is designed to help manufacturers increase their local content and is focused on the electronics sector as its first priority. This programme, with \$2.5 mn funding from the EU and the state budget, should raise the number of parts foreign investors purchase from Czech firms from the current 5 to 25 per cent or even 30 per cent.[8, 9]

Local governments

Local governments in CEE, jointly with MNCs, have become the most active agents for integrating FDI into the local economy. General and specific incentives on their own will not prompt MNCs to set up in CEE, but the favourable attitude of local governments willing to receive their manufacturing business is very appealing. Involvement of local government is the essential ingredient in strategic FDI policy.

EU policies and network alignment

European policy in electronics has been to trade imports for FDI, that is, Europe discouraged imports but tolerated and often 'directed' FDI (Linden 1998). Therefore, both US and Japanese electronics firms have made substantial direct investments in order to establish themselves as local producers in Europe. CEE countries that signed European Agreements have been affected by local content rules in many sectors, especially in the automotive industry. However, it seems that, due to the partial nature of subcontracting in electronics, the local content policy does not present an obstacle to non-EU foreign investors exporting to the EU from CEE.

The proximity and size of the EU market operate as strong attractors to locate in CEE. While MNCs were the key organizers or pushers of this process, EU demand during the 1990s determined the strength of the pull force. The overwhelming orientation of CEE electronics firms towards the EU makes the entire electronics sector very vulnerable to changes in EU demand. In this respect, growth in Russia may be seen as a necessary balance. However, once it happens it will very likely force CEE companies to move up the value chain as some of its assembly operations may one day move to Ukraine and to Russia.

EU accession is usually perceived as an important factor in motivating investors into CEE. Moreover, there is econometric evidence which suggests that the EU announcements on accession have had an important effect on investment decisions (Beavan and Estrin 2000). Even so, case study evidence suggests that the accession process plays a secondary role as the effective obstacles to trade and FDI have already been eliminated. In addition, the concentration of electronics on only three central European countries suggests that the effects of accession are either different across different candidate countries or are unrelated to the expansion of FDI in electronics. In cases of special or free economic zones, accession may slow down the process of investment as it means governments will lose an instrument which, thus far, has seemed important in the development of electronics in the CEE countries.

Morphology of networks and network organizers

As pointed out earlier, factors or resources alone do not explain network alignment. Favourable factors are only a conditional advantage, which operates only when network organizers and the alignment of different networks are in place. Favourable resources or factors may be transformed from conditional into real advantages only through network mobilization and the alignment of different networks. The alignment of networks framework helps us to understand which are the actors and networks involved and how their interactions influence international production integration in a specific sector.

However, Table 8.7 which presents network alignment elements still does not indicate who is the major actor or which is the dominant network. It assumes that all nodes of the framework are equally important. However, in reality, this is far from true. In order to understand the potential for network alignment, and to support complementarities between different networks and actors, the power structure of local networks should be recognized and these networks evaluated as to their objectives. As Benett and Krebs (1994) point out, a given network does not imply that all agents are equally important; often only one agent is the key animator of development (p. 132). The structure of power and control within networks is important in indicating the main network organizers.

The content of networking or, in our case, the strategies of actors, must be addressed as identical networks can function positively or negatively for economic or other performance reasons according to what is communicated (Fine 1999: 7). A great deal of the change that occurs in networks arises from single actors functioning as change agents or network organizers. The strategies of key actors will strongly shape the morphology of networks.

Radosevic (1999) concludes that network organizers in the post-socialist era could be any actor with the necessary capability and resources – a user or supplier firm, a bank, a holding company or a financial–industrial group, a foreign trade organization, a design institute, a foreign firm or even the state or regional administration. However, given the managerial, financial and technology gaps in CEE (Radosevic 1999) it is foreign companies that, for the time being, are the most active network organizers in CEE.

In the electronics industry the main driver of network alignment are MNCs (Figure 8.3). MNCs play a major role in shaping the way CEE integrates into global networks in electronics. However, EU demand is crucial in pulling MNCs towards further integration of CEE into their production networks.

Two other factors that are important for network alignment are the actions of local governments, specific incentives and the actions of national government. When compared to other regions, local industry networks, including large and small firms in CEE, do not play a significant role; they are, in the main, weak and undeveloped as network organizers. Also, the accession process does not seem to bring about a closer alignment of networks. Figure 8.3 tries graphically to summarize the power of individual actors/networks and the intensity of linkages in network alignment. Figure 8.3 depicts a situation that can be considered as

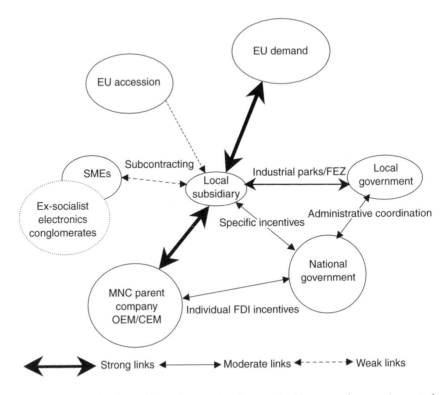

Figure 8.3 Stylized relationship and strength of network alignment elements in central
European electronics.

Source: Author.

'typical' for the region. It does not convey significant country differences, in particular coupling of national and local government policies in Hungary, compared to other countries. The figure illustrates a situation in which network alignment is driven by MNCs, is pulled by EU demand and is confined to local subsidiaries of MNCs. In Hungary and the Czech Republic (after 1996) local and national governments played a major role through subsidies and industrial park policies. As in the story of east Asian electronics dynamics (Hobday *et al.* 2001) the key finding is the critical role of foreign capital.

Conclusions

This chapter has analysed the electronics industry in CEE as an emerging production location using the alignment of networks framework. The application of this framework to explain the emergence and sustainability of upgrading CEE electronics generates several conclusions:

1   Foreign investment is the primary vehicle of integration of CEE electronics firms into global production networks and Hungary has moved furthest along this path, positioning itself as a major low-cost supply base in the region. Czech and Polish electronics industries are connected, in smaller but increasing degrees, to international electronics production networks. Other countries have much less integrated industries though this situation may change in the medium term, primarily through the activities of contract manufacturers.

2   The EU operates as the main source of demand for CEE electronics industries. This is the main pull factor which gives cohesion to the actions of MNCs and local and national governments in CEE. However, this also means that CEE electronics firms mirror to a great extent the strengths and weaknesses of EU electronics firms in terms of market segments and dynamics of growth.

3   Networks that are being built in CEE reflect the strategy of the dominant actor – the MNC. They are usually confined to subsidiaries with still limited local subcontracting, are export oriented and are expanding. Local subsidiaries have mastered production capabilities and several subsidiaries in Hungary are European mandate suppliers in their respective lines of business.

4   The layer of local firms in electronics is still very weak with very limited capabilities in core technologies. This is the key weakness for further alignment of networks in CEE electronics. The development in CEE still seems a long way behind that in East Asia where former manager from companies such as Intel and Hewlett-Packard have started some of the best local companies in the electronics sector. The weak financial systems of CEE countries, their still undeveloped capabilities in electronics technologies and lack of experience in competition in this sector, mean that local networks will continue to be very dependent on foreign investors.

Mastery of process technologies has primarily taken place within the foreign firms, but has also been achieved by a few of the more successful domestic firms. In some respects, the situation in central Europe in electronics is similar to the situation in Malaysia and Thailand (as opposed to Korea and Taiwan), where the overwhelming dominance of MNC investment is matched by the absence of major local exporting firms (Hobday *et al.* 2001).

Acknowledgement

I am grateful to Kate Bishop for research assistance.

Notes

1   We distinguish between central Europe (Poland, Czech Republic, Hungary, Slovenia, Slovakia, Baltic Economies) and eastern Europe (Romania and Bulgaria). Unless explicitly mentioned, we also include Russia and the Ukraine in CEE.

2 'Cranking up the volume', *The Warsaw Voice – Business*, No. 20 (395), 19 May 1996.
3 Based on actual data.
4 Information technology (IT) refers to the combined industries of hardware for office machines, data processing equipment, data communications equipment and of software and services. ICT refers to IT plus telecommunications equipment and services.
5 Peter Serenyi (February 2001): *Business: China's Cheaper, Why Mannesmann and Shinwa have defected east, Budapest Business Journal*, 26 February.
6 A significant number of engineers from the region are employed in several R&D labs and software centres owned by foreign firms in the Czech Republic.
7 'CzechInvest arrives in Silicon Valley', *Czech A.M.*, 6 December 2000.
8 'New fund to help small electronics suppliers', *Czech A.M.*, 20 March 2001.
9 For details see <www.czechcinvest.org/ci> (accessed 20.1.03).

References

Beavan, A. and Estrin, S. (2000) 'The determinants of foreign direct investment in transition economies', *Centre for Economic Policy Research Discussion Paper* DP2638.

Benett, J.R. and Krebs, G. (1994) 'Local economic development partnerships: an analysis of policy networks in EC-LEDA local employment development strategies', *Regional Studies*, 28(2): 119–40.

Deans, G. (2002) 'A Scottish strategy', *Electronics Weekly*, 6 March, p. 15.

Ernst, D. (2000) 'The economics of the electronics industry: competitive dynamics and industrial organization', *East West Center Working Papers*, No. 7, October.

Fine, B. (1999) 'The developmental state is dead – long live social capital', *Development and Change*, 30(1): 1–19.

Hobday, M., Cawson, A. and Kim, S.R. (2001) 'Governance of technology in the electronics industries of East and South-East Asia', *Technovation*, 21: 209–26.

Holland, D., Sass, M., Benacek, V. and Gronicki, M. (2000) 'The determinants and impact of FDI in CEE: a comparison of survey and econometric evidence', *Transnational Corporations*, 9(3): 163–212.

Kim, S.R. and von Tunzelmann, G.N. (1998) 'Aligning internal and external networks: Taiwan's specialization in IT', SPRU Electronic Working Paper Series No. 17, May.

Linden, G. (1998) 'Building production networks in central Europe: the case of the electronics industry', BRIE, Working paper 126. Available HTTP: <http://socrates.berkeley.edu/~briewww/pubs/wp/wp126.html> (accessed 16.1.01).

Mickiewicz, T. and Radosevic, S. (2001) 'Innovation capabilities of the six EU candidate countries: comparative data based analysis', Background paper for the study on 'Innovation Policy in Issues in Six Applicant Countries: the Challenges', EC DG Enterprise. Available HTTP: <http://www.cordis.lu/innovation-smes/src/studies3.htm#studies_candidate_countries> (accessed 29.9.02).

Radosevic, S. (1999) 'Transformation of S&T systems into systems of innovation in central and eastern Europe: the emerging patterns of recombination, path-dependency and change', *Structural Change and Economic Dynamics*, 10: 277–320.

Radosevic, S. and Auriol, L. (1999) 'Patterns of restructuring in research, development and innovation activities in central and eastern European countries: analysis based on S&T indicators', *Research Policy*, 28: 351–76.

Radosevic, S. and Yoruk, D.E. (2001) 'Videoton: the growth of enterprise through entrepreneurship and network alignment', *SSEES Department of Social Sciences Electronic Working Paper in Economics and Business*, No. 4, June. Available HTTP: <http://www.ssees.ac.uk/economic.htm> (accessed 19.6.03).

9 Policy and production integration in the central European electricity industry

Francis McGowan

Introduction

This chapter examines how the changing industrial architecture of Europe manifests itself in the electricity supply industries (ESIs) of central Europe, and focuses in particular on the interplay between policy integration and production integration. The interaction between these two dimensions of integration has been more apparent here than in other sectors examined in this book, not least because of the very significant changes that are taking place in the sector itself. While the central and east European (CEE) economies have undergone dramatic reforms of ownership, market structure, and trade and investment, the transformation has been particularly acute in the utility industries such as electricity supply. Moreover, the nature of the changes taking place has been focused as much on governments as on firms, with policy and regulation (at both national and European Union (EU) levels) having a higher profile than in other sectors.

The analysis shows that the processes of policy and production integration have encountered some difficulties over the last decade. While the formal overall alignment of national policies with the EU acquis and broader regulatory requirements has been relatively straightforward, there have been some significant criticisms of the ways in which national systems operate in practice. In each of the countries examined, there have been disputes over the conduct of policy, in some cases adversely affecting the prospects for foreign investment (indeed most of the disputes have been between foreign-owned firms on the one hand and the government or government-owned firms on the other). Although such friction may be an inevitable part of the transition process, it may also reflect more fundamental problems in the sector. Are the problems with integration in this sector a reflection of administrative shortcomings (such as a lack of regulatory resources), rent seeking by entrants and incumbents, or the assertion by states and their proxies in the sector of a more 'developmental' strategy?

The next section of this chapter provides a brief account of the way in which the industry has developed, focusing on the reforms of the last twenty years and the role of the EU in that process. The second part identifies some of the general issues raised by restructuring of the industry in the transition economies and highlights the contribution of policy and production integration in that process.

Three case studies – Poland, Hungary and Czech Republic – are examined to establish how processes of policy reform and industrial reorganization (particularly the role of foreign investment) have interacted over the last five years. The chapter concludes by considering what the dynamics of change explain about production and policy integration.

The European electricity supply industry

Electricity supply, like other utilities, was for much of its history regarded as a natural monopoly and as such was often subject to public ownership or government regulation (in Europe usually the former).[1] Over time there was a trend towards consolidation and integration across the processes of production, transmission and distribution to take advantage of economies of scale and coordination (Yarrow 1988). Given its capital intensity, long planning horizons, linkages to engineering and resource sectors and increasing importance as a source of energy, the sector was regarded as a strategic industry and government oversight of its development was extensive (McGowan 1993). For much of its history the industry was organized on a national basis: investment and planning were conducted nationally and predicated on the expectation that power requirements would be met from national sources of supply.[2]

In western Europe – as well as in other industrialized and industrializing regions – this pattern of governance began to be challenged in the 1980s. This was driven by a more general shift towards privatization and market liberalization as well as a related perception that the old model of industry development was not only failing to deliver the productivity gains of the past but was also being undermined by performance shortcomings from its monopolistic structure and government interference. Radical reform over the last fifteen years has impinged upon both organization and ownership. Privatization has been a feature of almost all electricity industries in Europe, often involving the participation of foreign investors. Organizationally the industry has been fragmented to enable competition wherever possible. Regulation to govern the behaviour of privatized utilities (for example on prices or on market conduct issues) has increased while government intervention in other respects has declined (though perhaps not as much as is often claimed).

Although these processes of reform have been conducted on a national basis, in the process of market restructuring a significant role has been played by the EU since the late 1980s. The development of an EU policy was largely motivated by a concern to complete the single market and extend it to the energy sectors. Commission proposals initially focused on trade between utilities, establishing a framework for permitting 'transit' of power and for increasing price transparency. Subsequently the Commission sought member state agreement on measures to increase competition in the sector as a whole, tackling the organization. The proposals originally outlined in 1991 faced considerable opposition from many member states, and it was only in 2003 that an agreement on full market opening was finalized (Official Journal of the European Union 2003). The liberalization project has been accompanied by an intensified role of EU authorities in the competition policy aspects of the sector. For more than a decade, the Commission has been monitoring conduct in the field and applying its antitrust, state aid and merger powers to the sector, becoming the 'regulator of last resort', and monitoring closely the implementation of reform.

At the same time as member states were adjusting to (or anticipating) EU policy reforms, the sector itself was becoming more integrated. Some of the largest European utilities have been engaged in mergers and acquisitions across (and beyond) the EU as barriers to investment have been removed. The arrangements for the transmission and trade of electricity have also been transformed as a European power market has emerged to replace the traditional systems of cooperation amongst utilities. Thus the processes of policy and production integration have been interacting even more intensively.

Electricity in CEECs – challenges and obstacles

It is in this context of change in the sector as a whole and in the EU in particular that we have to understand the reform of CEEC electricity supply. A broader shift in the culture of electricity supply and with it much more aggressive corporate strategies have led to internationalization as well as liberalization of the sector. The position of the CEEC sector has been that of a potential target for EU (and other) utilities seeking to diversify into new markets and possibly to take advantage of lower costs and/or weaker regulation to sell back to the EU market.[3] Electricity utilities in the CEECs have been 'interconnected' in both physical and corporate terms: the grids of CEEC networks have been synchronized with the west European network since 1996, and there has been a wave of investments through mergers and joint ventures (see Annex Table 9A.1). Accompanying such production integration is a process of policy integration. While many of the changes that have taken place in the ownership, organization and regulation of CEEC ESIs would have occurred as part of the general transition process, the character of that integration has been particularly shaped by the need to align regulatory regimes in anticipation of EU membership.[4] Such alignment has been in terms of the general economic and administrative adjustments required under the Copenhagen Criteria and the specific acquis surrounding electricity liberalization.

While arguably the 'old' ESI model was quite similar in both east and west Europe (in terms of the mix of public ownership structures, a long-term planning perspective and an engineering ethos), the technical condition of the CEEC ESI was inferior. The sector was characterized by under-investment on a scale much greater than seen anywhere in the west. Much of the capital stock was significantly older and more in need of refurbishment or replacement than in west European ESIs.[5] Moreover in a number of respects the operation of the industry was less efficient in both economic and energy senses.[6] The lack of price signals and internal controls led to inefficient operation and utilization of energy by both producers and consumers, contributing to serious local and regional environmental problems. Controls of emissions were particularly poor (exacerbated by the otherwise energy-efficient practice of district heat networks) and safety standards in sectors such as nuclear power were questionable.[7] Pricing problems have been most acute on the demand side, however. As part of the social wage, prices were kept well below the costs of production in many CEECs, while overall tariff design and accountancy principles undermined the financial base of the sector (Freund and Wallich 1997; Stern and Davis 1997; World Bank 1999).

Taken together, these factors not only presented serious problems to be solved in transition, but also constituted obstacles to reform in their own right, both financially and politically: concerns over the consequences of tackling pricing and employment levels have been a significant constraint on government action over the last decade. Beyond such substantive issues, moreover, there are issues of governmental effectiveness. Indeed it could be argued that the underdeveloped state of systems of administration and regulation in the sector – along with shortcomings in corporate governance and recurring political interventions – have been stumbling blocks to effective privatization, reorganization and regulation in the sector.

The redesign of the electricity sector in the transition economies has faced a number of problems in addition to those highlighted earlier. In particular there have been many problems regarding the sequencing of ownership changes and market restructuring. A primary problem has been the emphasis on privatization over market reform. The transfer of assets to private investors (local or foreign) before liberalization creates an important veto group, which can present a formidable political and legal obstacle to subsequent change (Kennedy 1999). Moreover, government interest in raising finance has tended to prevail over efficiency considerations, as is reflected in the mixed record of reform across the region. While in terms of adopting the acquis the basic conditions for market liberalization have been laid, in some cases there have been not only concerns over the capacity and resources of the regulatory authorities but also a number of problems in pursuing the spirit as well as the letter of the rules.

Restructuring electricity in Poland

Shortly after the transition, the Polish electricity sector began a process of restructuring which was to see the pre-existing vertically integrated regional utilities being split into a number of separate generation and distribution entities, organized as independent businesses reporting to the Industry Ministry. A separate national transmission company (Polskie Sieci Elektroenergetyczne SA – PSE) was established in 1990, while the country's 33 distribution companies were organized as joint stock companies in 1993. The reorganization of the production sector took rather longer, being completed only in 1999. These changes did little for the chronic under-investment which characterized the sector: over the period 1996–2010 it has been estimated that the Polish ESI required $50 bn of new investment in order to replace outdated equipment, modernize existing capacity and comply with tougher environmental rules (*Financial Times* 1996a).[8]

With regard to policy integration, the Polish authorities have made good progress in market liberalization, with national legislation transposing the EU rules agreed in 1997. However, in practice, securing that legislation was politically difficult, and in terms of market reorganization and regulation the process of alignment has been even more problematic. Proposals for change were subject to intense parliamentary scrutiny and faced opposition from trade unionists (in the coal as well as the electricity sectors), local governments and the energy sector itself. The 1997 Energy Law – which was under Parliamentary review for three years – laid out the principles for introducing competition into the electricity sector as well as setting up an independent regulatory authority for the sector. While this established the commitment to competition overseen by the Energy Regulatory Office (URE), the development of effective competition has proved difficult. This is partly due to the existence of long-term Power Purchase Agreements, which left little room for competition (European Commission 2002a; IEA 1998; OECD 2002), but it is also partly due to problems of regulation. While the Office of Competition has undertaken a number of actions against utilities' anti-competitive behaviour, the main regulatory mechanism has been regarded as relatively ineffective in tackling 'technical barriers' to competition that incumbents have imposed (OECD 2002).

The other important dimension of policy integration was that of ownership reform. While not strictly part of the acquis there has been pressure from the EU (and other international agencies) for privatization across the Polish economy, including the electricity sector. The government has continually restated that future investments will be sourced from the private sector and discussions on privatization took place throughout the 1990s – where foreign utilities, banks and consultancies were involved in defining the needs of the sector – but political opposition and uncertainties in government policy appeared to work against implementation of the policy.[9]

The government laid out its plans for a seven-year privatization process in a white paper in 1996 (*Financial Times* 1996b). In the meantime it was expected that there would be some restructuring and amalgamation of existing firms. In practice however, progress on privatization has remained very slow, with subsequent restatements of policy failing to meet their objectives. The policy has been undermined by political tensions within the government between the Finance and Economy ministries, the former seeking rapid privatization to raise revenue and the latter seeking prior restructuring of the sector (Allen 2002); while the political unpopularity of the programme has also made privatization difficult (*Power Economics* 2002).

Production integration has been closely related to the conduct of privatization: the government envisaged foreign investors as key partners in the privatization process and most of the privatizations in the sector have involved foreign utilities. The major European utilities soon acquired stakes in the sector, like Electricité de France's (EdF) purchase for $80 mn of a 55 per cent stake in the Elektrociepłownia 'KRAKÓW' (ECK) Combined Heat and Power (CHP) plant at Krakow in 1997, just as the legislation liberalizing Poland's energy markets was being finalized. EdF has since deepened its involvement in Poland with the purchase of a 45 per cent stake in the Wybrzeze power station in summer 2000 and with the acquisition of a number of smaller District Heating and CHP plants in the country. Vattenfall, the major Swedish utility, purchased a stake in the Warsaw CHP company Elektrocieplownie Warszawskie (EW) in 2000 for $235 mn, and outlined a ten-year investment plan for improving its operations. The venture followed a series of other moves to establish a presence in the Polish market, including the development of the Swepol link across the Baltic (in which it has a 48 per cent stake with PSE and Kraftnat, the Swedish transmission company). The Belgian utility Tractebel purchased a 25 per cent stake in the Polaniec plant in the south-east of Poland in early 2000, subsequently increased to 99 per cent in early 2003. In 2002 the US firm Public Service Electricity and Gas (PSEG) was able to acquire a 35 per cent stake in the Skawina power plant for $25 mn (and $56 mn investment commitment) (*Power in Eastern Europe* 2002b), and the German utility Rheinisch-Westfalische Elektrizitatswerk (RWE) acquired the Stoen distribution company. A number of District Heating and CHP plants have also been sold to foreign investors over the last few years.

However, in many other cases, privatization plans were not followed through. The overall process of privatization has been subject to considerable opposition within the Polish legislature and also from trade unions and local authorities. Perhaps the most serious obstacles have, however, emerged in the conduct of the privatization authorities themselves. In the case of the distribution company Górnoślaski Zakład Elektroenergetyczny (GZE) the Treasury apparently delayed negotiations with shortlisted companies only to seek a rapid settlement of the sale in autumn 2000: the foreign utilities pulled out complaining that they did not have sufficient time to complete 'due diligence' (*Power in Eastern Europe* 2000); the utility was eventually sold to Vattenfall in 2001. Even where privatizations have been successful they have been fraught with difficulties and political uncertainties.

Indeed, according to some accounts, the government elected in 2001 was thought to have adopted a more 'nationalist' approach to the issue, permitting a mix of vertical integration and horizontal consolidation amongst the Polish elements in the electricity sector, such as through the Poludniowy Koncern Energetyczny (PKE) consortium, formed in 2000 around a series of publicly owned and Silesian-based power stations (*Power in Eastern Europe* 2002b; *Power Economics* 2002). Although some further privatization took place in 2003 it appears that the political sensitivity surrounding utility privatizations, the problems encountered in following the process through, and a range of regulatory disputes have undermined the attractiveness of the Polish electricity sector (OECD 2002; *Utility Week* 2002).

Restructuring electricity in Hungary

Of the three countries examined in this chapter, Hungary was the most integrated into the west European economy prior to 1989. The process of change impacted relatively early upon the Hungarian electricity sector but in rather limited ways. The old company Magyar Villamos Müvek Reszvenytarsag (MVM Rt) – consisting of eleven power stations, six distribution companies, a transmission company and various repair and construction companies – was corporatized and reorganized in the early 1990s: in 1992 MVM ltd was created with fifteen subsidiary companies in which MVM ltd and the government each owned approximately 50 per cent of the shares (International Energy Agency 1995). In 1994 the government decided to privatize the distribution and generation companies. The transmission company would be retained in the public sector along with the country's nuclear power station, Paks. Between 1995 and 1998 most of the rest of the sector was sold, though some non-nuclear capacity remained in public hands (Bakos 2001).

How has the Hungarian government sought to align its policy towards the electricity sector with that of the EU? There have been two significant legislative changes since the initial reorganization of the sector. The 1994 Electricity Act set out the basic regime for the electricity sector, covering most operational and regulatory issues (OECD 2000). The Act leaves substantial powers with the Ministry for Economic Affairs as well as golden shares in all power companies. The Act also established the Hungarian Energy Office as a regulatory agency for the electricity and gas sectors. It is responsible for the preparation and implementation of Ministry decisions on licences, preparation of data for Ministry decisions on pricing, supervision of licence holders' operations, approval of contracts between MVM and other electricity companies and mediating disputes among them, as well as oversight of operational codes for grid, dispatch and distribution. In terms of policy integration therefore, the 1994 legislation set out the basic structures of the sector and in tandem with processes of privatization can be seen as bringing the Hungarian ESI into line with the EU. The 1994 Act did not address questions of liberalization *per se* – no competition for final consumers was permitted (except in very exceptional circumstances), though it did set out procedures for competitive tendering for new power plant capacity and for contractual arrangements between generators and distributors (Power Purchase Agreements).

The application of EU liberalization policy, after considerable dispute, emerged eventually in the form of the 2001 Electricity Act. The government began drafting the legislation in 1998 with the aim of bringing in liberalization at the start of 2001. The difficulties in finalizing the law meant that it was not passed by the Hungarian Parliament until the end of 2002, entering into force at the beginning of 2003. The law broadly follows the requirements of the EU's electricity directive, splitting the Hungarian market into utility and authorized segments: the former designed to meet the needs of domestic customers, the latter to operate competitively. The law allows for opening up to 35 per cent of the market in 2003 and full liberalization by 2010. The law also allows third-party access to the grid (MVM retains ownership of the grid, however). Much of the detail on the practical operation of the system was to be provided in subsequent government decrees (*Power in Eastern Europe* 2002a).

Policy integration in terms of aligning ownership followed the 1994 legislation, and over the subsequent three years the government sold stakes in a number of generation and distribution companies (Pesic and Urge-Vorsach 2001). The sales of distribution companies appeared to be relatively successful, with the six utilities attracting a number of investors from the European electricity sector. Initially it was planned to sell 50 per cent of shares to foreign investors and another 15 per cent to local investors (both institutional and individual). The sales were made on the basis of a guaranteed rate of return of 8 per cent with full management control passing to the foreign investors (OECD 2000). Sales of the generating companies were less successful: only two companies attracted investors in the first round though subsequent sales have taken place (part of the problem was its decision to bundle the generation companies together with neighbouring mines). In addition the government has authorized the sale of a number of CHP operators as well as some industrial cogeneration projects. Nonetheless, with its ownership of Paks (nuclear power) and stakes in three other power projects, the state-owned MVM remains the largest operator in the Hungarian market.

According to critics of the government's policy, the dominance of MVM remains a major obstacle to effective production integration of the Hungarian electricity sector. The process of policy integration has been subject to considerable criticism, with some representatives of the private sector alleging that the 2001 Electricity Act is designed to conform with the letter of the EU directive but not to permit any real competition to develop; the Commission itself noted some problems in the transposition process, though not enough to jeopardize the completion of negotiations on the energy chapter (European Commission 2001a). Even so, the initial experience of liberalization – with very limited take-up of the opportunities for competition – has been due to the very close links between the government and the main generator. In their review of regulatory progress in Hungary, the OECD (2000) saw the electricity regime as characteristic of shortcomings in the overall regulatory system in the country. While the regulatory office has been generally regarded as effective in its own right, there has been criticism of the government's unwillingness to give the office more powers over questions of licensing and price control (IEA 2003), with key aspects of governing the sector remaining in the hands of the Ministry of Economic Affairs.

Critics have argued that the government's apparent preferential treatment of MVM is evident in the company's willingness to exploit its market power *vis-à-vis* other stakeholders in the sector. A series of disputes between the foreign utilities on the one side and MVM/Ministry on the other have marked the sector's development. In some cases these disputes have been the subject of court actions, but where these have been addressed in Hungarian courts the government has always won. In one case – involving the US company Allied Energy Systems (AES) – the case was heard in the US, prompting MVM to settle the dispute (*Power in Eastern Europe* 2002a). Other foreign utilities, however, have opted to move out of the country in frustration at the government's closeness to MVM and the high level of politicization in the sector (*Financial Times* 2002).

Restructuring electricity in the Czech Republic

After 1989 the Czech electricity sector was reorganized by splitting the vertically integrated utility Ceske Energeticke Zavody (CEZ) into separate companies for production, transmission and distribution. CEZ remained responsible for production, accounting for 65–75 per cent of output within the country (the remainder is made up of industrial autogeneration, CHP and independent power projects). A new company Ceske Energeticke Prenosove Soustavy (CEPS) was established – as a 100 per cent subsidiary of CEZ – to own and operate the high-voltage transmission network, and distribution was vested in eight regional companies (International Energy Agency 1995).

The Czech electricity sector comprises over 15 GW of capacity, of which two-thirds is coal based (largely brown coal) and just over 10 per cent is nuclear power (with a further 2 GW to follow at the Temelin power station). CEZ is the second largest exporter of power in Europe (after EdF), partly as a result of its geographical location but also because of its surplus of power. The costs of its power are relatively low due to lower operating costs and nuclear capacity. Some critics have claimed that the costs are low due to poor environmental and safety standards and that western utilities seek to exploit this.[10]

Responsibility for energy policy rests with the Ministry of Industry and Trade under the 1994 Energy Act. A revised act in 2001 reformed the governance of the sector, leaving the Ministry of Industry and Trade to set energy policy and approve new power plants but giving a greater regulatory role to a new body, the Energy Regulation Office (ERO) (OECD 2001). The ERO is now responsible for price control and licensing and was granted considerable legal autonomy. The 2001 act was also designed to comply with the EU's programme of electricity liberalization, setting out a programme of phased market opening: 30 per cent of the market from 2002, rising to 100 per cent from 2006 (European Commission 2001b).

Privatization began relatively early in the Czech ESI. One-third of CEZ was sold as part of early voucher privatization schemes – the remainder is held by the National Property Fund (NPF). The NPF also owns large minority or majority stakes in the eight distribution companies, along with limited shares held by municipalities and in most cases a foreign utility as a strategic investor. In addition a number of district heating companies have been sold to foreign investors and in some cases foreign utilities have established Independent Power Project (IPP) ventures. The privatization and reorganization of CEZ has been at the core of the debate on power sector reform, however. A much postponed and controversial privatization was finally scheduled for early 2002 with the aim of completion before that year's elections (*Power in Eastern Europe* 2001a). The government not only left the structure of CEZ broadly unaltered but it also sought to lock the new owner of CEZ into a series of long-term obligations to retain the structure of the company and purchase coal from local suppliers (*Power in Eastern Europe* 2001b). Both attempts to reorganize CEZ have been criticized by a number of international authorities: the OECD called on the Czech government to restructure CEZ, arguing that the planned sell-off would hurt the development of competition (OECD 2001).

In the event, the planned privatization failed to materialize and a subsequent plan for CEZ to acquire controlling interests in the country's distribution companies has had to be scaled back in the light of widespread criticism and a ruling by the competition authority (*Energy in East Europe* 2003). As in other East European countries, the competition authority has been regarded as more effective than the sectoral regulator, which was for a time regarded as inadequately resourced and insufficiently independent (European Commission 2001b; International Energy Agency 2001). However more recently there are signs that the regulator has been willing to assert its powers, as manifest in its decision to permit distribution companies to import power despite the opposition of the transmission company (Energy Regulatory Office 2002; European Commission 2002b).

Concerns over the vertical integration of production and transmission have been intensified because it appears that CEZ retains a significant influence over the new company, CEPS. CEPS proposed curbing imports of power, though this was turned down by the regulator. Since then, increased trade has been the principal mechanism for taking advantage of liberalization, as distributors have sought to bypass CEZ and seek supplies from neighbouring states. The role of the competition authority in forcing CEZ to scale down its acquisition plans in the distribution sector is arguably another sign that regulation is becoming more effective. Earlier there had been concerns that the regulator was too close to the government and that the agency was under-resourced (*Power in Eastern Europe* 2001c). Indeed regulatory problems in the past have contributed to foreign investors' frustrations with the Czech electricity market. Two initial investors – the American firm Texas Utilities (TXU) and Vattenfall – have pulled out of the country, claiming that the system was biased in favour of CEZ and that CEZ would dominate the liberalized market. In 2001, the American power company Cinergy was reported to be considering selling its investments in the country in protest against the treatment of independent power producers (*Transmission and Distribution World* 2001). Whether subsequent assertions of autonomy by the industry regulator and the competition authority will be reassuring to investors remains to be seen.

Conclusions: policy integration and production integration in the CEEC ESI

The experience of reform in the Czech, Hungarian and Polish electricity industries illustrates the problems of policy and production integration and the key role of states in that process. In a sense, the strategic nature of the sector – and its links to a set of social issues – highlights the key role of governments and the tensions which can arise between them and foreign investors and international agencies. The problems have related less to the formal alignment of policy (though even here there have been some difficulties) than with day-to-day processes, perhaps reflecting more fundamental conflicts in the sector.

In Hungary an early commitment to privatization has not prevented subsequent disputes with investors over the conditions of sale and the commitment of the government. The regulator's lack of de jure or de facto autonomy only underlines the difficulty. Relations seem to have deteriorated since 1998. Moreover, the assertion by MVM of a national champion role seems to be condoned if not encouraged by the Ministry of Economic Affairs. What is less clear is whether this role is a real one or just a reflection of close links between government departments and the incumbent state-owned operator. It is clear that the tensions within the sector have been a factor contributing to delays in the liberalization process itself. Moreover, while legislation conforms to the requirements of the EU acquis there are many who doubt the law's effectiveness in practice.

In the Czech Republic legislation has had no immediate impact in the form of major switches between suppliers. However, more general concerns about the compatibility of planned production integrations with EU rules do exist (though as in the Hungarian case such misgivings were not sufficient to cause a delay in closing the energy policy chapter). Here the tensions have been as much about the details of restructuring as with the performance of the regulatory regime in practice (though there have been some disputes in this respect as well).

The Polish case seems to have provoked less controversy than the other two countries, but one is tempted to observe that this may be in part due to the slow pace of change (i.e. that events have not progressed far enough to permit such conflicts to take place). Certainly there have been a number of disputes surrounding aspects of government policy which have at least contributed to the slow pace of production integration. In part these can be regarded as failings in the 'spirit' of policy integration if not the letter. The uncertainties over the privatization programme reflect a series of conflicting objectives facing the Polish authorities. Support for the Polish coal industry and the requirements this imposes on utilities' fuel input costs have discouraged some investors. A more serious problem has been between the goals of market liberalization and privatization. For a number of years, the PSE concluded long-term contracts with generation companies, effectively as a means of guaranteeing a market and revenue flow to render them attractive to private and foreign investors. However, such arrangements worked to lock in supply and reduce the scope for competition. The tension between these objectives became more acute when the operations of the Polish Power Exchange revealed a very large difference between contract and wholesale prices. Although it appears that an alternative mechanism will be devised to bridge this gap (effectively liquidating the long-term contracts while providing some compensation for the affected utilities), the tensions between incumbents and entrants, domestic and foreign investors, and government and regulatory authorities have scarcely encouraged potential entry.

Policy integration defined as the incorporation of specific EU legislation into national law appears to have been achieved in all three cases. In some respects, the countries have gone further by setting timetables for full liberalization. Agreement has been difficult in some cases, however, there is some scepticism about the real impact of legal changes. The latter seems to a large extent due to problems in the wider process of policy integration. The limited resources and powers of regulators, the interventions of national ministers, lack of legal certainty in some cases and preferential position of incumbents, all cast doubt on the efficacy of this process, with consequences for the process of production integration.

Annex

Table 9A.1 Foreign investment in central European electricity industries

Investor	Czech Republic	Hungary	Poland
AES		Borsod (171 MW) Tisza (860 MW) Tiszapalkanya (250 MW)	
Cinergy	CHP Projects (148 MW)		
Electricite de France		27% Edasz c.61% Demasz 89% BERT (262 MW)	45% Wybrzeze (352 MW) 49% Wroclaw 50% Electrokrakow 35% Rybnik (1695 MW)
El Paso		50% EMA (70 MW) c.18% ECKG (350 MW)	
En BW	c.17% PRE	25% Elmu 25% Emasz 21% Matas (800 MW)	15% Wroclaw
Enron			ENS (116 MW)
E.On	28% SME 42% VCE 45% JME 37% JCE 5% SCE	c.91% Dedasz 28% Edasz c.83% Titasz	
International power	96% EOP (539 MW) 7% Vychodeceska Energetika 45% PT (135 MW)		
MEAG			53% Bedzin (55 MW)
NRG		50% ECKG (350 MW) 100% Csepel (505 MW)	
PSEG			35% Skawina 90% Chorzow (220 MW)
RWE	35% STE 43% Skode Energo	51% Elmu 52% Elmasz	
Tractebel		c.74% Dunameti (2000 MW)	25% Polaniec
Horizon	c.84% United Energy (236 MW)		
Vattenfall			25% GZE 55% Warszawski (984 MW)

Source: OECD, *Power in Eastern Europe.*

Notes

1 See Joskow and Schmalensee (1983), Vickers and Yarrow (1985) and Foster (1992) on the monopolistic characteristics of the sector and the implications for reform. See Kennedy (1999) on the 'misconception' of electricity supply as a monopoly.
2 Trade in power constituted a relatively small proportion of power supply for most countries until relatively recently (see McGowan 1999).
3 Although most accounts of the transition have underplayed the potential of social/environmental 'dumping' into the EU market, some commentators suggest that west European utilities have contracted to import 'dirty electricity' from east European partners/subsidiaries (see Greenpeace 2001). However, given the medium-term prospect of both environmental compliance and the likelihood of closer alignment of electricity prices, such claims may be overstated.
4 As well as to obtain EU funds for administrative and infrastructure development.
5 Though one perverse effect of the wider economic restructuring is its impact upon energy and electricity demand. As a result of the reduction in demand (compounded by the closure of energy-intensive industries) CEECs do not have the immediate pressure of building new capacity to meet supply needs (though of course there are compelling environmental reasons to do so in many countries). See Kennedy (1999).
6 Lewington (1997) offers a rather more positive view of the performance of one CEEC power sector (East Germany).
7 There are conflicting views on this. Some such as Thomas (1997) highlight the overall strong performance of nuclear power in the former socialist states while most international organizations, western utilities and environmental organizations have expressed concern over the level of safety regulation in the sector.
8 The heavy reliance on coal and lignite has caused serious environmental damage but has been hard to overcome, given the political sensitivity of that industry.
9 Attempts to modernize capacity were initially undermined by uncertainties over government policy on privatization with government oscillating between sell-offs, foreign partners and local partners (see *Financial Times* 1990a,b, 1992).
10 Indeed Greenpeace has levied a campaign against imports of Czech power on the grounds of its reliance on nuclear power, and succeeded in persuading E.On to cancel its contract. More generally some governments have lobbied the Czech authorities to improve safety standards at its nuclear plants, with the Austrian government making such improvements a condition of accession.

References

Allen, Z. (2002) 'A fork in the road', in M.E. Burdett (ed.) *Power in East Europe*, London: Platts, pp. 25–28.
Bakos, G. (2001) 'Privatizing and liberalizing electricity: the case of Hungary', *Energy Policy*, 29: 1119–32.
Energy in East Europe various years, 16th May 2003.
Energy Regulatory Office (2002) *Report on the Activities and Financial Management of the Energy Regulatory Office for 2001*, Prague: ERO.
European Commission (2001a) *Regular Report on Hungary's Progress towards Accession, 2001*, Brussels: Commission of the European Communities.
European Commission (2001b) *Regular Report on the Czech Republic's Progress towards Accession 2001*, Brussels: Commission of the European Communities.
European Commission (2002a) *Regular Report on Poland's Progress towards Accession, 2002*, Brussels: Commission of the European Communities.
European Commission (2002b), *Regular Report on the Czech Republic's Progress towards Accession 2002*, Brussels: Commission of the European Communities.

Financial Times (1996a) 27th March.

Financial Times (1996b) 13th March.

Financial Times (2002) 10th June.

Foster, C. (1992) *Privatisation, Public Ownership and the Control of Natural Monopoly*, Oxford: Blackwell.

Freund, C. and Wallich, C. (1997) 'Public sector price reforms in transition economies: who wins? who loses? The case of household energy prices in Poland', *Economic Development and Cultural Change*, 46(1): 35–59.

Greenpeace (2001) *Cheap and Clean? How Imported Electricity will Undermine EU Environmental Standards*, London: Greenpeace.

International Energy Agency (1995) *Energy Policies of Hungary*, Paris: IEA.

International Energy Agency (1998) *Energy Policy Review: Poland*, Paris: IEA.

International Energy Agency (2001) *Energy Policy Review: Czech Republic*, Paris: IEA.

International Energy Agency (2003) *Energy Policy Review, Hungary*, Paris: IEA.

Joskow, P. and Schmalensee, R. (1983) *Markets for Power*, Cambridge, MA: MIT Press.

Kennedy, D. (1999) *Competition in the Power Sectors of Transition Economies*, London: EBRD.

Lewington, I. (1997) 'The transformation of the East German electricity sector: an economic analysis', unpublished DPhil thesis, University of Sussex.

McGowan, F. (1993) *The Struggle for Power in Europe*, London: RIIA.

McGowan, F. (1999) 'Internationalization of large technical systems', in O. Coutard (ed.) *The Governance of Large Technical Systems*, London: Routledge, pp. 130–48.

Official Journal of the European Union (2003) Directive 2003/54/EC of the European Parliament and of the Council of 26 June 2003 concerning common rules for the internal market in electricity and repealing Directive 96/92/EC, OJ L176, Brussels: EC.

Organisation of Economic Cooperation and Development (2000) *Regulatory Reform in Hungary*, Paris: OECD.

Organisation of Economic Cooperation and Development (2001) *Regulatory Reform in the Czech Republic*, Paris: OECD.

Organisation of Economic Cooperation and Development (2002) *Regulatory Reform in Poland: From Transition to New Regulatory Challenges*, Paris: OECD.

Pesic, R. and Ürge-Vorsatz, D. (2001) 'Restructuring of the Hungarian Electricity Industry', *Journal of Post-Communist Economies*, 13(1): 85–99.

Power Economics (2002) 30 September.

Power in Eastern Europe (2000) 20 October.

Power in Eastern Europe (2001a) 3 September.

Power in Eastern Europe (2001b) 9 November.

Power in Eastern Europe (2001c) 11 June.

Power in Eastern Europe (2002a) 4 January.

Power in Eastern Europe (2002b) 4 February.

Stern, J. and Davis, J. (1997) 'Economic reform of the electricity industries of Central and Eastern Europe', *CERT Discussion Paper 97/25*.

Thomas, S. (1997) 'East European Nuclear Performance', *Power in Europe*, 27 March.

Transmission and Distribution World, June 2001.

Utility Week (2002) 8th November.

Vickers, J. and Yarrow, G. (1985) *Privatising the Natural Monopolies*, London: Public Policy Centre.

World Bank (1999) 'Non-payment in the electricity sector in Eastern Europe and the former Soviet Union', *World Bank Technical Paper no 423*, Washington, DC: World Bank.

Yarrow, G. (1988) *Some Economic Issues Surrounding the Proposed Privatisation of Electricity Generation and Transmission*, London: Prima Europe.

10 Foreign direct investment and indigenous industry in Ireland

A review of the evidence

T. P. O'Connor

Introduction

This chapter considers the development of industry in Ireland, highlighting the contributions of Foreign Direct Investment (FDI) and networks. It examines the way in which the Irish government adapted its industrial policy to foster inward investment, and explores the linkages between indigenous industry and multinational corporations (MNCs) in Ireland.

Ireland's embrace of foreign investment as the mainstay of its development strategy came relatively early. Economic problems in the post-war period forced the abandonment of its previous protectionist policy; mass emigration and a balance of payments deficit led to a severe financial crisis in 1956 and a reorientation of economic policy to stimulate export-led growth. An important component of the new policy was the establishment of the Industrial Development Authority (IDA), which identified key sectors such as electronics, pharmaceuticals and chemicals and set about attracting the strongest companies in these sectors, particularly from the United States.

Since the 1970s, an important factor in attracting foreign investment has been Ireland's membership of the European Union (EU): MNCs have considered the country a good location for offshore plant, providing them with access to the large EU market. In addition to the market access advantages of EU membership, Ireland has received considerable structural assistance from the European Regional Development and Social Funds. This support was used to develop physical infrastructure and human resources (education has been another priority for the government in developing a skills and knowledge base).

Although the country has been successful in attracting investment, economic development from 1960 to 1990 was mixed. Following a serious financial crisis in 1987, however, there has been a dramatic turnaround in the economy with the country experiencing substantial growth through the 1990s. Foreign investment remains at the core of that economic success, with FDI now accounting for over two-thirds of total net output in manufacturing, approximately half of manufacturing employment and just short of two-thirds of total exports. The overall health of the Irish economy is, in fact, dependent on the foreign-owned manufacturing sector. The major FDI inflow to Ireland in the 1990s came mainly from the

United States. It would appear that Ireland's location on the periphery of Europe is not a disadvantage for US MNCs seeking an offshore location. This is especially true for the so-called 'weightless' products (electronics, pharmaceuticals, software, etc.) where transportation costs are not a significant factor. Cultural similarity with the United States and the fact that English is the spoken language are seen as important advantages in attracting US FDI to Ireland.

Indigenous industry after the protectionist period consisted of a large number of small, weak and uncompetitive companies. Initially, industrial development grants only applied to exporting companies, so indigenous companies were effectively excluded. Many companies went out of business in the 1960s, and membership of the EU in 1973 brought intense competition from Europe. Large numbers of indigenous companies curtailed their operations or closed down completely in the 1980s. Following a major review of industrial policy in 1982, a number of very effective programmes (including the National Linkage programme) were set up to rectify the inherent weaknesses of indigenous industry (i.e. management, financial control, marketing, technology and research and development (R&D)). Indigenous industry has witnessed a revival since 1988 with increases in employment, output and profitability. Many new companies now have strong linkages with MNCs (in Ireland and Europe). They are exporting, have offshore locations and are internationally competitive. The low-skill, low-pay employment of older firms has in effect been replaced by high-skill and high-pay employment (though with a few exceptions in fields such as food processing, building materials and banking, there are not many large indigenous companies in Ireland).

Ireland's economic success in the 1990s is primarily due to its success in attracting FDI. Good industrial policies implemented by a very professional organization, EU membership, an effective education system, the recent growth in the US economy, improved communications, changes in the underlying geography of the world economy, tight fiscal control, national wage agreements and an English-speaking workforce, are all contributory factors to Ireland's success. Making these factors successful has been achieved through networks, both formal and informal, of government policy makers, state agencies with their worldwide network of offices, the education system, MNCs in Ireland, the EU, the unions and employers.

The evolution of Ireland's outward-oriented development strategy

Like governments in many other developing countries, in the 1930s, the Irish government introduced a policy of economic self-sufficiency and the development of indigenous industry behind protective barriers. This industrialization strategy was initially successful in the pre-Second World War years, but the limits of protectionism became widely recognized in the 1950s, a time when the whole western world was moving to restore free trade. As Kennedy notes,

> The chief benefit of protection was that it led to the establishment of many firms that would not have existed without it. Indeed in the troubled world economic conditions of the 1930s it is doubtful if any other approach would

have achieved as much. Nevertheless, the hasty and indiscriminate application of the strategy resulted in an industrial base that was weak and vulnerable. There was no vision about how to progress further once the potential of the small home market was fully exploited.

(Kennedy, 1998: 79)

The financial crisis of 1956 and emigration, which peaked at 2 per cent in 1957, precipitated a fundamental change in government policy. A new outward-looking strategy emerged thereafter.

There were three main elements to this new outward-looking strategy:

- capital grants and tax concessions to encourage export-led manufacturing;
- the IDA was given the task of attracting foreign firms to Ireland; and
- protection was gradually dismantled in return for greater access to markets abroad, culminating in Ireland's accession to the European Economic Community in 1973.

Policy was reoriented to stimulate export-led growth, with the emphasis on freeing trade, giving incentives for exports, providing fixed investment grants to industry and expanding capital formation through the public capital programme. Ireland was one of the first countries to adopt such a strategy.

Industrial policy and the IDA

Irish Industrial Development Policy has remained constant in its fundamental thrust since the late 1950s. In response to reviews and criticisms over the years there have been changes, but these have not affected the main objectives of employment and exports, nor the use of grants and tax concessions.

The IDA was established in 1949 as part of the government's Department of Industry and Commerce and with limited powers and objectives. However, the Industrial Development Act 1969 brought about radical changes in policy and the IDA was given a powerful statutory mandate to act under the Minister for Industry and Commerce 'as a body having national responsibility for the furtherance of industrial development'. A rapid expansion followed and within a few years the IDA had established offices in most major industrialized countries.

During the 1970s, the IDA perfected its approach by targeting selected industries, and high-performing companies within those industries. Electronics and pharmaceuticals were the first industries to be identified by the IDA as offering the best opportunities for Ireland's drive to industrialize through FDI. These sectors remain to this day the two most important sectors of FDI in Ireland. Subsequently, other sectors were seen as having good potential for Ireland including healthcare, and more recently software and financial and other computer-based services.

Ruane and Gorg (1999) highlight three key characteristics of Irish policy towards FDI: a focus on employment as the major requirement for FDI projects (though more recently policy has shifted to emphasize profits, technology and linkages to domestic firms); the provision of tax incentives and discretionary supports, and the maintenance of policy certainty and a positive investment climate. Although the orientation of policy has remained fairly consistent overall, in the last few decades Irish policy has become more discretionary in the provision of support (with grant levels related to the number of jobs created) and more selective in the types of projects being sought (with greater emphasis on market niches, where growth potential is greatest, and the development of industrial clusters).

While foreign industry expanded in Ireland in the 1960s and 1970s, indigenous industry faced decline, a decline that was to continue for another decade. Matters became much worse in the early 1980s when the flow of foreign industry fell and there was a loss of 10,000 jobs in the foreign companies. The government took action by initiating a comprehensive review of industrial policy.

The Boston-based Telesis Consultancy Group carried out this review, and published its report in 1982. This report criticized the over-reliance on foreign industry and favoured a better balance between overseas and indigenous industry. It recommended a modification to the outward-looking strategy to give priority to building up a select group of Irish firms to serve world markets using 'sticks as well as carrots' for the purpose. In its subsequent 1984 White Paper on Industrial Development, the Irish government accepted much of this diagnosis and many of its recommendations. The White Paper highlighted problems in Irish industry such as the weak calibre of management, a lack of attention to R&D, the failure of Irish companies to maintain their share of the home market or to diversify exports beyond the United Kingdom, and the lack of links between Irish businesses and the education system.

The White Paper outlined a shift in priorities for Irish industrial policy. Industrial incentives and state assistance would be applied selectively to both domestic and foreign-owned firms (with priority given in the latter instance to projects which would perform key business functions in Irish factories). There would be a shift in government resources from investment in fixed assets to technology acquisition and export marketing. The government would also provide tax incentives for the development of a risk capital market for investment in internationally traded manufacturing and service industries.

The IDA responded to the White Paper by adjusting policy implementation regarding FDI and by introducing a series of programmes aimed specifically at the problems inherent in Irish indigenous industry, for example, the National Linkage Programme, and Company Development Programmes. At approximately the same time initiatives were taken by other state agencies to tackle the problems of product and process quality. Over the ensuing years up to the mid-1990s a large number of firms, both foreign and indigenous, achieved registration for the prestigious ISO 9000 Quality Standard.

Since it was established, Irish government ministers and Members of the Dail (i.e. the Irish Parliament) have identified very closely with the activities of the IDA in attracting FDI to Ireland. In addition, the Irish Government has reacted posi-tively to problems and opportunities identified by the IDA, for example, the upgrading of the telecommunications system, advanced banking and financial systems to cater for the needs of US corporations, tax agreements with the US Internal Revenue Service, etc. This close relationship between the Irish government and the IDA is irrespective of political party affiliation and has existed since the early days of the IDA in 1960. This network of Irish government, IDA and MNCs is important in the continuing efforts of the IDA to attract suitable FDI to Ireland. Executives of MNCs in Ireland attest to the advantages of Ireland as a foreign location and discuss their positive experiences of setting up in Ireland with executives of corporations considering foreign locations.

Education and training

The introduction of free secondary education in 1967 became, in due course, an important factor in laying the foundations for future rapid growth and was to have far-reaching economic consequences in later decades. Over time, further education and training reforms have raised the skills base. The government has demonstrated its long-term commitment to education and training with a major overhaul and expansion of the system at all levels. This could not have been achieved without the involvement and close co-operation of all the relevant actors: government, Department of Education and Science, state agencies (the FAS, IDA, Enterprise Ireland, etc.), universities, institutes of technology, secondary education system, employers and unions.

Third-level education was expanded considerably with the establishment of nine Regional Technical Colleges (RTCs) – now institutes of technology, two National Institutes of Higher Education (NIHEs) – now universities, and the expansion of facilities at the existing universities (according to Lee (1998), the establishment of new institutions encouraged older universities to adapt and develop). All the universities and colleges of technology now work closely with local and national industry, thereby providing the much-needed R&D resources for industry.

Ireland did not have research institutes (such as are found in many other countries) which support industry. This weakness was addressed by the Programmes in Advanced Technology (PAT) – partnerships between the third-level sector and the government's Department of Enterprise and Employment and its agencies. Technological expertise resided in the third-level sector, but was widely dispersed and needed to be organized as a more coherent entity. The PATs were set up to provide strategic expertise in certain key technologies to support industry. Nine PATs were set up between 1988 and 1991 in the following technology areas: bio-research, advanced manufacturing technology, opto-electronics, software, materials, power electronics, microelectronics and telecommunications.

In addition to the improvements in the third level described above, Vocational Education and Training (VET) was identified as a priority and substantial resources were committed to the task of training and retraining. FAS, the Training and Employment Authority, was established in 1987. Attention was given to training for the unemployed, and as a regionalized organization FAS made training more relevant to local demand. Human Resources received major support in the National

Development Plans for 1989–93 and 1993–99. Furthermore, and following various critical reports, the government's 1997 White Paper defined strategies and programmes to encourage and support Irish business to improve its overall skills base and to foster the knowledge and skills of individuals in the labour market.

Economic development from the mid-1970s and the impact of EU membership

From 1974 to 1979, Ireland experienced strong economic growth, followed by a downturn in the period 1979–86. The growth in employment, which had commenced in the late 1950s, was brought to a sharp halt with the recession of 1980–81. In the early 1980s, there was a marked decline in FDI, as well as failures of established foreign companies and the continuing closures of indigenous Irish companies. This resulted in decreases in employment, which were to continue until the late 1980s. It was clear that the expansionary policies of the previous decade were unsustainable and had contributed to a serious fiscal crisis. In response the government and opposition adopted an aggressive policy of retrenchment – backed by national agreements between employees and employers – to stabilize the economy. This policy, along with the improved external environment (particularly the thriving US economy), helped to bring about a dramatic improvement in the Irish economy. Moreover, longer-run factors (such as improved infrastructure, demographic trends, structural transformation and the development of scientific and technological capabilities) also contributed to the economic growth of the 1990s.

One of the key factors in transforming the Irish economy since the 1970s has been membership of the EU. Prior to joining the EU, Ireland's external economic relations were characterized by a dependent relationship on the United Kingdom. All this changed in 1973, when Ireland became a member of the EU. The focus of attention shifted from the United Kingdom to a new multilateral world, where Ireland was legally, and *de facto* equal, to all other members of the EU. This changed environment within the EU not only strengthened Ireland's economic independence, but it also provided new ideas, a stimulus to look at a wider world, and a knowledge that there were different ways of achieving the desired social and economic objectives.

Since entering the EU, Ireland has received structural assistance from the Regional Development and Social Funds (ERDF and ESF) as well as from the Guidance section of the Agricultural Guidance and Guarantee Fund (FEOGA). In 1988, as the move to market completion started in earnest, the range of structural funds was reformed, reorganized and expanded. This entailed the development of the Community Support Frameworks (CSF) as coherent multi-year programmes, agreed between the Commission and national authorities, with the aim of promoting economic and social cohesion throughout Europe. These programmes were aimed at developing the country's physical infrastructure and human capital and assisting private development in investment, marketing and innovation. The Economic and Social Research Institute (ESRI) estimated that of the funding, 36.3 per cent went to physical infrastructure, 28.4 per cent to human resources,

25.8 per cent to the private sector and 9.5 per cent to income support. The EU Structural and Cohesion Funds amounted to a mini Marshall plan to help the Irish economy out of recession, adding to growth and clearing bottlenecks in infrastructure and education and training. It has been estimated that the EU CSF expenditures may have raised GNP by 3 to 4 percentage points above what it otherwise would have been (Barry *et al.* 2001).

Of more long-term importance, however, have been the effects of economic integration and in particular the single-market programme. The latter initiative was designed to provide a competitive 'shock' to the economies of member states by removing a number of non-tariff barriers to an internal market, improving productivity through greater scale economies and reducing prices through greater competition. Although Ireland's status as one of the poorer member states meant that it was viewed as vulnerable to the effects of the single market (many expected it to increase income disparities in the short run), in practice Ireland benefited from the industrial restructuring effect of the programme. According to Barry *et al.* (2001) the single market may have added as much as 3.5 per cent to Irish GDP. Others see the single-market programme and European integration more generally as reinforcing a flexible model of development, which has been attractive to foreign investors (though some such as O'Hearn (1998) question the sustainability of this approach).

FDI – Ireland's experience

FDI has been central to Irish economic development since the abandonment of protectionism in the 1950s. Much of the history of the Irish economy since then can be explained in terms of the quite phenomenal growth of export-oriented FDI in manufacturing. The Irish domestic market is of no significance to foreign firms; they locate in Ireland to produce for export. Foreign firms also tend to be larger, more productive and more profitable than indigenous firms – five times as productive and eight times as profitable. In 1993, FDI accounted for over two-thirds of total net output in manufacturing while employment in foreign-owned industries as a percentage of total manufacturing employment was 44.7 per cent in 1993. All foreign-owned firms had very high percentages of exports, with chemicals at 96.3 per cent and instruments at 94.4 per cent. As a considerable amount of FDI is in the high-technology sectors it comes as no surprise that skill levels in foreign industry are higher than in indigenous industry. Similarly, the data show that R&D of foreign firms accounted for 64 per cent of R&D spending.

Gorg and Ruane (2000) assert that Ireland's recent success in attracting FDI in manufacturing has been influenced by the process of European integration. They further claim that economic integration may impact positively on the periphery of the EU through the location decisions of internationally mobile firms. The authors argue that an MNC will find it profitable to locate in the periphery if the costs of producing goods there and shipping them to the core of Europe are less than the cost of producing the same goods at the core. This is especially true for goods with high value-to-weight ratio, that is, 'weightless' goods.

However, other countries in the periphery, such as Portugal, Spain and Greece, have not had the same success as Ireland in attracting US investment. The authors conclude, therefore, that economic integration may be one of a number of necessary conditions for a peripheral country to be able to attract FDI, but it is certainly not in itself a sufficient condition.

Krugman (1997) argues that changes in the underlying geography of the world economy resulted in trade becoming less influenced by transportation costs but being more critically dependent on communication. Many authors have argued recently that one of Ireland's current advantages for foreign MNCs is the existence of agglomeration economies and the presence of some of the major companies in electronics and pharmaceuticals. Further, it has been shown theoretically that firms that are linked through production inputs tend to agglomerate geographically. These agglomerations can occur either within narrowly defined industrial sectors or across all industries.

Since many key players in both electronics and pharmaceuticals are present in Ireland, it has become an attractive production base for other firms in the same sector because of the availability of pools of common inputs, such as infrastructure, skilled labour and intermediate inputs. For example, computer firms located in Ireland include Apple, Compaq, Dell, Gateway, Hewlett-Packard, Xerox and IBM, while the semiconductor manufacturers Intel and NEC as well as software companies such as Microsoft, Lotus and Oracle also have production facilities in Ireland. If key players have located abroad successfully, their decision signals to other firms that the chosen location is favourable and, thus, triggers the location of these 'followers' in the same locale (ibid.).

Indigenous industry

If FDI has driven Ireland's development, it has been to some extent at the expense of domestic industry. Over the twenty-year period from 1960 to 1980 there was no employment growth in Irish indigenous industry. The 1960s' improvement in the Irish economy led to an increase in demand in the Irish market, which was met by imports. After 1980, with demand falling, imports continued to make inroads. In 1986, there was a slump in domestic demand which had catastrophic effects on indigenous industry with large numbers of firms closing and reductions of staffing levels in others. Table 10.1 shows that between 1980 and 1988 employment in

Table 10.1 Permanent full-time manufacturing employment 1980–97

Year	Irish	Foreign	Total
1980	143,000	88,400	231,700
1988	110,918	82,381	193,299
1997	120,700	107,173	228,873

Source: IDA/Forfas Employment Survey.

Irish-owned manufacturing firms dropped from 143,300 to 110,918, or by almost 23 per cent. After 1988 came the first indication of an increase in employment numbers. This may not appear to be spectacular but when one considers the performance of indigenous Irish industry over these years it actually represents the most successful period of growth under conditions of open international competition. The very substantial growth in foreign-owned manufacturing industry over the same period has masked the quite remarkable growth in indigenous industry, with much of the growth occurring in the high-technology sectors of software, medical instruments, office machinery and data processing equipment, electronics, telecommunications and pharmaceuticals. Irish indigenous industry had for a long time been under-represented in these sectors compared to the industrial structure of the EU. This is still the case for the most part, but the growth in these sectors means that, rather than building on traditional relative strengths, Irish indigenous industry has showed signs of developing new areas of competence and this has been matched by increases in expenditure on R&D.

The reversal of the decline in indigenous manufacturing has been matched by growing contributions to economic output – gross output increased from £7.2 bn to just under £10 bn between 1985 and 1995 (1985 prices). Profitability also increased over the 1990s: whereas profits expressed as a percentage of sales were 3.9 per cent in 1989, they increased to 4.3 per cent in 1995 and an estimated 6.2 per cent in 1996.

It is a generally accepted fact that from the late 1950s until the 1980s indigenous industry was neglected. This was partly because the attention of policy makers was distracted from indigenous industry by the high profile attached to the attraction of multinationals, but it was also because there was little that could have been done for the bulk of weak and uncompetitive indigenous industry which had grown up under the protectionist policies in place until the early 1960s. Since the mid-1980s, however, indigenous industry has shown a remarkable turnaround and has been able to improve its competitive performance. This has been shown by O'Malley (1998) to be due to a variety of reasons:

- Most if not all of the uncompetitive companies which grew up under the protectionist years had already gone, leaving only the more competitive ones.
- Changes in industrial policy which focussed on the problems of indigenous companies in the marketplace started to have an effect.
- There were more existing indigenous companies expanding than new companies being formed.
- The companies were predominantly in high-tech areas.
- Backward linkages developed into indigenous firms, with Irish-economy expenditure per employee in foreign firms rising by 50 per cent from 1983 to 1995.

Linkages

The question of 'linkage' between indigenous and foreign firms has been a contentious point in Irish industrial policy. According to Kennedy (1991), the strategy of attracting foreign investment has not succeeded in 'encouraging link-ages with the rest of the economy'. An analysis of data from the 1974 census of firms in Ireland suggested that new foreign-owned enterprises tended to have lower linkages than new domestic enterprises and that linkages tend to increase over time in new enterprises and particularly in foreign-owned enterprises. Following the ever-increasing criticisms of poor linkages between FDI and indige-nous Irish industry, and the continuing poor performance and ongoing closures of the latter, action was taken in the mid-1980s to address the problems of indigenous Irish industry. Kennedy (1991) identified the four critical deficiencies that needed to be overcome to meet the supply needs of foreign multinationals:

- lack of quality control, and inadequate product standards;
- low productivity and efficiency;
- lack of customer support services, resulting in late deliveries etc.; and
- inadequate financial control.

The solution put forward was the National Linkage Programme (NLP), which was a co-ordinated approach by industry and state agencies to finding solutions to these real problems/deficiencies of Irish industry. An objective of the NLP was the development (by target companies) of plans, including milestones to be reached in terms of quality, service and technology improvements, to meet the international standard required.

The NLP also focussed on upgrading local suppliers by improving their technical know-how and ability – initially in the electronics sector where the potential was largest and where industry itself was keen. An evaluation of the NLP by Crowley (1996) concluded that there was an increased capacity and competence in supply companies serving the needs of MNCs.

Quality became a key issue for indigenous Irish industry in the late 1980s and 1990s. State agencies actively promoted ISO 9000, and offered practical support to companies seeking registration. The net effect was a huge number of registrations of companies in Ireland for ISO 9000 over the ensuing years, as can be seen from Table 10.2. The quality of Irish goods and services, which was a major problem for Irish indigenous industry in the years up to the late 1980s, has also been corrected.

According to the study by Ruane and Gorg (1998) of linkages in the electron-ics sector, indigenous firms in this sector appear to have higher linkages with domestic supplier firms than foreign firms, although the gap seems to be narrow-ing, particularly since the 1990s. Indeed, by the early 1990s, foreign firms sourced 24 per cent of their raw material inputs locally (compared with the Scottish expe-rience of 14 per cent in 1991). Large firms and expanding firms have lower linkages than other firms, *ceteris paribus*. This may be due to large or growing firms being better able to internalize their operations, that is, expand vertically rather than create more backward linkages. Alternatively, it may be due to the fact that Irish suppliers do not have the necessary scale for supplying big firms, especially where corporate policy is to source inputs globally from a small number of suppliers. Overall, however, firms increase their linkages over time, which may

Table 10.2 ISO 9000 registrations in Ireland

Date	ISO registrations
1993 January	100
1993 September	893
1994 June	1,132
1995 March	1,410
1995 December	1,617
1996 December	2,056
1997 December	2,534
1998 December	2,854
1999 December	3,100

Source: International Standards Organization (ISO).

indicate that once foreign firms get accustomed to the local market, they also source more of their inputs locally.

Kennedy (1998) and others argue that, with an increasingly integrated European Community, Ireland is becoming more akin to a small region within a large country. He goes on to point out that it would not be sensible for a region, in developing sub-supply industries, to focus only on purchases within the region, it must also concentrate on sub-supplies to other regions, or as in this case to enterprises in other member states of the EU. The sub-supply strategy of the NLP is not just to supply multinationals in Ireland, but to use them as a platform for developing sub-supply to enterprises in Europe and beyond. The NLP also promotes the development of a number of integrated contract manufacturing companies who can meet customer trends towards reduced numbers of vendors by offering a more comprehensive range of services, including management of lower tier suppliers, purchasing of sub-components, etc.

Significant linkages of indigenous Irish industry with FDI have taken many years. This was because of the poor state of indigenous industry from the 1960s to the mid-1980s. Even today linkage with the pharmaceutical industry is very small. However, by 1996 foreign enterprises in the manufacturing sector were responsible for nearly as much Irish economy expenditure as their Irish-owned counterparts.

Conclusions

The success of the Irish economy over the last decade has received much favourable comment. Considering that Ireland has come from the economic doldrums of the 1950s, through initial success with FDI in the 1960s and early 1970s, followed by recession and financial crisis in 1987, the performance of the Irish economy over the last ten years is remarkable. All commentators agree that Ireland's success in attracting FDI is the key factor that has led to the major economic success in the last decade. However, since Ireland is just one of many countries that have focussed on FDI as a strategy to industrial development, the question must be asked, what are the factors that have made Ireland such an attractive location for FDI? While the

Irish economy has been able to benefit from a variety of internal factors ranging from its position as a low-cost English-speaking country to its demography, and from external factors such as membership of the EU and the overall health of the world (particularly the United States) economy, the government's role has been of central importance. As well as focusing on the development of education and infrastructure, providing a stable labour relations policy and establishing a flexible economic policy, it has pursued a strategic industrial policy – with the establishment of a professional IDA pursuing a targeted approach to attracting investment.

In all of these actions the state has built on existing networks, thereby strengthening and enhancing them, or has evolved totally new networks particularly in the case of industrial policy and national wage and salary agreements. Arguably networks, and the alignment of these networks, have played an important role in Ireland's drive towards industrialization at a variety of levels. Networks consisting of government departments and ministers, the IDA, Irish embassies, MNCs already in Ireland, universities and institutes of technology, have worked together with the objective of attracting FDI into the state. The IDA, industry (both MNC and indigenous), education policy makers and the education system have worked together to produce major improvements in education and training. The NLP can be considered as an alignment of networks, which included policy makers, state development agencies, private consultants and MNCs in Ireland. This alignment has assisted the development of linkages between indigenous industry and MNCs, and together with the National Standards Authority of Ireland (NSAI) and quality system consultants, these networks have also contributed in a significant way to the revival of indigenous industry. Government, unions and employers worked together in partnership to produce a series of national wage and salary agreements giving industrial stability, moderate pay increases and the basis for the growth in the 1990s. EU and government networks have helped to improve infrastructure and develop human resources.

Ireland faces a number of threats in the future. It is vulnerable to changes in technology, competition from other European locations particularly Eastern Europe, and the possibility that other EU member states could force changes in Ireland's taxation and wage rates. Furthermore, for Ireland to continue to be attractive as a location for FDI, it must remain competitive. Difficulties with the most recent National Wage and Salary Agreement, strikes in the public sector and the highest inflation rate in the EU, all suggest that maintaining competitiveness will be difficult. The government and development agencies constantly monitor Ireland's competitive position, and introduce change in policy and incentives as required. A good example is the recent initiative of the IDA in encouraging senior management of multinational subsidiaries to adopt a more genuinely strategic approach to development and thereby enhance the subsidiary mandate.

References

Barry, F., Bradley, J. and Hannan, A. (2001) 'The single market, the structural funds and Ireland's recent economic growth', *Journal of Common Market Studies*, 39(3): 537–52.

Crowley, M. (1996) 'National Linkage Programme: Final evaluation report', Industry Evaluation Unit, Department of Enterprise and Employment, Dublin.

ESRI, *Medium-Term Reviews 1997–2003 and 1999–2005*, Dublin: Economic & Social Research Institute.

Gorg, H. and Ruane, F. (2000) 'European integration and peripherality: lessons from the Irish experience', *World Economy*, 23(March): 405–21.

Government Publications Office (1984) *White Paper on Industrial Development*, Dublin: Government Publications Office.

Kennedy, K. (1991) 'Linkages and overseas industry', in A. Foley and D. McAleese (eds) *Overseas Industry in Ireland*, Dublin: Gill and McMillan, pp. 62–74.

Kennedy, K. (1998) *From Famine to Feast: Economic and Social Change in Ireland 1847–1997*, Dublin: Institute of Public Administration.

Krugman, P. (1997) 'Good news from Ireland: a geographic perspective', in A. Gray (ed.) *International Perspectives on the Irish Economy*, Dublin: Indecon.

Lee, J.J. (1998) 'Education, economy and society', in K. Kennedy (ed.) *From Famine to Feast: Economic and Social Change in Ireland 1847–1997*, Dublin: Institute of Public Administration, pp. 82–105.

O'Hearn, D. (1998) *Inside the Celtic Tiger: The Irish Economy and the Asian Model*, London: Pluto Press.

O'Malley, E. (1998) 'The revival of Irish indigenous industry 1987–97', *Quarterly Economic Commentary*, April, Dublin: The Economic and Social Research Institute.

Ruane, F. and Gorg, H. (1998) 'Linkages between multinationals and indigenous firms: evidence for the electronics sector in Ireland', *Technical Economic Series*, Paper No. 98/13, Dublin: Trinity College.

Ruane, F. and Gorg, H. (1999) 'Irish FDI policy and investment from the EU', in R. Barrell and N. Pain (eds) *Investment, Innovation and the Diffusion of Technology in Europe*, Cambridge University Press, pp. 44–64.

Telesis Consultancy Group (1982) 'A review of industrial policy', NESC Report No. 64, Dublin.

11 Integration of Slovenia into EU and global industrial networks

Matija Rojec and Andreja Jaklič

Introduction

Slovenia is a small and open economy, for which internationalization of operations is a critical factor for creating a competitive corporate sector. The need for intensive internationalization is additionally strengthened by the final stage of the transition process and accession to the European Union (EU). Such integration into the EU/global economy can largely be achieved through corporate networking and foreign direct investment (FDI). Of all internationalization modes FDI, with its backward and forward linkages to home and host economies, seems to remain the most efficient integration tool for, as yet, non-integrated countries.

The aim of the chapter is to review the existing evidence on the internationalization of the Slovenian economy. The first part of the chapter briefly outlines the scale and dynamics of industry integration of Slovenia into EU/global industrial networks through foreign trade, outward and inward processing trade (OPT), and subcontracting and FDI. The second part analyses the integration of the Slovenian car components industry into international industrial networks. The third part concentrates on the motivation and strategies of foreign investors in Slovenia and Slovenian investors abroad. The chapter utilizes available statistical data and existing research and especially ongoing research undertaken at the Center of International Relations of the Faculty of Social Sciences, University of Ljubljana.

Industry integration of Slovenia into EU/global industrial networks

Foreign trade

Slovenia remains a very open economy measured by its participation in foreign trade, with exports ranging from 52 to 63 per cent of GDP over the years 1992–2000 and imports from 55 to 64 per cent (Statistical Office of Republic of Slovenia, various issues). There was a deteriorating but not severe current account balance over this period. In the EU, Slovenia's market share remained almost unchanged in spite of real appreciation of the Slovenian Tolar (SIT). On the other hand, Slovenia lost competitiveness in relation to Central European Free Trade

Table 11.1 Exports and imports of goods by country groups, 1996 and 1999, %

	Exports		Imports	
	1996	*1999*	*1996*	*1999*
Total	8,310 mn USD = 100%	8,546 mn USD = 100%	9,421 mn USD = 100%	10,083 mn USD = 100%
Developed countries	70.3	72.5	77.8	79.8
EU	64.6	66.1	67.5	68.9
EFTA	1.0	1.3	2.6	2.4
Other developed countries[a]	4.7	5.1	7.6	8.5
Developing countries	29.6	27.4	22.2	20.2
CEFTA countries[b]	5.4	7.3	6.5	8.4
Successor countries of former Yugoslavia	16.7	15.2	7.5	5.7
Other European developing countries	5.1	2.6	2.9	2.0
Other developing countries	2.5	2.5	5.3	4.1

Source: Statistical Office of the Republic of Slovenia.

Notes

a In 1999, Republic of Korea is included; in 1996, it was in 'Other developing countries'.

b In 1999, Romania and Bulgaria are included; in 1996, they were in 'Other European developing countries'.

Agreement (CEFTA) countries, which increased their market share in EU by 60 per cent. The geographical structure of Slovenia's foreign trade reveals a high concentration on EU countries, and on the export side in particular on successor countries of the former Yugoslavia (see Table 11.1).

The structure of foreign trade demonstrates the strong involvement of Slovenian manufacturing in intra-industry trade, with intermediate goods being the most important foreign trade item. Highly processed goods dominate the structure of foreign trade by degree of processing.

Inward and outward processing transactions

This large share of intermediate goods in foreign trade suggests that OPT is important for Slovenia. Nevertheless, similar to other transition countries, the overall involvement of Slovenian manufacturing in OPT has been declining since the early 1990s, especially in textiles and certain other sectors, mostly due to increased labour costs or technological changes. The increasing importance of OPT is however evident for wood products, non-metallic mineral products, medical products and optical instruments (Majcen 1998) (see Table 11.2).

Four processing transaction categories can be distinguished: exports after inward processing (so-called active transactions), exports for outward processing (passive

Table 11.2 Share of inward and outward processing in Slovenian exports and imports, 1992 and 1997, in selected manufacturing industries

	Total		EU15	
	1992	*1997*	*1992*	*1997*
Exports				
Manufacturing	14.8	11.1	21.8	15.2
Mfr. of textiles	39.4	27.4	51.8	31.5
Mfr. clothing apparel; dressing fur	83.4	81.4	88.0	86.6
Leather tanning; mfr luggage etc.	21.7	20.8	31.4	24.8
Mfr. coke, refined petroleum products, nuclear fuel	0	32.2	0.0	94.7
Imports				
Manufacturing	15.7	6.9	19.9	8.4
Mfr. of textiles	28.0	17.8	34.7	19.9
Mfr. clothing apparel; dressing fur	84.9	68.6	95.7	78.6
Leather tanning; mfr luggage etc.	32.3	18.3	47.9	21.3
Mfr. coke, refined petroleum products, nuclear fuel	47.3	2.1	40.5	6.7

Source: Majcen (1998).

Notes
Industries with 10% or higher share of inward and outward processing in total exports in 1997.

transactions), imports for inward processing and imports after outward processing. For Slovenian foreign trade, inward processing transactions are traditionally the most important, dating back to the pre-transition period. The EU was the most important region for these transactions in 1992–97, and especially Germany (Pellegrin 2001).

Foreign direct investment

Inward FDI

The FDI stock in Slovenia at the end of 2000 amounted to US$2,808.5 mn (Table 11.3), and continued to rise thereafter, following a slowdown between 1998 and 2000. Record inflows in 2001 and 2002 were predominantly the consequence of several relatively big foreign acquisitions.

As can be seen from Table 11.3, the share of inward FDI stock in Slovenian gross domestic product (GDP) doubled between 1993 and 2000. The 15.5 per cent ratio in 2000 is still relatively low compared to developed market economies and to other most successful transition economies. Foreign investment enterprises (FIE,

Table 11.3 Inward and outward FDI[a] in Slovenia, 1993–2000[b], US$ million

	1993	1994	1995	1996	1997	1998	1999	2000
Inward FDI								
Year-end stock	954.3	1325.9	1763.4	1998.1	2207.3	2765.8	2656.5	2808.5
Annual inflow[c]	112.6	128.1	177.4	194.0	375.2	247.9	181.2	175.5
Stock as % of GDP	7.5	9.2	9.4	10.6	12.1	14.1	13.2	15.5
Outward FDI								
Year-end stock	280.6	354.0	489.9	459.5	459.4	608.3	605.0	794.0
Annual outflow[d]	−1.3	2.9	5.1	−6.3	−35.6	1.7	−37.5	−66.0
Stock as % of GDP	2.2	2.5	2.6	2.4	1.5	3.1	3.0	4.4

Source: Bank of Slovenia.

Notes

a FDI whereby a foreign investor holds a 10% or higher share in a company.

b From 1996 onwards direct investments with indirectly affiliated enterprises are also included.

c Inflows are in principle smaller than changes in stocks since international payments transactions comprise only part of the changes in stock; most notably, inflow data do not include changes in net liabilities to foreign investors, nor data on indirectly affiliated companies. From 1995 onwards data on reinvested earnings are also included in inflows, and thus in the balance of payments.

d Minus sign means outflow.

enterprises with 10 per cent or higher foreign equity share) nevertheless represent a significant segment of the Slovenian economy. In 2000, FIEs accounted for only 13 per cent of total assets and 10 per cent of all employees in the Slovenian non-financial corporate sector, but 16.7 per cent of total net sales, 20 per cent of total operating profits and 29.7 per cent of total exports. In the manufacturing sector, FIEs accounted for 26.3 per cent of total sales and 34.2 per cent of total exports. In the 1995–2000 period, the level of foreign penetration (measured by share of FIEs' assets in total assets) in the manufacturing sector increased from 12.5 to 22 per cent.

Investors from EU countries dominate FDI in Slovenia. At the end of the year 2000 no less than 84 per cent of total inward FDI stock was accounted for by EU countries, the major investors being Austria (45.6 per cent share), Germany (12.5 per cent), France (10.7 per cent) and Italy (5.4 per cent). Proximity of Slovenia to the EU and traditionally strong economic co-operation with Austria, Germany, Italy and France account for this pattern.

Manufacturing, with 43.1 per cent of total 2000 end-year FDI stock, is the most important recipient of FDI in Slovenia; elsewhere, FDI is concentrated in trade (12.4 per cent), financial services (25.4 per cent) and other business services (12 per cent). The industrial distribution of FDI is mostly determined by a handful of large (for Slovenia) FDI projects. Foreign investors in Slovenia have been far more attracted by individual Slovenian companies than by particular industries.

Outward FDI

At the end of 2000, the stock of Slovenian outward FDI was US$794 mn, but with a record US$104.2 mn outflow to follow in 2001. Slovenian investors in the

1994–99 period were mostly consolidating their existing investments abroad, while in 2000 and more particularly in 2001, new FDI projects were being established, mostly related to the successor countries of the former Yugoslavia. Croatia had as much as 45.1 per cent of Slovenia's end-2000 outward FDI stock; others included Macedonia (8.3 per cent) and Bosnia-Hercegovina (7.8 per cent) (Svetličič *et al.* 2000). Except for a few multinational firms that succeeded in developing global production, regional production networks are the most important.

In the 1993–2000 period, the share of outward FDI stock in Slovenian GDP doubled (Table 11.3). In 1998, companies investing abroad represented only about 1.3 per cent of the total number of companies in the Slovenian non-financial corporate sector, but they employed 27 per cent of all employees, and realized 25 per cent of total sales, 30 per cent of total value-added and as much as 37 per cent of total exports. In the 1994–98 period these figures increased (Jaklič 2001b). International integration through outward FDI has therefore significantly influenced domestic economic performance and involves a significant part of the domestic economy. As much as 54.4 per cent of Slovenia's end-2000 outward FDI stock is in manufacturing.

The major outward FDI manufacturing industries, as a rule, started internationalization through exports. The first entrants using exports were also the first to adopt more complex modes of doing business abroad. These industries were also more deeply penetrated by inward internationalization, especially in terms of subcontracting, licensing, contract manufacturing and partial projecting.

Integration into EU/global industrial networks via FDI

Inward FDI

Motivation for investing in Slovenia

It is reasonable to distinguish between FDI motivated by gaining access to the Slovenian market (market-seeking FDI) and FDI motivated by Slovenian national competitive advantages, that is, to establish efficient production for a regional or global market in Slovenia (factor cost-seeking). Factor cost-seeking FDI directly increases the competitiveness of a host economy, while market-seeking FDI for a host country is directed primarily at achieving greater consumer satisfaction; the effect on the competitiveness of local producers is indirect, being through increased competition in the local market (Caves 1971, 1982; Dunning 1993).

Table 11.4 shows that access to the local market is the most important single motive for foreign investment in Slovenia; however, the frequency of other motives – like access to markets of South-east Europe, favourable quality and price of labour force – shows that foreign investors in Slovenia are increasingly attracted by the possibility of establishing efficient export-oriented production. This is strongly confirmed by data on the export propensity of FIEs in Slovenia: in 2000, FIEs in Slovenia on average exported 48.1 per cent of their sales, the ratio in the manufacturing sector being as much as 72.7 per cent though only 15.0 per cent in non-manufacturing sectors.

Table 11.4 Motives of foreign investors in Slovenia

Motive	% of FIEs quoting individual motive
Access to Slovenian market	59.4
Long-term cooperation	40.6
Access to markets in South-east Europe	32.4
Labour force quality	30.5
Low cost of labour force	19.5
Technology and know-how	12.5
Recognized trade mark(s)	10.5
Purchasing of material and parts	9.4
Access to EU markets	7.0
Other	6.6

Source: Gral iteo in Agencija RS za gospodarsko promocijo Slovenije in tuje investicije pri Ministrstvu za gospodarstvo (Trade and Investment Promotion Agency) 2001.

Notes
257 FIEs answered the question. Each respondent was allowed to quote multiple motives.

Case studies support these statistical findings, although suggesting that foreign investors tend to be influenced by a combination of market-seeking, factor cost-seeking and strategic motives (Rojec and Stanojević 2001).

Wages as a determinant of FDI in Slovenia

As far as labour is concerned, it is the quality rather than the low cost of labour that motivates foreign investors in Slovenia. This is reflected also in the tendency of FDI to locate in capital rather than labour-intensive manufacturing industries. Moreover, FIEs tend to use capital-intensive techniques much more than do domestic enterprises (DEs) within particular manufacturing industries.[1] On average, FIEs in the manufacturing sector use 2.33 times more machinery and equipment per employee than DEs. On the other hand, FIEs pay on average only 17 per cent higher labour costs per employee than DEs. It seems that the more capital-intensive production techniques of FIEs are rather standardized and, in principle, do not require more skilled labour. FIEs use more or less the same pro-portion of skilled labour as do DEs and pay somewhat higher wages, but as a result of these higher wages are able to achieve much greater labour productivity. The indicator of value-added per labour cost is very persuasive in this regard: with 1 SIT of labour costs, manufacturing FIEs are able to produce 1.84 SIT of value-added, while DEs obtain only 1.38 SIT (1999 data).

So far as the foreign investor is concerned, the price of labour in Slovenia is lower, that is labour cost per employee, than any of the major EU investing coun-tries, but Slovenia lags well behind in terms of productivity, that is, quality of labour measured by value-added per employee. The foreign investor has to be confident

Table 11.5 Value-added and labour costs per employee in Slovenian manufacturing and major EU investing countries in 1998

	Value-added per employee (€)	Labour costs[a] per employee (€)	Value-added per labour costs (ratio)
EU – 15	48,800	33,400	1.46
Austria	58,072	34,736	1.67
Germany	56,120	39,078	1.44
Italy	38,552	27,722	1.39
France	62,952	38,744	1.63
Slovenia	16,680	10,624	1.57
FIEs[b] in Slovenia	22,565	11,784	1.92

Source: Eurostat 2000; Statistical Office of the Republic of Slovenia 1999.

Notes
a Remuneration in the case of EU countries and compensation of employees in the case of Slovenia.
b Calculated by applying FIEs/All enterprises indexes from company financial statements data (Institute for Macroeconomic Analysis and Development; based on Bank of Slovenia and Agency for Payments data) to national accounts data for Slovenian manufacturing as a whole.

of achieving approximately the same productivity as at home but at lower labour costs. Thus, the value-added per labour cost ratio in foreign manufacturing FIEs in Slovenia is much higher than in any of the major EU investing countries in Slovenia (Table 11.5).

Restructuring and development impact of inward FDI

Major findings from the analysis of FIE vs DE performance and operating characteristics (Rojec 1998, 2000b) are: (i) FIEs perform much better than DEs for the vast majority of individual manufacturing industries in which FIEs are involved, as well as overall; (ii) FIE activities are distributed in a radically different pattern from DEs, indicating that FIEs bring about considerable industrial change; (iii) apart from ownership-specific advantages brought by foreign investors, there seem to be four major areas in which FIEs show distinctively different operating indicators that might explain their superior performance: company size, level of capital intensity, structure of assets and level of export orientation. Compared to DEs, FIEs are much larger in size, more capital-intensive, have a better asset structure and are more export-oriented. FIEs in the Slovenian manufacturing sector export a significantly larger portion of their output than DEs and buy significantly more inputs abroad than DEs (Rojec 2000b; Rojec *et al.* 2000).

FDI occurs mainly in capital-intensive (56 per cent) and labour-intensive (37 per cent) industrial groups (Majcen 1998).[2] In terms of exports, the capital-intensive orientation of FIEs is even more pronounced. On the other hand, DEs could be characterized mainly as producers of labour-intensive and human capital-intensive products. Majcen concludes that FDI has had a positive role in the restructuring process in Slovenia.

Case studies of FIEs focus on the restructuring in a company after the entry of the strategic foreign partner (Agens 1999; Rojec and Svetličič 1998a–c; Svetličič and Rojec 1998). Even before foreign acquisition, most of the interviewed enterprises had been at a reasonable technological level that made them appealing to foreign investors. Most would have encountered much greater difficulties with their survival and further development without the input of strategic foreign investors. Restructuring of the acquired companies usually took place relatively smoothly and speedily. In some cases, strategic foreign investors did not produce dramatic overnight changes but speeded up existing restructuring efforts. In all cases, foreign partners brought new technology, know-how, finance and the means for the company to gain access to western markets. The changes that most frequently occurred following a take-over of a company by a strategic foreign investor include:

- product quality upgraded as a result of changes in production and technology, and accentuating product quality issues;
- production programmes improved, with the range of products mostly being reduced so as to concentrate on core activities;
- organizational structure changed to reflect western business methods;
- considerable initial and continuing increase of training for management and also for workers;
- new systems of accounting and financial reporting set up which conformed to international accounting standards; much more emphasis on information gathering and dissemination as crucial for competent decision-making; large amounts of resources invested in internal information and control systems;
- managers in general retained their jobs (a great deal of importance was attributed to the stability of management), but in most cases there was a redundancy of workers, in principle accomplished by soft methods (early retirement, help to establish private business, etc.), with remaining workers generally better paid and more productive than in comparable domestic enterprises;
- subsidiary–parent company relations depend on the nature of the organization of a parent company, with strategic decisions generally being made at the foreign partner's headquarters, although in day-to-day operations the subsidiaries interviewed were largely autonomous;
- role and quality of marketing substantially improved;
- foreign partners generally instrumental in introducing environmentally better products and processes.

Outward FDI[3]

Motivation and strategies of Slovenian investors abroad

The analysis is based on a survey of 32 Slovenian companies, holding about 16 per cent of the total stock of Slovenian outward FDI. Market-seeking motives were found to be the most important, followed by strategic asset-seeking, increased efficiency and, lastly, resource-seeking motives, using the categories of Dunning (1993).

That most Slovenian outward FDI is clearly market seeking and can easily be explained by the loss of the former Yugoslavian market after Slovenia gained independence, the smallness of the domestic market with increasing competition from foreign companies and stage of economic development (Dunning 1993). It also reflects the fact that export commodity composition is concentrated in those commodity groups for which foreign demand is growing at less than average rates. FDI is then employed to retain existing market shares as well as to expand or acquire them; thus, outward FDI is also a means of 'market protection'.

Although Slovenia is a poor country in terms of factor endowments, resource-seeking motives appeared to be the least important. Production factor costs were also assessed as an unimportant motive for most of the sample companies, although labour costs are relatively high in Slovenia and much lower in some major host countries of Slovenian outward FDI, most notably successor countries of the former Yugoslavia. This is perhaps partly explained by the low labour productivity and higher risk in those successor countries, despite low hourly labour costs.

The fact that market potential outweighs factor price differences (or labour cost, or natural resources) as a motivation for investing abroad suggests that Slovenian multinational enterprises (MNE)s are more of a horizontal than a vertical type. Slovenian affiliates abroad are also more trade than production oriented. As the survey showed, only 11 per cent of foreign affiliates of the interviewed companies are involved in manufacturing, while more than 90 per cent of them are in sales and marketing. The modest share of resource-seeking motives is consequently understandable.

Strategic asset-seeking is the second most important motive for Slovenian investors abroad. Company growth and strengthening overall competitive position were assessed as particularly important motives for investing abroad. Two issues are especially related to strategic asset-seeking FDI: first, firm-specific strategic advantages; second, acquisitions and mergers.

Firm-specific strategic advantages represent specific products adapted to and already affirmed in markets of penetration. The companies going abroad seek to capitalize on technology that is not very new but is suited to the needs of local factor configurations. Quite a number of Slovenian firms are investing abroad in kind, transferring to their affiliates their own technology while, at the same time, starting to upgrade their own. Such investment offers first-time foreign direct investors the opportunity to gain competitive strength in an unfamiliar market.

Although acquisitions increase the speed of growth and asset creation of a firm and offer fast technology and knowledge transfers, companies at the beginning of the internationalization process are often unable to cope with acquisitions. They are quite rare in the case of Slovenian outward FDI. According to the survey in 1999, 85.4 per cent of foreign affiliates of the sample companies were established as greenfield, only 11.7 per cent through acquisitions and 2.9 per cent through mergers.

Often, strategic asset-seeking motives are closely related to efficiency-seeking motives, which, in our survey, follow strategic asset-seeking motives in terms of importance. The efficiency-seeking motivation for outward FDI can only be realized after a parent company has already established some foreign affiliates. Through central supervision of geographically spread activities, this type of investment aims to increase yields by specialization, economies of scale and scope and risk diversification. Although the affiliate network of the average sample company is expanding (according to the survey, on average from two to four in the 1992–98 period), there are only a few *star companies* in Slovenia that are in a position to invest abroad for this reason. Although Slovenian MNEs are on average bigger and more experienced than Slovenian companies without direct investments abroad, they are still small and inexperienced compared to western MNEs.

Impact of outward FDI on investing firms and the home economy

The Slovenian foreign investors interviewed mostly reported positive effects of outward FDI for the investing companies. Outward FDI greatly increases the investing companies' market shares, exports and domestic production levels, but the effect is much less on domestic employment and imports (Table 11.6). This reflects the predominantly market-seeking motivation of Slovenian foreign investors. More specifically, investing companies assess that outward FDI has stimulated them to introduce new products and to increase their range of products (71 per cent of sample companies) and to increase quality (65 per cent). Direct presence in a foreign market has helped them respond to customers' needs more rapidly. By investing abroad, firms also achieved other positive asset-creation effects. They have improved their image (93 per cent) and enhanced and broadened their marketing, management and organizational skills (60 per cent), all of which are important learning effects. Technological learning has been more modest since the majority of host countries are less developed than Slovenia. In short, most of the interviewed companies assess that outward FDI has increased their efficiency (81 per cent) and restructuring (59 per cent).

Firm-level effects spill over to the whole domestic economy and influence trade balance, level and structure of industrial production and investment and employment, all with related development implications. Outward FDI was found to be complementary to exports; it has not crowded out domestic investment. Investing

Table 11.6 Effects of foreign affiliates on the parent company (% of investors)

Effects on	Strong increase	Increase	Unchanged	Decrease	Strong decrease
Market share	26	53	18	3	0
No. of employees	0	24	59	12	6
Exports	9	74	18	0	0
Imports	0	29	53	6	12
Production volume	9	68	24	0	0

Source: Survey.

firms have the highest growth potential, while exposure to foreign competition forces them to pursue high quality adaptations and innovations, which are also introduced in the home economy. Slovenian foreign investors believe that their outward FDI (strongly) improves or speeds up the competitiveness and transformation of the Slovenian economy, as well as its EU integration.

Integration of the Slovenian car components industry into EU/global industrial networks[4]

As an example of the integration of Slovenian firms into EU/global industrial networks, we examine the case of the car components industry, concentrating primarily on two aspects, namely the pattern of relations with suppliers and customers and technology transfer. The analysis is based on a questionnaire survey of the major car component manufacturers in Slovenia. Questionnaires were sent to thirty-nine companies that are members of the Slovenian Automotive Component Manufacturers Association, twenty-six of whom replied. It should be noted that, on average, members of the Association perform much better than manufacturing enterprises; they have higher returns on equity and higher value-added per employee. According to 1998 data, Association members are more than ten times bigger than the average manufacturing enterprise, they are also more capital-intensive and much more export-oriented.

Products and sales

The interviewed companies produce a wide variety of car parts and components. Almost three-quarters consider their products to be of very high or high complexity, and only one company classed its products as low or very low complexity.[5] All three foreign companies responding make products of very high complexity (Table 11.7).

The companies interviewed on average export more than 80 per cent of their production, the export propensity being the highest in the case of high complexity products, closely followed by very high and medium complexity products. Foreign companies seem to be more export-oriented than mixed and domestic

Table 11.7 Complexity of product and type of ownership

	Domestic	Foreign	Mixed	Total
1. Very low complexity	1	0	0	1
2. Low complexity	0	0	0	0
3. Medium complexity	4	0	1	5
4. High complexity	2	0	4	6
5. Very high complexity	6	3	4	13
Complexity not defined	1	0	0	1
Total	14	3	9	26

Source: Survey. Data refer to number of companies.

companies, but the small number of cases surveyed must be taken into account. The EU is ranked as by far the most important market for the interviewed companies, followed well behind by the domestic market, then other markets (including Central and Eastern European (CEE) and Commonwealth of Independent States (CIS) countries), which are of relatively low significance.

Suppliers and customers

The companies interviewed usually source from both foreign and domestic suppliers (eighteen out of twenty-six) or from foreign suppliers only (eight). None of the companies sourced only from domestic suppliers. There are no major differences between types of companies (domestic/foreign/mixed, or MNE/independent) in terms of supplier patterns.

The relationships between the companies and their suppliers are assessed on average as strong, more so for high complexity products (higher than for very high complexity products), mixed companies and where companies are a part of an MNE (Table 11.8). This is probably explained by the higher integration of highly export-oriented subsidiaries into a foreign parent company's network.

Much the most frequent buyers of Slovenian automotive components manufacturers are final assemblers, followed by other suppliers and retailers. In as many as

Table 11.8 Relationships with suppliers by product complexity, type of ownership and MNE participation, average scores

	Relationships with suppliers
Nature of product	
1. Very low complexity	n.a.[a]
2. Low complexity	—
3. Medium complexity	3.00[a]
4. High complexity	4.33
5. Very high complexity	3.78[a]
Complexity not defined	3.50
Type of ownership	
Domestic	3.55[a]
Foreign	3.00[a]
Mixed	4.11
MNE participation	
Part of MNE	4.20[a]
Non-part of MNE	3.63[a]
Average	3.78[a]

Source: Survey.

Notes
Score 1 = very weak relationships, 5 = very strong relationships.
a Not all interviewees in this category answer the question.

84.6 per cent of the cases, MNEs are among the customers. Final assemblers seem to be relatively more frequent buyers from domestic rather than foreign and mixed companies.

R&D and technology transfer

The vast majority (88.5 per cent) of the interviewed companies undertake some R&D (see Table 11.9). The frequency of R&D does not seem to depend greatly on the product complexity, as proportions of all complexity categories from medium upwards are high. On the other hand, foreign companies and companies that are part of MNEs have lower frequency of R&D.

In the questionnaire, we concentrated on two streams of technology transfer: that from interviewed companies to their suppliers and that from buyers to the

Table 11.9 R&D and transfer of technology by nature of product, type of ownership and MNE participation

	R&D undertaken		Technology transfer to suppliers		Technology transfer from buyers		Importance of technology transfer[a]
	Number	Propn.	Number	Propn.	Number	Propn.	
Nature of product							
1. Very low complexity	0	0.0	0	0.0	0	0.0	1.00
2. Low complexity	—	—	—	—	—	—	—
3. Medium complexity	5	100.0	4	80.0	4	80.0	3.00
4. High complexity	5	83.3	6	100.0	5	83.3	4.00
5. Very high complexity	12	92.3	8	61.5	6	46.2	3.55
Complexity not defined	1	100.0	1	100.0	1	100.0	4.00
Type of ownership							
Domestic	13	92.9	9	64.3	7	50.0	3.00
Foreign	2	66.7	1	33.3	0	0.0	3.00
Mixed	8	88.9	9	100.0	8	88.9	4.22
MNE participation							
Part of MNE	5	71.4	6	85.7	6	85.7	4.14
Not part of MNE	18	94.7	13	68.4	9	47.4	3.18
Total	23	88.5	19	73.1	15	57.7	3.46

Source: Survey numbers of companies.

Notes
Number = no. of reporting companies;
Propn = proportion of all companies of this kind.
a 1 = very low importance; 5 = very high importance of technology transfer for upgrading.

interviewed companies. The first characteristic observed is that transfers to suppliers are much more frequent (73.1 per cent of cases) than transfers from buyers (57.7 per cent). In relation to the level of product complexity, the most outstanding feature is that in very high complexity products transfers in both directions are much less frequent, conforming to the general belief that transfer of technology happens not at the technology frontier but somewhere inside it. At the leading edge, firms keep their knowledge to themselves. For the firms on the receiving end this means they do not receive disembodied technology but completed products. Technology transfers in both directions are relatively more frequent for companies with foreign equity participation (particularly those that are part of MNEs) than for domestic companies.

Companies were also asked to assess the importance of technology transfer for upgrading what they make and how they make it (Table 11.9, final column). In general, companies attach much importance to technology transfer in the above sense; however, there was little correlation between the frequency of technology transfer and the level of importance attached to the transfer, so frequency does not imply importance. This seems to be influenced by the fact that own R&D is important for the domestic companies interviewed.

The interviews show that companies with high frequency of R&D also have high frequency of technology transfer in both directions, supporting the notion of 'absorptive capacity' (Cohen and Levinthal 1989). Foreign companies, which demonstrate the lowest frequency of R&D, also demonstrate the lowest frequency of technology transfer in both directions. There are two main exceptions: (i) in very high complexity products the frequency of R&D is high but the frequency of technology transfer is much lower; (ii) companies not part of MNEs show much higher frequency of R&D undertaken than companies that are, but at the same time have much less frequent technology transfer than the latter.

Another interesting issue is whether there is any link between frequency of technology transfer to suppliers and type of suppliers, or similarly from buyers Technology transfer to suppliers is relatively much more frequent in the case of companies having foreign as well as domestic suppliers (83.3 per cent of cases) than in the case of companies having only foreign suppliers (50 per cent). The interviews indicate that the capabilities and competencies of suppliers and the strength of the relationships between suppliers and buyers, do not seem to have much influence on whether or not the technology transfer to suppliers will occur.

In the case of technology transfer from buyers, the transfer is relatively more frequent in the case of retailers as buyers (75 per cent of cases), than final assemblers (61.9 per cent) and other suppliers as buyers (59 per cent), and more frequent in the case of MNE buyers (60.9 per cent) than non-MNE buyers (33.3 per cent). This confirms the expectation that MNE buyers more frequently transfer technology to their suppliers to make them produce according their blueprints.

Conclusions

Slovenia is a small economy, for which internationalization of operations is a critical factor in creating a competitive corporate sector. Relatively high shares of exports and imports in GDP indicate that the economy is heavily dependent on foreign markets and inputs. This orientation is additionally strengthened by the final stage of the transition process and accession to the EU. To become viable actors in the internal market of the EU and globally, Slovenian companies undoubtedly need to increase the internationalization of their activities via all possible modes, but especially FDI.

Traditionally, the major method of internationalization of Slovenian companies has been foreign trade. With the beginning of transition and disintegration of the former Yugoslavia, it was precisely the ability of the Slovenian corporate sector to reorient sales to EU markets that helped the companies cope with increased competition in the domestic market and with the loss of the former Yugoslavian market.

In these respects, Slovenia is gradually losing its traditional competitive advantages, based on a relatively cheap but reliable and quality labour force, and is still lagging behind with regard to restructuring the economy towards higher value-added activities. This results in the market shares of Slovenia abroad remaining unchanged, which jeopardizes existing export competitiveness, removes the rationale for OPT (which is losing importance) and advances FDI as the major Slovenian internationalization challenge for the future. This holds for inward as well as for outward FDI. The evidence suggests that inward FDI helps in restructuring the corporate sector towards industries with higher value-added per employee and, thus, increases national competitiveness. On the other hand, outward FDI, by establishing a direct presence in foreign markets, promotes exports and enables restructuring of the investing firms by relocating some lower value-added, labour-intensive activities abroad. Inward and outward FDI directly foster the internationalization of the Slovenian corporate sector and also indirectly stimulate it, by a positive impact on the restructuring process and hence national competitiveness. For these reasons, intensification of inward and outward FDI is the main challenge for the internationalization of the Slovenian economy in the future.

Outward FDI activity by the Slovenian corporate sector has been relatively low since the beginning of transition and has started to emerge only recently. This coincides with the concluding phase of defensive, transition-related enterprise restructuring in an increasing number of companies. Outward FDI is motivated by market-seeking as well as efficiency-seeking factors and is directed towards the countries of the former Yugoslavia and, to a lesser extent, other transition countries. Outward internationalization via FDI is expected to strengthen in the future and to tackle the EU countries as well, related to the EU integration process of Slovenia.

In the past, Slovenia has not been very successful in attracting FDI from abroad, and this has been an important reason for the slow restructuring of the Slovenian corporate sector and stagnation of its export competitiveness. The explanations for FDI inflows not being as high as in countries like Hungary and Czech Republic include: (i) the small local market; (ii) the mass privatization concept in industry and trade which implicitly favoured internal (employee and management) buy-outs; (iii) hesitance over privatization of state ownership until recently in the financial and public utilities sector; (iv) administrative barriers to investment and operation of companies; (v) problems in acquiring industrial locations; (vi) relatively rigid and protective labour legislation; and (vii) policy for promoting FDI long being rather passive (Dedek and Novak 1998; FIAS 2000; Rojec 1998).

Internationalization of operations is increasingly becoming a critical factor for creating and stimulating a competitive corporate sector in Slovenia. To strengthen the internationalization processes, policy should focus on lifting barriers to internationalization. As far as inward FDI is concerned, Slovenia should promote FDI in companies being privatized under the mass privatization scheme, open up the privatization of state-owned assets to strategic and institutional foreign investors, stimulate all kinds of foreign investments in the sector of business services, encourage private investments in industrial estates where the state has provided appropriate infrastructure and establish an institution for the promotion of FDI with a clear legal mandate, professional supervision and appropriate staff and budgetary funding. The state should also assist potential Slovenian investors abroad by: using consulates and embassies to collect and provide information about investment opportunities and make preliminary contacts with potential foreign partners; improving the climate and regulatory framework for direct investments abroad; and promoting the establishment of risk-capital funds to facilitate activities related to investment abroad.

Notes

1 Of twenty manufacturing industries with FDI participation, no less than seventeen FIEs have higher machinery and equipment per employee than DEs (1999 data).
2 Majcen distinguishes between capital-intensive, labour-intensive, human capital-intensive, and R&D and human capital-intensive industrial groups.
3 This part is based on Jaklič (2001a,b); Svetličič and Jaklič (2002).
4 This part is based on Rojec (2000a).
5 No exact definition of product complexity was given to the interviewees. They were just asked to give their own view on the subject.

References

Agens (1999) Tuje naložbe v podjetjih SRD (Foreign Investment in Companies of Slovenian Development Corporation), *Agens*, No. 66, pp. 6–7.

Caves, R.E. (1971) 'International corporations: the industrial economics of foreign investment', *Economica*, 38(2): 1–27.

Caves, R.E. (1982) *Multinational Enterprise and Economic Analysis*, Cambridge UK: Cambridge University Press.

Cohen, D. and Levinthal, D. (1989) 'Innovation and learning: the two faces of R&D', *Economic Journal* (September).

Dedek, F. and Novak, J. (1998) *Raziskava podjetij s tujim in mešanim kapitalom (Research of Companies with Foreign and Mixed Capital)*. Ljubljana: Gral iteo, Urad za gospodarsko promocijo in tuje investicije pri Ministrstvu za ekonomske odnose in razvoj.

Dunning, J.H. (1993) *Multinational Enterprises and the Global Economy*, Wokingham: Addison-Wesley.

Eurostat (2000) *Statistics in Focus – Economy and Finance*, Theme 2 – 23/2000. Luxembourg: Eurostat.

FIAS (2000) *Administrative Barriers to Foreign Investment in Slovenia*, Washington, D.C.: Foreign Investment Advisory Service.

Gral iteo in Agencija RS za gospodarsko promocijo Slovenije in tuje investicije pri Ministrstvu za gospodarstvo (Trade and Investment Promotion Agency). 2001. 'Raziskava podjetij s tujim in mešanim kapitalom v letu 2001' (Research of companies with foreign and mixed equity in 2001), Ljubljana, Mimeo.

Jaklič, A. (2001a) 'Internationalisation of Slovenian companies during transition', in Liuhto Kari (ed.) *East go West – The Internationalisation of Eastern Enterprises*, Lappeenranta: Lappeenranta University of Technology, pp. 380–403.

Jaklič, A. (2001b) *Outward Internationalisation by Direct Investment*, Study prepared within Phare ACE project P97-8073-R. Ljubljana: Faculty of Social Sciences.

Majcen, B. (1998) *Industrial Growth and Structural Changes in the Associated Countries – the Case of Slovenia*. ACE Research Programme (Project no. P96-6148R) 'Trade between the European Union and the Associated States: prospects for the future', Ljubljana: Institute for Economic Research, Mimeo.

Pellegrin, J. (2001) *The Political Economy of Competitiveness in an Enlarged Europe*, Basingstoke: Palgrave.

Rojec, M. (1998) *Restructuring with Foreign Direct Investment: The Case of Slovenia*, Ljubljana: Institute of Macroeconomic Analysis and Development.

Rojec, M. (2000a) 'Car components manufacturing in Slovenia', Ljubljana: Faculty of Social Sciences, Mimeo.

Rojec, M. (2000b) 'Restructuring and efficiency upgrading with FDI', in G. Hunya (ed.) *Integration Through Foreign Direct Investment*, Cheltenham, UK, Northampton, USA: Edward Elgar in association with The Vienna Institute for International Economic Studies (WIIW), pp. 130–49.

Rojec, M., Damijan, J.P. and Majcen, B. (2000) 'Export propensity of foreign subsidiaries in Slovenian manufacturing industry', *Globalisation and European Integration*. 6th EACES Conference, Barcelona, 7–9 September.

Rojec, M. and Stanojević, M. (2001) 'Slovenia: factor cost-seeking FDI and manufacturing', in G. Gradev (ed.) *CEE Countries in the EU Companies' Strategies of Industrial Restructuring and Relocation*, Brussels: European Trade Union Institute, pp. 137–71.

Rojec, M. and Svetličič, M. (1998a) 'Sarrio Slovenija Ltd. – Cartonboard-producing company in the control of Saffa S.p.A. from Italy', *Eastern European Economics*, 36(6): 29–54.

Rojec, M. and Svetličič, M. (1998b) 'Tobačna Ljubljana, d.o.o. – cigarette producing company with the majority share of Reemtsma, Germany, and Seita, France', *Eastern European Economics*, 36(6): 55–97.

Rojec, M. and Svetličič, M. (1998c) 'Biterm d.o.o.: Thermostat-Producing Company of Gorenje GA (Slovenia) and Danfoss International A/S (Denmark)', *Eastern European Economics*, 36(5): 73–93.

Statistical Office of Republic of Slovenia (various issues) *Statistical Yearbook of the Republic of Slovenia*, Ljubljana: SORS.

Svetličič, M. and Jaklič, A. (2002) 'Internationalisation through outward FDI – the case of Slovenia', in M. Marinov (ed.) *Internationalisation of Central and Eastern Europe*, Chelthenham: Edward Elgar.

Svetličič, M. and Rojec, M. (1998) 'Kolektor', *Eastern European Economics*, 36(6): 5–28.

Svetličič, M., Rojec, M. and Trtnik, A. (2000) 'Strategija pospeševanja slovenskih neposrednih investicij v tujino (Strategy of Promoting Slovenian Outward FDI)', *Teorija in praksa*, 37(4): 623–45.

12 FDI and industrial networks in Hungary

Judit Hamar

Introduction

The goal of this chapter is to review some of the main effects of FDI inflows and of the presence of the subsidiaries of multinational companies (MNCs) on Hungarian economic development in the last decade. The chapter summarizes some of the key findings of our research on the macro- and microeconomic effects of foreign direct investment (FDI) (Hamar 2000; Hamar and Nagy 2001). It focuses on the impact of MNCs on development and on industrial and trade restructuring, and represents a first attempt to draw a map of industrial networks in Hungary. Its primary aim is to try to answer the question of whether the rapidly increasing presence of MNCs did, and will, increase the gap between indigenous and foreign-owned firms in Hungary.

Foreign investment in Hungarian industry is at a level equivalent to that in Ireland, and achieved over a much shorter period (cf. Chapter 10). Moreover, the first signs of dualistic economic development, with foreign-owned firms taking preferential positions compared to indigenous firms, emerged earlier (in 1996) than in the cohesion countries, such as Ireland, Portugal, or Spain. In the wake of this development indigenous manufacturing firms have also recorded rapid improvement in performance, in export capability and in productivity. However, the gap in some important economic indicators between indigenous and foreign-owned companies had not diminished by 1999; in fact, in some cases it had even increased.

As the time of Hungary's accession to the European Union (EU) approaches, a new wave of FDI can be expected. However, as liberalization of trade and FDI inflows took place ten years ago, the gains and losses may be much smaller now than in countries that had previously joined the EU. The outcome of accession will depend much more on the ability of indigenous firms to overcome their disadvantages compared to foreign-owned firms and close the gap in their performance. Policy-makers will have to contribute by balancing the attractions of further FDI through generous incentives, against fostering the development of local indigenous enterprises and capital accumulation, including positive discrimination in favour of the local small and medium enterprise (SME) sector (even though their ability to do so may be circumscribed by the conditions of EU membership).

FDI, trade and development

The role of policy changes

The attractiveness of Hungary for FDI is well known. This is partially due to 'first-mover advantages', as Hungary was the first country in the region to create the political and legal conditions for FDI inflows. In addition, relative political and economic stability and the Hungarian mode of privatization have encouraged high FDI inflows. The maintenance of economic liberalization over the whole period – even in the face of pressures for protection – has added to the positive outcomes.

Economic policy together with the investment attractiveness of the host country are the main determinants of the activities and results of MNCs (Markusen 1997). Trade and FDI liberalization can be identified as the necessary first conditions for fostering competitiveness, changing the market structure and developing an export orientation. The economic stabilization process launched in 1995 was essential for closing the gap between export performance and import intensity of the country,[1] as shown by the data on market and product structure of foreign trade. Following trade liberalization, the openness of the Hungarian economy intensified greatly, with shares of exports and imports in Hungarian GDP reaching higher levels than in the cohesion economies at the time of their accession to the EU. Growing economic openness and a more stable economic environment influenced MNCs to change their strategy toward greater export orientation. Since then, export-led economic growth has become crucial, but has not resulted in deterioration of the external balances.

While the first recovery from the transition crisis in 1993–94 followed the traditional pattern of Hungarian economic development – an upturn in growth and investment rapidly increased the foreign deficit (fed mainly by public consumption) – after economic stabilization this old pattern of development was broken and an export-led sustainable period of growth began. FDI inflows helped to finance the modernization of the Hungarian economy throughout the 1990s (with the exception of 1993–94). Annual average FDI reached about 4 per cent of GDP during the period, with peaks coinciding with the launch of specific privatization initiatives.

Economic development and structural change

Indices of real GDP show a declining trend in the 1980s, a deep transition crisis in the early 1990s, recovery after 1992 and significant growth from 1995. Since agriculture is still shrinking, dynamic growth has been led by manufacturing, mainly engineering, though recently the service sectors have also contributed to the high level of GDP growth.

The product structure of Hungarian foreign trade also changed dramatically in the 1990s. Engineering products greatly increased their share in exports (from 21 per cent in 1992 to 60 per cent by 2000) and in imports (from 30 to 51 per cent over the same period), clearly illustrating the extent and speed of restructuring. The rapid market reorientation is demonstrated by the fact that EU countries already accounted for more than half of Hungarian exports and 45 per cent of imports by 1992, and these levels increased to three-quarters of exports and two-thirds of imports by 2000.

FDI and the increasing presence of MNC subsidiaries played a leading role in these changes. The rapid market reorientation and restructuring of production and exports are due mainly to the firms operating with foreign capital (Table 12.1). By analysing the trends of foreign-owned firms in the whole economy, we can conclude that the transition crisis would have been deeper and continued for longer, the unemployment level would have been higher and the salary and wage levels lower without foreign investment (see Table 12.2).

Table 12.2 shows that the relative number of foreign firms started to diminish in the second half of the 1990s, but their dominance in the economy and in foreign trade continued to grow. The rising shares of foreign firms in exports and imports were increasingly due to newly emerging foreign firms (in 2000, for instance, the shares of foreign firms excluding new participants was only 68.9 per cent in exports and 67.9 per cent in imports).

The trend towards a relative decrease in the number of foreign firms, combined with an increase in their share of assets, could be recognized in all sectors of the economy. It was most evident in trade, where company structure became much

Table 12.1 The role of foreign firms[a] in Hungarian foreign trade ($ base, %)

Shares of foreign firms	1992	1993	1994	1995	1996	1997	1998	1999	2000
Exports	30.4	38.1	39.5	55.2	68.3	73.4	74.4	74.0	77.3
Imports	32.8	38.7	43.7	61.0	70.1	72.9	71.8	71.2	74.8

Sources: Tax Office, financial reports of double-entry accounting firms, and Ministry of Economics (GM), customs statistics, author's calculations.

Note
a Partially or totally foreign-owned (double-entry accounting) firms, existing in the previous year.

Table 12.2 The share of foreign firms in the Hungarian economy, %

	No. of firms	Assets (AS)	FDI/ AS	Investment	Net income relative to sales (NIS)	Exports[a]	Employment	Wages
1989	9.3	7.1	1.7	11.0	4.7	10.0	No data	3.9
1992	21.4	17.8	10.1	30.2	24.4	37.3	15.3	19.1
1995	21.1	47.0	28.3	61.8	45.0	66.0	33.0	37.1
1998	16.2	49.1	37.6	61.1	51.6	79.0	31.7	45.3
1999	15.4	58.2	49.9	71.0	53.4	82.2	31.6	46.0

Sources: APEH (Tax-office), Double-entry accounting firms, tax reports, author's calculations.

Note
a Export shares here are different from those in the previous table. Here, 100 per cent represents the exports of all double-entry accounting firms, while custom statistics include *all* firms.

more concentrated. In manufacturing, changing regulations gave the incentives for MNCs to merge their Hungarian joint ventures. The expansion of foreign firms (especially according to invested capital) was significant in real estate, in consulting and even more so in the financial sector, while education and healthcare lost their relative attractiveness to foreign investors.

Overall, while the scale of FDI inflows, as well as some privatization scandals, provoked certain negative effects and sentiments, on balance the effects of FDI have been positive. The higher than average investment- and export-intensity of foreign-owned firms (see Table 12.2) speeded up structural changes and made them the 'engines' of export-led economic growth.

Dependency and changing modes of linking to global corporate networks

The high level of economic openness and the dominant shares of foreign-owned firms in a number of economic activities and in foreign trade, certainly increased the sensitivity of the Hungarian economy to external demand, prices and volatile capital markets. However, radical changes in the product and market structures of foreign trade have improved the ability of the economy to withstand and overcome crises, as the Russian financial collapse in 1998 proved. This seeming contradiction is resolved when we consider the evolving links of exporters to global corporate networks, resulting mainly from FDI.

At the beginning of transition, it was mostly those firms that had direct, long-term subcontracting links (often as outward processing trade, OPT), especially with German firms, that could rapidly increase their exports to western markets. These firms were able to benefit from the first wave of foreign investment, too. However, OPT was also highly sensitive to the recession in the EU in late 1992 and 1993. Hungarian exports fell by 18 per cent in 1993, owing to a sudden decrease in OPT turnover, mainly as a result of falling external demand. The strict bankruptcy law introduced in 1992 also aggravated the export positions of Hungarian firms.

As the share of foreign-owned firms in Hungarian foreign trade has increased, the role of the more traditional modes of direct linkage to the global (EU) corporate networks (such as OPT) has diminished. The Free Trade Zones (FTZs), especially after the economic stabilization in 1995, offered additional flexible advantages for firms to participate in intra-industry trade, as part of global corporate networks. This is why the FTZs became the main locations for new greenfield investments by MNCs, especially in engineering, and became the main tools of fast integration into global (EU) corporate networks (Table 12.3).

Expected gains and losses from joining the EU

The openness of the Hungarian economy is illustrated by the share of exports (54 per cent) and of imports (56 per cent) of goods and services to GDP in 2000, figures that

Table 12.3 The role of OPT in the total Hungarian exports, 1992–2000 ($ base, %)

	1992	1993	1994	1995	1996	1997	1998	1999	2000
Shares, total exports = 100									
OPT exports	23.5	19.1	22.8	24.1	23.7	20.3	20.9	20.2	18.6
FTZ exports	n.d.			11	19	27	36	43	45
Annual growth in percentage terms									
Total exports	0	−18	20	22	22	22	20	9	12
Shares, total imports = 100									
OPT imports	17.0	12.3	12.3	16.3	17.6	16.5	16.0	15.9	14.7
FTZ imports	n.d.			8	14	19	25	31	32
Annual growth in percentage terms									
Total imports	0	12	16	7	17	17	21	9	15

Sources: Ministry of Economics (GM), Custom statistics; author's calculations. n.d. = no data.

are much higher than for Spain (exports and imports together 44 per cent), Portugal (69 per cent) or Greece (55 per cent) when they joined the EU. The EU average was 61 per cent at that time. Hungarian exports are already concentrated on the EU to a higher degree than was the case with the cohesion countries (with the exception of Portugal) in 1995.

The fact that the Hungarian economy has already substantially changed its sectoral structure in order to adjust to rapidly increasing international competition will generate *advantages* for EU accession. Most domestic firms are already accustomed to the presence of MNCs and to their competitive threat in global and local markets. Companies which could not adjust to the radically changing conditions have gone bankrupt, or have become foreign-owned and undergone a restructuring of their production profiles and markets. Besides foreign firms, an increasing number of indigenous private firms have been able to enter global markets (even small private firms); however, they still suffer from clear disadvantages in terms of capital and creditworthiness. The presence and extent of foreign-owned firms in Hungary certainly will ease accession to the EU, because many of them operate as an integrated part of global MNCs or their networks (see later). The already high level of intra-industry trade will also lessen the effects of the losses caused by a new wave of necessary restructuring following accession.

The *disadvantages* of the presence of MNCs relate to their dominance in some economic activities. This dominance inhibits potential entrants (even new foreign investors) from entering the local market. As MNC strategies are formed abroad, this will further reduce the room for Hungarian economic policy-makers to influence microeconomic performances. Increasing dependence on international capital markets and on the global strategies of MNCs is the price of rapid catch-up. Policy-makers, however, should recognize that further reduction of the modernization deficit from outside sources will be increasingly difficult and costly.

Company performance: rapid improvement but emerging dualism

The massive FDI inflows had significant effects on the level of company performance and, especially since 1995, on closing the gap between export capability and import intensity. But, as a result of dominant foreign control, Hungarian manufacturing started to show the first alarming signs of a dual economy as early as 1996, with foreign-owned firms strongly forging ahead of indigenous private firms. Since then, under stable growth, indigenous firms have begun to catch up, but the gap in several aspects has not reduced.

The period of recovery

After the deep transition crises (1989–92), all economic indicators demonstrated a clear improvement in productivity and company performance from as early as 1992–96. This improved performance was linked mainly to the increasing export orientation of firms. The firms that defined this trend were mainly foreign owned with higher capital endowment and investment capability, with more possibilities for getting investment credits and with better market links and knowledge. The growth rates of foreign-controlled firms were extraordinary, especially relative to indigenous manufacturing firms, during these four years.

It is worth noting that the share of indigenous private ownership, which increased at almost the same pace as that of foreign firms during 1989–92, had lost pace by 1995 and even decreased in 1996. The relative share of foreign-owned firms by numbers did not increase in 1992–96, but their share in industrial investment almost doubled from 43 to 83 per cent, while in assets it increased from 29 to 71 per cent and in exports from 32 to 79 per cent. With less than 41 per cent of all employees in manufacturing, they generated 86 per cent of profits before taxation and 91 per cent after tax in 1996. Foreign firms' higher productivity levels enabled them to pay relatively higher wages and salaries (55 per cent of the total wage bill compared to a 41 per cent share of employment).

By contrast, indigenous firms, with almost 60 per cent of manufacturing employees, but paying less than 45 per cent of total manufacturing wages, produced only 14 per cent of profits before taxation and 9 per cent after tax in 1996. They accounted for only 17 per cent of investment and just 28 per cent of the capital stock. They generated almost half of domestic sales, but their relative share in exports decreased from 68 to 21 per cent in 1992–96. The lack of capital, their modest and even decreasing level of investment activity, in the context of their limited creditworthiness and rapidly increasing level of debt, proved clearly that private indigenous firms were at a disadvantage.

The period of export-led economic growth

The expansion of foreign-owned firms slowed down after recovery from the transition crisis. The relative number of foreign firms fell away, but their leading position in manufacturing was reinforced. Their aggregate exports still tripled and their investment and profits more than doubled in 1996–99.

The most important and, for the future, the most encouraging changes, however, occurred in the indigenous company group between 1996 and 1999. The 100 per cent Hungarian-owned firms recorded profits before taxation 2.5 times and after taxation by 3.5 times higher. Their investments also increased by 78 per cent, and their exports by 41 per cent, similar to domestic sales. Although total assets in this group hardly increased and employment further decreased, for the latter this was at a slower pace than previously.

The productivity and profitability indexes also show important improvements in the indigenous company group. Profit rates on assets in this group increased from 16 to 24 per cent in 1996–99 (author's calculation from KOPINT-APEH). In addition, net income per capita rose by more than 50 per cent (from 4 to 6.4 billion HUF per employee). This means that the general view that productivity growth was due only to a few multinational companies cannot be fully sustained.

In 1999, for the first time, increases in employment came much more from indigenous firms than from foreign-owned ones, and the level of investment activity of the 100 per cent Hungarian-owned firms surpassed that of the foreign-owned group. They achieved a spectacular improvement in profitability, as their profits before tax reached 24 per cent of assets and 31 per cent after taxation, while the foreign-owned group on average showed worse results than in earlier years. This was partially due to the Russian financial crisis, which affected the results of some food producers and pharmaceutical firms belonging to large MNCs.

The final balance for the decade is that, despite the improved performance of the indigenous company group, most of the economic indicators for foreign firms (in unit values) remain superior to those for the indigenous group, even though some degree of convergence can be detected. The gap between the two groups in favour of the foreign-owned firms remained significant and, for some indicators, the differences actually widened.

Modest but increasing role of indigenous firms in industrial restructuring

The rapidity of Hungarian restructuring is illustrated by the fact that the output and exports of traditional 'labour-intensive' activities lost share, while the modern, mainly 'knowledge-intensive' activities gained rapidly.

The share of the *food industry*, for instance, decreased from 25 to 17 per cent in manufacturing output and from 14 to 7 per cent in exports between 1996 and 1999. The output of *electrical machinery*, on the other hand, increased by more than three times and its share grew from 12 to 21 per cent, and in exports from 20 to 33 per cent. The output and export share of the *transport equipment* industry at least doubled, while traditional *mechanical engineering* lost 1.9 percentage points in output, 6 points in employment and its exports shrank by one half.

As an overall result, it is evident that the foreign-owned firms speeded up output growth and structural change, significantly improved their employment levels and the growth rate of exports, and became the 'engines' of growth. More detailed analysis, however, shows a more sophisticated view: even in some of the most dynamic sectors, indigenous firms showed spectacular development, while foreign-owned firms increased output, employment and export shares even in those activities that lost share in manufacturing during 1996–99.

Industrial networks: MNCs and links between foreign and indigenous firms

For the purposes of the project on which this book is based, a series of in-depth interviews was conducted with subsidiaries of MNCs, focusing on the degree of their globalization and effects on links between different types of firms. How deeply were the firms operating with foreign capital integrated into the global MNCs? What kind of SMEs could link to them? We asked about product life cycles, technological level, and demand and market functions – input and output links – of the firm. We compared the results with the ownership structure and the main features of the parent firm. Further questions focused on their strategic role (where and by whom strategy is made), and on the potential effects of barriers, and tools of adjustment to meet the requirements of EU accession.

Despite the small sample of twenty-four firms, our research results delivered some interesting insights. The most important finding was that dependence on foreign headquarters, or on the network of the parent firm, was much heavier than expected. We found hardly any independent firms even among SMEs. The parent firms – according to their Hungarian subsidiaries – were not the most competitive at a global level in several respects, especially in the case of foreign investors that owned SMEs. From the policy perspective, it is important, therefore, to bear in mind that the managers of Hungarian firms have little room for manoeuvre in strategy formation.

The sample

The large MNC subsidiaries were selected from the list of the 100 largest exporters and importers. Few turned out to have backward links with indigenous SMEs, the alternative being that their network was dispersed with thousands of suppliers (in the food industry, for instance). Their purchases and sales were also organized mainly by, and with, their parent firms or their company groups. Therefore, the SMEs co-operated only occasionally with MNC subsidiaries: only one SME had direct links to an MNC subsidiary (its parent was also in the sample). We also visited indigenous firms which did not (or could not) participate in an MNC network. All the firms in the sample, with the exception of one SME, had been established in the first half of the 1990s (one-third of large firms and one-fifth of the SMEs by privatization; all others by 'greenfield' investment).

Table 12.4 The distribution of the sample

No. of firms	All	MNC	Export	Import	Both	Location of HQ				
						Budapest	W	C	NE	S
Large	9	8	7	6	2	5	2	1	1	0
Small	15	9	10	12	11	3	3		4	6
All	24	17	22	18	13	8	5	1	5	6

Source: Author.

Notes
MNC = for simplicity, means the firms belonging to an MNC.
W = West.
C = Central.
NE = North East.
S = South.

As a result of our selection method, the large firms all participated in foreign trade, but the SMEs were also highly export-oriented (one-third of them operated exclusively in domestic markets) and for the most part were foreign connected. Table 12.4 shows the size and distribution of the sample by ownership, market-orientation and geographic location.

Market structure

The predominantly export-oriented firms usually purchased and sold through their parent firm, or at least through the global network of the parent firm. Only one-third of the MNCs mentioned that they had suppliers other than their export partners, and only in two cases did the partners not belong to the company group of the parent.

The relative importance of *indigenous suppliers* varied sharply between firms. One firm, for instance (with a Hungarian parent), did not import directly, so its share of indigenous suppliers was 100 per cent. One food producer purchased 90 per cent of its inputs in Hungary, another global market-oriented firm 60 per cent. At the opposite end, the two largest exporters had almost no indigenous suppliers (0–5 per cent). Half of the suppliers of the domestic-market oriented – but also service – sample firms were located in Hungary, but some of them were owned by the same parent company. The firms with a higher proportion of Hungarian suppliers mostly had networks with indigenous small and medium-sized firms, or entrepreneurs.

The *regional distribution* of both input and output markets in the sample was dominated by the developed (mainly EU) countries, but, typically, not Germany. One of the German-owned large firms, for instance, purchased 70 per cent of its inputs from the USA, while an American subsidiary bought inputs from everywhere in the world for further processing and exported through Germany to the rest of the world. Few firms indicated markets outside Europe as important direct export targets: one food producer mentioned the American – and to a smaller extent the Korean and Japanese – markets and only two of them the ex-socialist countries. The Russian market was significant for one food producer, however, its share shrank dramatically (from half of its output to 8 per cent in 1997–99). One clothing firm, with an 80 per cent export share, stopped exporting directly to Russia because it became part of a global MNC and has exported through the parent firm's headquarters in Brussels since then. All the firms (except one) had had continuous contract links with their export partners since their establishment and only one exported a small fraction under OPT. The market structure of the SMEs was very similar: the only difference was that 40 per cent of them had dominant shares of indigenous suppliers. Their external market relations were almost wholly based on the European networks of the parent firms. Only one Japanese-owned firm had some minor links with Asian and ex-socialist markets.

Development

Surprisingly, the activities of the subsidiaries of MNCs in the sample had hardly changed over the period covered, though some of them had supplemented them with new ones. More than half of these companies mentioned that their export products had scarcely changed at all since the formation of the firm, while the rest indicated mostly increases in the intensity of capital, technology and R&D (knowledge) (one food processor stated that its production had become more labour intensive).

Table 12.5 demonstrates the development of large firms. By comparing the two parts of the table, the most export-oriented firms can be seen to be the most dynamic in terms of output growth. Only one-third of them were able to attain high growth along with a significant increase in the number of employees. The less export-oriented firms had hardly increased (and in some cases even decreased) employment, even when their export shares in output had grown somewhat.

Dynamic growth in the SME group was also linked to the level of export orientation: more than half of them, with high (70–90 per cent) export shares, doubled or almost doubled their output in three years. These firms were able to increase their employment, but at a more modest rate relative to the MNC group. Those that were totally or mainly domestic-market oriented could not extend their employment level, and in some cases even reduced it.

Product structure, market position and production organization

The managers' opinions about the main features of their products might partially explain the close correlation between the growth of output and export orientation. Results from the MNCs and the SMEs showed more similarities than differences; however, the product structure and the level of technology of the SMEs were clearly inferior to that in the MNCs in the sample.

Life cycle of products

The large exporters considered their products to be mainly in the mature stage of their life cycle. The mainly domestic-market-oriented firms judged their products to be in an earlier growth stage. Only one large firm indicated that a small proportion of its output relocated to Hungary could be attributed to the introductory period of

Table 12.5 The size of the subsidiaries of MNCs

(a) According to the number of employees

The sample of 'MNCs': in decreasing order of export sales	No. of employees					Growth (%)
	1990[a]	1996	1997	1998	1999	1999/96
Transport equipment manufacturer		1,011	2,204	3,425	4,312	426.5
Manufacturer of spare parts for computers		1,500			6,000	400.0
Manufacturer of lighting equipment	14,297	10,500	10,300	10,200	11,000	104.8
Chemicals manufacturer	6,532	4,159	3,439	3,267	3,304	79.4
Food processing firm	2,000	1,700	1,650	1,600	1,600	94.1
Clothing firm[b]						No data
Manufacturer of spare parts for trains		80	286	409	429	536.3
Manufacturer of communication equipment and electrical machinery			Falling[c]		1–2,000	No data
Communications service company		506	611	595	559	110.5

Source: Author.

Notes
a Data of the acquired firm. The last two firms are only importers.
b Firm No. 6 did not give data for employment.
c Firm No. 8 was privatized through a workers' buy-out.

(b) According to net income from sales (million HUF)

Firm	Net income from sales, million HUF					Growth (%)	Export/output ratio (%)	
	1990[a]	1996	1997	1998	1999	1999/96	1996	1999
1		52,829	178,749	479,160	729,000	1,380	100	100
2[b]						No data	100	100
3	2,000	6,000	8,000	10,000	12,000	200	90	95
4	33,349	65,550	90,425	85,187	89,905	137	45	47
5	6,300	13,600	17,900	18,600	17,800	131	50	54
6		7,362	8,573	9,096	9,464	129	66	80
7		388	2,912	6,985	7,402	1,908	99.6	99.7
8		12,600	16,000	27,000	40,000	318	3.6	1.5
9		20,104	26,534	28,132	35,848	178	6	11

Source: Author.

Notes
a As for the previous table.
b Firm No. 2 did not give data on output.

the life cycle. Two-thirds of the SME group considered their products to be in the mature stage and two SMEs had products in the final declining stage.

Value-added

The large exporters (transport equipment, computer spare parts, lighting and electronics firms) and most of the domestic-market-oriented firms judged their products to be in the high value-added (or high-tech) category. Only one food producer indicated the low value-added category, and one chemical and one railway spare parts producer rated their products with medium value-added. By contrast, more than a quarter of the SMEs had main products belonging to the low value-added (price-sensitive) category, while all others considered their products to be medium value-added.

Type of demand

Two-thirds of the MNCs answered that they could dynamically increase exports of products primarily in markets with medium levels of demand. One-third of them (and the same proportion of the SMEs) possessed products of dynamic demand, but a quarter of the SMEs had products for which demand was sluggish.

Type of technology

Firms with products facing increasing demand stated that their technological level had improved. Firms in the food and clothing industries, along with the domestic-market-oriented firms, judged their technology to be at the medium level. Eighty per cent of SMEs also operated with medium-level technologies; two had old technology.

Production organization

Production organization was similar in both groups. Two-thirds of the MNCs and 40 per cent of the SMEs had an R&D department, but the two largest exporters and one clothing company did not have their own R&D. All firms conducted some training activities, while the outsourcing of such activities was rare. Most often accounting and payroll administration, warehousing and advertising were outsourced. In one case (a clothing factory) marketing, and in another case custom-administration, logistics and transporting activity were contracted out to a small service firm (in the SME sample). Only two firms could give data on the costs of their outsourcing activities.

Company strategy

Very few firms in the sample had any likelihood of being able to change product structure or market position on their own. Most companies had virtually no influence at all over the strategy decided by the parent firm. Among the MNCs, only one indicated that local management was fully in control of strategy. In another case, the regional and local strategies were decided in the Hungarian headquarters of the firm, while global strategy was in the hands of the parent firm. In one case, the management co-operated closely with the owners, which were international institutional investors. Among the SMEs, more (one-third) were able independently to formulate their own strategy, the others were able to influence strategy process to some extent.

Most of the MNCs and more than half of the SMEs, considered their firms to be an integrated part of a global company group. Only two MNCs were able to determine the main features of their own firms. One judged it as dynamically developing, but expansion or relocation of production to low-cost regions was not appropriate to improve their competitive position. One food producer saw its firm as·stagnating. More SMEs than MNCs were able to describe their main characteristics. One-third considered they were meeting particular needs, one as an innovator, one as a follower supplier and one as competitive when compared to other agricultural firms.

EU accession

There were differences regarding the effects of the EU accession within and between both company groups. Among the MNCs, only one (a transport equipment producer with American interests) emphasized the advantages of a larger market. One-third of them thought that they would face increasing competition both in domestic markets and abroad. Food producers expected worse conditions, while others foresaw fierce competition in the home market. Two firms had no particular expectations.

The SMEs also had varying views in relation to the expected effects of EU accession: one-fifth did not anticipate any particular effects, considering that they were already in the EU. Another fifth (the mainly domestically oriented) were expecting deteriorating conditions in domestic markets, and most of them expected the same abroad. Among the SMEs, however, a larger proportion (40 per cent) of firms clearly foresaw better prospects, mainly because of decreasing bureaucratic barriers, the simplification of trade and customs regulations and the advantages of access to larger markets.

In general, the firms (both MNCs and SMEs) did not foresee major problems in their preparation for EU accession. Most of them considered themselves as 'EU-mature' (one large MNC complained that the parent firm already treated them as a 'member-firm'). Two of them did not have a strategy because they did not have any opportunity to influence it. For some SMEs, the lack of capital and information about the changing conditions in relation to EU accession were the most important barriers to successful preparation; some were scared that large firms with capital strength could make it difficult for them to enter EU markets.

Conclusions

The ten years of restructuring the Hungarian economy have been sufficient to achieve the same or even higher levels of openness and of presence in EU markets, and similar trade structures, as in the southern EU economies that joined earlier. Since the 1995 stabilization and austerity programme, export orientation has increased rapidly, even in those company groups that earlier were not characterized by a high export share. The catching-up process has been accelerated by FDI inflows and has been based on close integration into European corporate networks. The importance of OPT has faded, while greenfield investment in the FTZs (especially in the engineering sector) has fostered the development of intra-industry trade and strengthened the export capability of the country without damaging the external balance.

On balance, the FDI inflows and the presence of MNCs can be considered as positive. The transition crisis would have been deeper, the unemployment higher, the restructuring and adjustment in the economy and especially in foreign trade would have certainly been much slower and less successful. Since 1995, the subsidiaries of MNCs have become the 'engine' of export-led, fast and sustainable growth.

Policy changes have helped enable such rapid growth of FDI, but this has also led to alarming signals of a dual economic development in manufacturing. Yet together with the signs of the dual economy, some hopeful changes could be recognized in the indigenous company group, too. Domestically controlled firms have improved their performance, though the gap between them and foreign-owned firms did not diminish.

It remains open whether the negative effects of dualistic economic development could be revised or at least moderated by economic policy. In regard to policy, it is important to bear in mind that the most dynamic firms (even large global multinationals) were not the same over the whole period. This means that targeting the dynamic effects of governmental policy and foreseeing the future role of MNCs need more sophisticated tools than just giving generous advantages to large MNCs to attract FDI. In addition, even the small sample of interviewed firms shows how narrow the path is for policy-makers to influence the strategy of firms with dominant foreign equity, which are highly integrated into global corporate networks.

The main policy conclusion coming out of our findings is that further development in terms of the catch-up process, and the balance between gains and losses of EU accession, depend primarily on the ability of indigenous firms to close the gap with the foreign-owned firms. For this, the SME sector needs extra support from central and local governments rather than the large global MNCs' investments.

Note

1 For reasons of space, the indicators cannot be shown here in detail, but are available from the author on request.

References

Hamar, J. (2000) 'Hungarian Foreign Trade and the EU accession', *Külgazdaság*, no 6.
Hamar, J. and Nagy, Á. (2001) 'The role of the FDI in the Hungarian economic development', KOPINT-DATORG, Manuscript, p. 190.
Markusen, J.R. (1997) 'The theory of multinational firms and its relevance to transition', (Budapest, MTA).

13 Industrialization and internationalization in the Spanish economy

Jose Molero

Introduction

This chapter examines how internationalization affected the industrialization of the Spanish economy. First, we briefly review the overall changes in the structure of the Spanish economy particularly after the shift from an import substitution strategy to one which sought to integrate Spain into the international economy. Second, we concentrate on the relationship between domestic innovation activities and foreign direct investment (FDI) in this development process. Third, we analyse policy attempts to enhance domestic technological activities that would complement foreign technology imports.

Spanish industrial development: some stylized facts

Growth and structural change

The consolidation of Spain's industrial development did not occur until the second half of the twentieth century. As late as 1951, value-added in agriculture was greater than in manufacturing and mining. Nevertheless, from that point on industrial production came to represent the foundation on which the dynamism of the Spanish economy was built. Thus, the sector that expanded most rapidly between 1954 and 1974 was industry, with its share of gross domestic product (GDP) rising from 17.6 to 28.4 per cent over the same period. Subsequently, economic problems impacting on the industrial sector resulted in a reversal of this trend but for the period as a whole it is clear that value-added in the industrial sector increased at a faster rate than in the rest of the economy, and its contribution to the growth of the economy correspondingly increased (to 26.8 per cent). The composition of industry changed in response to market opportunities and the uneven incidence of technological change. Growth was initially focused on manufacturing, as elsewhere in Europe, and was facilitated by the process of import substitution. Indeed, in the earlier period exports were generally only a marginal aspect of production although a few exceptions can be mentioned, such as shipbuilding and publishing. The main sources of dynamism in the economy – sectors such as chemicals, metal machinery, processed rubber and plastics, non-metal mineral products and paper and printing – were the recipients of a remarkable proportion of FDI.

The dynamism of this period implied a degree of convergence with the industrial structures of the principal west European economies, including those of the European Economic Community (EEC). There remained – and still continue to be – significant differences between Spain and the other European economies, however. By the end of 1975, one of the most notable characteristics of the manufacturing sector was the importance of non-metallic mining derivatives and clothing, textiles and footwear, and the low share of capital goods and machinery. In this sense, the Spanish economy suffered from an excessive specialization in the production of consumer and intermediate goods of low technological sophistication, while at the same time capital goods industries were under-represented (Buesa and Molero 1988, 1998).[1]

The crisis of the mid-1970s, which abruptly ended the dominant model of accumulation prevalent since the civil war, transformed the sectoral patterns of growth described earlier. From the perspective of industry, the most significant impact was the change in relative prices caused by the hike in energy prices and the instability associated with the crisis in the international monetary system. This led to a dramatic reduction in the demand for manufactured products, particularly in such sub-sectors as metallurgy, heavy machinery and electrical materials. As a result of the introduction of new technologies, demand simultaneously increased in sectors such as electronics, precision instruments and the automobile and aeronautical industries. Over the period 1975–95, there was a profound transformation in the structure of the Spanish manufacturing sector. Many of the earlier sources of dynamism faced crisis, reversal and stagnation. Overall, however, these structural changes amounted to a reversal in the previous tendency towards greater structural convergence with the large European economies (Table 13.1). This divergence is slight and gradual, but clearly discernible.

Opening up, specialization and international competitiveness

These adjustments reflected changes in the relative specialization and international competitiveness of different sectors in the Spanish economy. There was an overall trend towards greater specialization as the economy was integrated into international markets (Buesa and Molero 1998, 2000). At the beginning of the period, the level of production was greatly limited by the size of the domestic market and the paucity of international transactions: the value of the exports reached only 1 per cent of production, and imports only 2 per cent of local demand.

Nevertheless, in the aftermath of the Stabilization Plan of 1959, the Spanish economy was gradually liberalized. Progress was hesitant up to the crisis in the mid-1970s, but more rapid thereafter, especially once Spain became a full member of the European Union (EU). The pace of liberalization was reflected in a growing propensity to export (with only one break at the end of the 1980s) and a reduction in the coverage of the domestic market, due to the growth of imports. All of this resulted in a greater degree of specialization of the Spanish economy.

In order to understand the process of specialization better, it is useful to analyse the trends within manufacturing, according to the technological content of the sectors (Figure 13.1). Sectors with a high technological content have developed

Table 13.1 Percentage distribution of value-added[a] in Spain and the EU-4, 1970–95, by industrial sector

Industrial branch	1970		1975		1985		1995	
	ES[b]	EU-4[c]	ES	EU-4	ES	EU-4	ES	EU-4
Energy products	16.7	13.6	14.7	14.1	19.1	19.7	22.7	18.1
Ferrous and non-ferrous mineral products	6.8	5.8	6.2	5.2	5.1	3.5	2.9	3.0
Non-metallic mineral products	7.0	4.8	6.5	4.7	5.9	3.9	6.5	4.2
Chemicals and chemical products	7.7	6.8	7.6	7.1	8.4	7.5	6.4	7.8
Metallic products	5.1	8.1	8.5	7.6	5.9	6.6	6.1	7.5
Machinery and mechanical equipment	4.5	8.8	3.3	9.6	3.3	8.6	3.4	8.0
Office machinery, precision instruments	0.4	2.5	0.6	2.5	1.4	2.6	1.2	2.6
Electrical and electronic machinery	3.5	7.5	5.3	8.1	5.4	8.5	5.6	8.3
Vehicles and transport equipment	5.6	7.6	6.6	8.1	7.6	8.6	7.9	8.8
Food, beverages and tobacco products	13.7	12.8	12.4	12.0	17.2	11.1	17.8	11.3
Textiles, clothing, leather and footwear products	14.1	8.9	12.4	8.0	9.0	6.7	6.9	5.4
Pulp, paper and products	5.0	5.6	6.3	5.7	4.5	5.9	5.0	7.2
Rubber and plastic products	3.4	2.8	3.2	3.0	3.2	3.0	3.5	3.8
Other industrial products	6.5	4.3	6.3	4.4	4.0	3.8	4.0	4.1

Source: Buesa and Molero (2000) and EUROSTAT data.

Notes
a Gross value-added at market prices valued in ECUs at current prices and exchange rates.
b ES: Spain.
c EU-4: Germany, France, United Kingdom and Italy.

only marginally. Yet, strangely, this has not generally been incompatible with a good competitive performance of Spanish industry at the international level, as revealed by the high export propensity since the 1980s and especially the 1990s. As we shall see in the next section, a crucial part of the explanation is the presence of MNEs in these sectors, to the extent that they controlled a large proportion of sectoral production. Progress in some sectors, such as automobiles, came about because of an industrial policy aimed at attracting the entry of new multinationals and market liberalization (especially after the crises in the 1970s).

The effect of greater liberalization in less technological sectors was mixed. Hitherto they had operated in conditions of relatively high levels of protection and, while some sectors were able to sustain their competitiveness, others were less able to adjust to the increased competition which followed from membership of the European Community (EC). The long period during which they had been living under a protective umbrella combined with technological backwardness

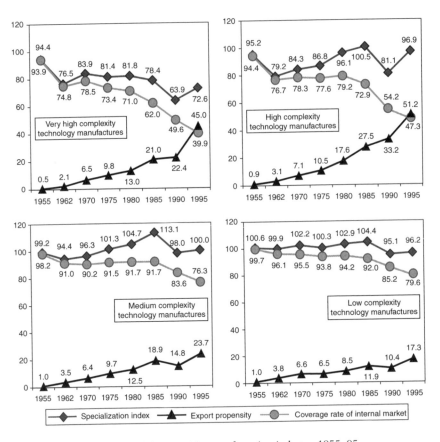

Figure 13.1 Specialization of the Spanish manufacturing industry, 1955–95.

Source: Buesa and Molero (2000).

imposed a very heavy burden that only a number of successful firms and specific sectors were able to overcome. The presence of FDI was less abundant than in more advanced sectors and did not permit a general transformation of the sector as a whole. Even today, the need for modernization is alive in these kinds of activities. In more advanced sectors, competitiveness problems persisted due to the limited role of Spanish affiliates in multinational enterprises (MNEs) and the lack of effective domestic firms.

The role of internationalization in the modernization of Spanish industry

Antecedents

The period of economic nationalism and autarky was accompanied by an important reaction against the 'de-nationalization' of the Spanish economy, because of the strong presence of foreign capital. Legislation after the civil war restricted foreign investments even more, as the international context of the world war naturally limited transnational investments. Nevertheless, it did not take long for voices to be raised in favour of a change in the legislation towards liberalization (Muñoz *et al.* 1978).

The United States emerged from the Second World War as the undisputed leading investing country; in Europe the Marshall Plan reinforced the position of US firms. While Spain did not participate directly in that Plan, the signing of the Madrid Pact in 1953, which permitted the establishment of American military bases on Spanish soil, had a similar effect as far as the opening of Spanish legislation was concerned. The implications of the Madrid Pact went far beyond its direct military consequences: it involved important technological collaborations, provided the basis for the 'productivity movement' and entailed a certain liberalization of the Spanish economy, especially with regard to the reduction of legal obstacles to investments by US firms. However, while there were some important developments in the wake of the Madrid Pact, substantial internationalization only occurred in the wake of the Stabilization and Liberalization reforms of 1959.

Development, liberalization and the first great wave of investments

These changes marked a definitive shift in policy towards foreign investments, bringing Spanish policy gradually into line with the majority of other European countries (Braña *et al.* 1984). From that point on, FDI helped to initiate a period of extraordinarily high growth that would slow down only with the onset of the economic crisis of 1973 and the political transition (Buesa and Molero 1988; Muñoz *et al.* 1978). The favourable conditions that the reforms established consisted of a new and stable legal framework and a range of incentives for foreign investors. Their positive impact was reinforced by the dynamism of the Spanish economy after 1959, with GDP rising by an average of 7 per cent annually from 1960 to 1975 and industrial production more than tripling over the same period. Moreover, in the wake of the first reforms, Spain underwent a steady if gradual opening of its economy, with reforms to trade policy, exchange controls and foreign investment. A major milestone in this process was the signing of the 1970 preferential agreement with the EC.

In this context, foreign investment grew rapidly from Ptas 2 bn in 1960 to Ptas 19 bn in 1975, as firms sought to take advantage of low labour costs and growing markets and to overcome the remaining trade barriers. In terms of the origin of investments, in the initial period US firms constituted the principal investors, accounting for nearly 30 per cent of investment (though the aggregate share of EC states was larger). Sectorally, investment was concentrated on the manufacturing sector (more than 75 per cent of the total in 1960–75 though investments in services were increasing towards the end of this period) with most of it in the most dynamic industrial sectors.

The effect of this investment in technological capabilities is hard to estimate with any precision but a reasonable approximation can be made. With regard to *embodied* technologies, foreign firms were superior to domestic for practically every indicator considered (Rodriguez de Pablo 1980). This would seem to support the hypothesis that the presence of foreign firms raised business standards in Spanish industry during the boom period. With respect to *disembodied* technologies, the importance of the contribution of foreign firms can be confirmed by census data for 1977, which reveal that firms with foreign capital over 20 per cent made almost 60 per cent of the total payments for foreign technologies, and also by analysis of the contracts for technology transfer, which shows that a significant share was carried out by foreign firms, frequently with their respective parent companies (Molero 1982). There was a strong correlation between control of the firms and technology imports, especially in technologically more advanced sectors like electric materials, chemicals and vehicles.

From the outset, with a few exceptions, foreign firms integrated quite well with local conditions and economic power. This can be seen from analysing participation in pro-active industrial policies, and second, the relative position reached by MNCs' subsidiaries within the core of Spanish economic forces.

On the former point, a detailed microanalysis of the firms that received state aid in many different ways and through a large variety of programmes in the period 1963–77 (Braña et al. 1984) allows the importance of foreign firms in state aid within each sector and the generosity of the benefits they received to be measured (Buesa and Molero 1988). For a nucleus of three very important sectors – chemicals, electronic equipment and vehicles – both generosity in benefits and the importance of firms receiving state aid reached very high levels. A large number of firms with foreign capital or technology received state aid. The kind of incentives offered to foreign firms included tax reductions, incentives for exporting, facilities for importing intermediate inputs, flexibility for investment amortizing, aids for labour force training, cheap and well-organized land, and so on.

Second, the position of foreign firms was evaluated by Muñoz et al. (1978) through a detailed analysis of the 300 largest industrial firms in 1973. As early as 1973 their role was comparable with large Spanish industrial firms in terms of sales (particularly) and employees. However, such penetration came in different ways; just under half of the firms with foreign capital acted separately, otherwise they joined different fractions of Spanish capital (private or public). These mixed examples added more economic value than the exclusively foreign firms.

Recovery, economic integration and a new wave

Transformation of the external and internal framework

The period between 1974 and 1985 can be considered as a transitional period towards a new growth model that was to become firmly established in the second half of the 1980s. In this period, foreign investment inflows experienced a period of stagnation, followed by a recovery. But the most significant changes were qualitative rather than quantitative. Prior to this period the model of development in Spain had been principally a Fordist one, characterized by specialization based on the chemical and metal-mechanical sectors. The internationalization of firms corresponded to the classical model of cost reduction, growing markets and firm-specific capabilities acquired in the home country. During the crisis, this model of internationalization, however, became increasingly precarious. In order to adapt to a more volatile international business climate, firms were forced to adopt more flexible strategies in the face of new international competitors and technical change (especially the growth of information technology).

For Spain itself, the crisis had a particularly strong economic impact. The problems facing many industrial sectors required radical restructuring. This process of adjustment was marked by a more intensive opening-up of the economy, notably more liberal foreign investment and trade regimes. The prospect of EC membership reinforced and required these policy shifts. In addition, two other basic changes affected Spanish industrial development. The first was related to the diminished importance of industry in terms of both its absolute impact on the macroeconomy and its contribution to growth. The second change had to do with a deep process of industrial restructuring, which led to a shift in the structural composition of the economy away from some of the leading sectors during the 'development' period, and towards new sectors.

General FDI trends and sectoral distribution

From the 1980s on, the country's policy on FDI was increasingly liberalized. The government embarked on a gradual and continuous process of reducing the remaining barriers, as part of a programme to completely liberalize capital movements. Moreover, the fast growth of the economy in the second half of the 1980s led to a massive trade deficit, which needed to be balanced. In this process, FDI inflows were seen as crucial and were stimulated through high interest rates. From a micro perspective, both the state and regional governments established important incentives regarding land acquisition, personnel training, tax reductions, subsidies for specific purposes and so on. As a result, the level and quality of FDI was transformed. From the mid-1980s to the early 1990s, the levels of FDI grew rapidly, reflecting both the worldwide boom in FDI in the period and the capacity of the Spanish economy to attract international investment. However, in the second half of the 1990s, a significant decline occurred, reflecting a reduction in total EU-based inward FDI. At the same time, outward investment from Spain grew rapidly, especially during the 1990s. Indeed, in recent years, outward investment has exceeded inward investment. While services accounted for an increasing share of foreign investment in this period (as well as for much of Spanish foreign investment), the bulk of investment remained concentrated in the industrial sector.

Three conclusions can been drawn from Figure 13.2, which graphs the industrial data in relative terms. The first is the weak capacity of low-technology sectors to attract FDI relative to their economic dimension (value added). Second, sectors of the highest level of technology (very high technological complexity) basically receive FDI proportional to their overall economic importance. Third, the group of sectors of 'high' technological complexity stands out as the group that receives, relatively, the most foreign investment, particularly motor vehicles, which in the last

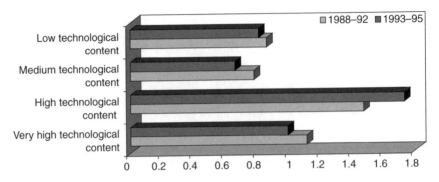

Figure 13.2 Relative FDI by categories of sectors.

Source: Author's own elaboration.

Note
The ratio measures the percentage of FDI received by each category of sectors relative to the value-added percentage they account for. Thus, an index > 1 indicates that FDI is greater than value added and < 1 that it is smaller.

period has consolidated a solid position in Spain. This example demonstrates the particular combination of production costs, which were neither as low as previously nor as low as in other less developed countries; and productivity, which was not as high as in the most advanced countries.

MNC strategies

These changes were accompanied by a significant shift in the kind of strategy adopted by firms. The most notable was the change in the balance between domestic and external markets. In recent years, a great number of multinationals with a presence in Spain have consolidated their strategies of using the country as an export platform. The adoption of such strategies explains to a large extent the aforementioned improvement in export performance. The increasing export activity does not mean that foreign markets have completely replaced domestic ones; on the contrary, the available studies confirm that domestic sales are still clearly the first objective of most firms, although in some cases exports are nearly as important as domestic sales. However, in spite of the growing importance of export strategies the trade balance remains negative. The reason for this resides in the fact that imports have also expanded very rapidly; moreover, all the available studies concur that companies with foreign capital have a higher import propensity than those with domestic capital. The result of all this has been a deficit in the foreign trade balance.

Another fundamental element of MNC strategies has been their technological activities, playing a very significant role in the Spanish research and development (R&D) system. According to OECD (1997) estimates, MNCs represent more than one-third of total Spanish business R&D and more than half of R&D financed by firms (Molero *et al.* 1995). More detailed information can be obtained from the

Table 13.2 Technological activity of foreign firms, 1994

	Percentages of foreign groups in			Percentages of companies with technological activities in each group		
	Total number of firms	Innovatory firms with R&D	Innovatory firms with R&D centres	Innovatory activities	R&D activities	R&D centres
Firms of a foreign group from EU	3.80	9.50	11.63	47.24	62.33	52.11
Firms of a group from other countries	0.86	2.48	3.22	53.16	72.31	64.10
Total firms	100	100	100	10.71	24.94	17.83

Source: Author's own elaboration on data from the Spanish Innovation Survey (1994), INE (1997).

first Spanish survey on innovation carried out in 1994. As can be seen from Table 13.2, foreign firms are 4.66 per cent of the total, but represent 14.85 per cent of those with R&D centres. Their contribution to the national system of innovation (NSI) is more visible when we compare their technological activity with national averages. Thus, while only 10.7 per cent of national firms can be classified as innovative, in foreign firms this ratio rises to around 50 per cent. Similarly, about a quarter of national firms in the sample declare having R&D activities, against 62 – 72 per cent in the case of foreign companies. Finally, less than 18 per cent of national firms have R&D laboratories, compared to 64 per cent in the group of non-EU firms.

This superiority in innovatory activity is one of the most general findings of recent research (Bajo and López 1996; Circulo de Empresarios 1995; González 1997; Martín and Velázquez 1996; Merino and Salas 1996; Molero 1995); however, there are underlying factors – apart from nationality – that could explain a considerable part of those differences. In fact, all available studies confirm two basic causes of the distance between Spanish and foreign enterprises: the size and sector of activity. When both elements are controlled for, the technological effort is quite similar between the two clusters (Martín and Velázquez 1996; Merino and Salas 1996). Nevertheless, it is misleading to assert that MNCs do not represent any special contribution to technological development. In fact, MNCs constitute a central part of the Spanish NSI because they usually have a longer tradition of organizing innovative activities, are of a size more adequate to carry them out and are more active in sectors that focus on current technological developments, notwithstanding the fact that Spanish companies can face firm-to-firm comparisons when they enter the same sphere.

The situation is different if we consider technology importation. In this case, all studies reveal that MNCs import foreign technology more intensely (González

1997; Martín and Velázquez 1996; Merino and Salas 1996; Sánchez 1984). Leaving aside other factors, what is most critical is the special link they have with their mother companies, which constitute the first external source of technological know-how (Molero 1982; Molero *et al.* 1995; Pellegrín 1997).

A last point to highlight is that the presence of foreign firms in the Spanish market has increased considerably; they now constitute one of the most efficient and powerful groups of industrial firms. As has been recently noted (Buesa and Molero 1998), the presence of foreign affiliates among the leading firms in each sector doubled between 1982 and 1992. If we look at the way in which they execute their control over the firms we also can find substantial changes in the period. Thus, in 1982 foreign firms had absolute control in 53.3 per cent of all their subsidiaries, another 26.3 per cent was under majority control, and in 20.4 per cent of cases it was a minority one, implying the existence of important Spanish partners. Ten years later absolute control was exercised in 75.6 per cent of cases, majority control affected 17.2 per cent and minority control was reduced to 7.2 per cent of firms. In other words, the strategy of association with national economic forces was considerably reduced, while the integration into multinational groups advanced in the same period.

Technology policy, modernization and internationalization

Development and crisis (1960–80)

In the first period of strong industrial growth that commenced in the 1950s, the technological requirements of industry grew almost exponentially from a position of backwardness, while at the same time the difficulties in paying for imported technologies were eased by income from tourism, foreign investments and remittances from workers abroad. Unfortunately, this was accompanied by an almost complete lack of policy initiatives to address the structural problem of the lack of technical know-how. The results were three-fold: a lack of resources dedicated to the creation of technology, the continuing need to import foreign technologies and the absence of effective policies to tackle this situation.

Measured in constant 1970 pesetas, expenditure on R&D went from Ptas 5,593 mn in 1970 to Ptas 17,038 mn in 1980, equivalent to a 0.23 per cent to 0.44 per cent increase in GDP. Despite this substantial increase, in comparative terms Spain was still underperforming, with comparable countries such as Ireland or Italy dedicating as much as 0.77 and 1.12 per cent, respectively, in the early 1980s. The results for patenting activity are similar: whereas in Spain the number of patents per 10,000 inhabitants went from 13 in 1965 to 4 in 1983, the average figures for the OECD countries were 36 and 47 for the same years. These figures include public institutions and universities.

Arguably, a better idea of the technological state of industry is obtained from data that refer only to firms. In general terms, companies contributed around half of R&D, rising from 0.10 per cent of GDP at the beginning of the 1970s to 0.25 per cent in 1983. From a qualitative point of view, the precarious nature of the situation is revealed by the following facts:

- At the beginning of the 1980s, barely 500 companies carried out any R&D at all.
- Only 23 companies had a team of researchers (or their full-time equivalents) greater than 25 people.
- More than 90 per cent of the expenditure on R&D carried out by firms were directly financed by the firms themselves; public resources accounted for only a little over 5 per cent.
- Most R&D has been concentrated in a few products, leaving a wide range of products where there is little or no R&D involved at all. Radios and radio apparatus, motor engines, non-ferrous metals and electrical machinery accounted for more than 40 per cent of the total R&D resources in 1983.

While R&D is only one indicator of technology acquisition, the lack of resources devoted to this activity was symptomatic of a broader innovation problem among domestic firms. By contrast, the import of technology increased steadily during the 1960s and 1970s. In the 1980s, technological sales abroad grew, but they still only accounted for 25 per cent of imports – a much lower figure than for most other developed countries (Sánchez 1984). This imbalance between technology purchases and sales has been a characteristic of Spanish industrial development right up to the present day (Casado 1995; COTEC 1999; Molero 1996). The contracts for the transfer of technology published by the Ministry of Industry and Energy permit a more detailed analysis. This data source confirms the tendency towards an increase in imports, from an average of 350 contracts annually in the mid-1960s to more than 700 a decade later, and between 800 and 900 by the mid-1980s (Braña *et al.* 1984; Buesa and Molero 1988). The most obvious repercussion was an increase in liabilities from 1978 to 1982, rising from Ptas 30.5 bn to Ptas 78 bn a year (Gil Peláez 1983). But the importance of the contracts goes far beyond their number – they reveal the unequal situation under which they were drawn up. Contracts often incorporated multiple clauses which seriously limited the assimilation of the technology, a situation declared 'abusive' by various international organizations. For instance, subcontracting of the acquired technology was sometimes prohibited, restrictions were placed on the export of the products manufactured using the transferred technology and purchases of other goods were 'tied' to the sale of technology.

The effect of foreign technology on Spanish industry can be estimated from the Ministry of Industry's data on the largest industrial firms. In previous studies (MINER 1983) it was estimated that production based on foreign technology was more than 23 per cent for the whole group of firms – a figure that was much higher for firms in *high technological content* sectors. These sectors were characterized by the strong presence of foreign investments, foreign firms being crucial for the import of technology (Molero 1982; Sánchez 1984).

As has already been noted, from a policy perspective the quantitative restrictions on the purchase of external technologies became progressively less important in a macroeconomic context characterized by an enhanced capacity to attract foreign savings. With regard to the lack of applied research with relevance for industry, in the National Council for Scientific Research (CSIC) and universities, few changes were perceptible. Nor was much effort made to provide incentives for Spanish firms to perform R&D. While there was a growing awareness that something had to be done to address the problem of the lack of national sources of innovation, the initiatives taken made little or no improvement to the overall technological capacity of Spanish industry (Molero 1982).

Recovery, integration and active technological policies

Throughout the 1980s, some significant changes occurred in both the level of technological activity of Spanish firms and the general orientation of policy. First, the consolidation of a strong cyclical boom was associated with an unprecedented increase in the internationalization of the economy. This was associated with the economic reform efforts of the socialist government that came to power in the early 1980s. The new government also introduced measures to reform the institutional framework for technology policy and scientific activity, including the establishment of national R&D plans as a basic instrument to increase domestic technological resources and the reorganization of the Centre for Technological and Industrial Development (CDTI) as an agency to stimulate the innovative activity of firms (a range of incentives for R&D was also introduced at the level of the autonomous communities). The University Reform Law provided an institutional framework to put university research in touch with the business community and the sectoral plans of the Ministry of Industry and Energy were reorganized. The policy implemented in 1973, designed to improve the process of technology imports, was definitively abandoned, not just because the results were poor but because of the challenge and opportunity of entry into the EU in 1986. This certainly facilitated a more favourable institutional framework for promoting technological innovation and enabled Spanish firms and researchers to take part in a range of international collaborative programmes.

Against this background there were some significant – though not sufficient – changes in the technological capacity of the Spanish economy. Throughout the 1980s, the share of R&D in GDP almost doubled, but stagnation in the 1990s meant that on average R&D stood at 0.9 per cent of GDP. While this indicator shows that the gap with the rest of Europe has narrowed, it still remains substantial. In respect of other indicators (such as number of patents and levels of importation of foreign technology) there appears to have been little change. While the lack of change in these respects may reflect more general internationalization trends in respect of technological activities (European Commission 1998), the Spanish case stands out for two reasons: first, the high initial level of dependency and second, the relatively low dynamism of technological exports generated in the Spanish economy.

Overall then, the wide-ranging reforms have helped to improve the situation with regard to Spain's innovative capacity (notably in education) and technological dependence. Yet, in the new international context, R&D performance is still far from satisfactory. Technology policy needs to be reconsidered, bearing in mind the need to relocate resources within an institutional structure that is more responsive to contemporary demands. Improving absorptive capacities starts from devoting more resources (in both R&D and education) and increasing tacit efforts. In this last period, those favourable conditions fared better, because of the much more intense international competition and the internationalization of the economy as described in the previous section.

Summary

We have shown the intensity and speed of the transformations that Spanish industry has experienced, paying special attention to the role played by international forces. Since the 1950s, the country has undergone a transformation from conditions of backwardness, with the share of industry increasing over that period. While the share has declined in more recent decades it remains of fundamental importance. Within industry, there has been some shift towards sectors with a higher technological content, particularly motor vehicles, with FDI playing an important part in consolidating activities. Yet overall, there continues to be real competitiveness issues, due substantially to problems of technological weakness, which have become more acute as the economy has become more internationalized. While foreign investment has led progress in some sectors, there is still a lack of domestic innovative capacity. As a result, there is still a high dependence on foreign technology (even if there is a higher capacity for absorbing foreign technologies as a consequence of the upgrading of local technological effort and capabilities).

The role of FDI and the ways in which it connected with Spanish institutions and firms changed substantially between the two basic periods used in this study. To summarize these changes four types of links can be differentiated: property relations, technological activities, participation in public policies and those derived from the economic activity of the foreign companies themselves.

Starting from property relations, the first modification has to do with the relationships maintained with the mother company and other firms within the group. While, in the period before the 1970s crisis, it was a subordinated relationship corresponding to a traditional hierarchical pattern, in the last period there have been more interactive relations with the group as a whole. A second change in this field refers to the participation in joint ventures with different business groups, mainly financial institutions and public companies. In the first stage, a remarkable number of these ventures were organized in order to avoid investments of over 50 per cent of the capital. Since the 1980s, the trend has been clearly towards the reduction in the number of such joint ventures and to the consolidation of exclusive or dominant positions in a vast majority of firms.

In terms of technological activities, two other stylized changes can be highlighted. On the one hand, the relationships with research centres and universities, in order to create new technological capacities on a domestic basis, were almost non-existent in the first period. However, in the most recent period, some linkages have been established due to the upgrading of the local resources and the new more active role of the MNE subsidiaries. On the other hand, importation was the main source of technology acquisition before the crisis. However, the high economic costs and other restrictive clauses associated with that importation constituted a large barrier to its effectively spilling over into the national system.

The relations with the state and regional administration have also been a relevant way to create local linkages. Between the 1950s and 1970s, MNE subsidiaries participated very actively in many programmes created by the state to foster the industrialization process; in a significant number of cases that participation was carried out jointly with Spanish companies. The most significant change that has occurred in the most recent period has to do with the consolidation of regional governments as decreed in the democratic Constitution. Most of them have put into operation a large variety of new promotion instruments, adaptation to which has made interactions with public powers more complex and territorially diverse. This complexity has been compounded by European integration. There is no doubt that the policy of economic liberalization, initiated in the 1950s and underpinned by EC membership in 1986, has provided the context in which production integration has taken place. The particular effect of European integration has been to provide financial support in the form of funds for infrastructure development and research partnerships and to reinforce economic openness through regulatory commitments.

Finally, there is a heterogeneous number of other networking activities, which have arisen along with the economic activity of the firms itself. A good example is relationships with local suppliers. In fact, the low technological level of most of them at the beginning of the process led to the establishment of simple relationships with little value added, corresponding to firms' organization patterns characterized by integrating a large number of activities within the company. Nevertheless, the fast development of the economy upgraded the technological level of the Spanish companies, allowing them to participate in a more profound way in the production plans of MNE subsidiaries and to take advantage of the strategies for externalizing an increasing part of their activities.

Note

1 Significant differences arise in comparing Spain with each of the four countries. Italy and France are more similar to Spain whereas Germany shows the greatest difference and the United Kingdom is an intermediate case. Interestingly enough, Italy's industrial structure is today more different from that of Spain than two decades ago (Buesa and Molero 1998: 46).

References

Bajo, O. and López, C. (1996) 'La inversión extranjera directa en los procesos de innovación tecnológica. Un análisis del caso español', *Economía Industrial*, n° 306.

Braña, J., Buesa, M. and Molero, J. (1984) *El Estado y el cambio tecnológico en la industrialización tardía. Un análisis del caso español*, Fondo de Cultura Económica, Madrid-México.

Buesa, M. and Molero, J. (1988) *Estructura Industrial de España*, Madrid: Ed. Fondo de Cultura Económica.

Buesa, M. and Molero, J. (1998) *Economía Industrial de España. Organización, Tecnología e Internacionalización*, Madrid: Ed. Civitas.

Buesa, M. and Molero, J. (2000) 'La industrialización es la segunda mitad del siglo XX', in L. Velarde (ed.) *1900–2000, Historia de un Esfuerzo Colectivo*, Barcelona: Planeta.

Casado, M. (1995) 'La capacidad tecnológica de la industria española. Un balance de la transferencia de tecnología', *Información Comercial Española*, No. 740.

Circulo de Empresarios (1995) *Actitud y comportamientos de las grandes empresas españolas ante la innovación*, Madrid.

COTEC (1999) *Informe COTEC 1998. Tecnología e Innovación en España*, Madrid: Fundación Cotec para la innovación tecnológica.

Donges, J.B. (1976) *La Industrialización en España. Políticas, Logros, Perspectivas*, Ed. Oikos-Tau, Barcelona.

European Commission (1998) *Internationalisation of research and technology: trends, issues and implications for science and technology policies in Europe*, Working paper, ETAN, Brussels: European Commission.

Gil Pelaez, J. (1983) 'Transferencia de tecnología. Un canal de abastecimiento a las empresas', *Economía Industrial*, No. 230.

González, X. (1997) *Capital extranjero y actividad tecnológica. Una aplicación a las empresas manufactureras españolas.* Documento de Trabajo, n° 9711. Fundación Empresa Pública, Madrid.

INE (1997) *Encuesta Sobre Innovación Technológica en las Empresas 1994*, Madrid: Instituto Nacional de Estadistica.

Martín, C. and Velázquez, J. (1996) 'Factores determinantes de la Inversión Directa en los países de la OCDE: una especial referencia a España', *Papeles de Economía Española*, n° 66.

Merino, F. and Salas, V. (1995) 'Empresa extranjera y manufactura española: efectos directos e indirectos', *Revista de Economía Aplicada*, n° 9.

MINER (1983) *Las grandes empresas industriales en España, 1980–81*. Ministerio de Industria y Energía, Madrid.

Molero, J. (1982) *Tecnología e Industrialización*, Madrid: Pirámide.

Molero, J. (ed.) (1995) *Technological Innovation, Multinational Corporations and New International Competitiveness. The Case of Intermediate Countries.* Harwood Academic Publishers. Reading.

Molero, J. (1996) 'La exportación de tecnología como factor estratégico de desarrollo industrial', *Información Comercial Española*, No. 752.

Molero, J., Buesa, M. and Casado, M. (1995) 'Technological strategies of MNCS in intermediate countries: the case of Spain', in Molero, J. (ed.) Technological Innovation, Multinational Corporations and New International Competitiveness. The Case of Intermediate Countries. Harwood Academic Publishers.

Muñoz, J., Roldán, S. and Serrano, A. (1978) *La Internacionalización del Capital es España*, Madrid: Edicusa.

Pellegrín, A. (1997) *La Inversión Exterior Directa de Japón: comportamiento de la inversión manufacturera en España*, Doctoral Thesis. Universidad de Barcelona.

Rodríguez de Pablo, J. (1980) 'Consideraciones generales sobre los resultados del censo'. *Información Comercial Española*, n° 563.

Sánchez, P. (1984) *La Dependencia Tecnológica Española. Contratos de Transferencia entre España y el Exterior*, Madrid: Ministerio de Economía y Hacienda.

14 Markets and networks in Romania

Systemic unrest or life after disorganization?

Geomina Turlea and Cezar Mereuta

Introduction

As elsewhere in central and eastern Europe (CEE), the starting point of Romanian post-communist transformation lay in artificially constructed industrial networks that were formed administratively between big or very big companies and industrial platforms. In order to become integrated into the world economy these networks had to transform themselves into authentic value chains formed spontaneously between independent agents which operate in competitive markets and follow utility maximization objectives (Blanchard and Kremer 1997). The problems for Romania were particularly acute because, prior to 1989, the country had probably the most centralized production system in CEE while its political economy was not conducive to rapid systemic change.

This chapter analyses some key aspects of the restructuring of Romanian industrial networks during the transition. Our hypothesis is that, after a stage characterized as an *incomplete disorganization* of the requisite value chains, Romania has found itself in a situation we describe as *systemic unrest* where the growth of the private sector has not compensated for the decline in state sector output, and a permanent and complex process of adaptation by economic agents to pronounced uncertainty prevails. Both vertical and horizontal links between economic agents operate in conditions of strongly asymmetric information and moral hazard that pervade the domestic market. Because of high levels of uncertainty in the domestic market, local economic agents have strongly reoriented towards the foreign market, the key driving force for growth and recovery. In this respect, international integration has compensated to a certain extent for the anti-developmental nature of local networks and for widespread network failure at the national and regional levels.

In discussing the potential impact of this systemic unrest on domestic growth, we conclude that foreign direct investment (FDI), although still at a rather low level, is crucial to support clusters, around which a more ordered system could evolve. As emphasized in Chapter 3, this may not be a sufficient condition for network realignment, but we argue here that in the present circumstances it is very likely a necessary one. To the best of our knowledge this issue has not been yet analysed in Romania and, hence, our chapter can only define the problem and suggest perspectives for understanding it.

The domestic market context is examined in the next section and the world market in the one that follows it. In the section 'FDI – agent of alignment' FDI is targeted as the agent of integration between these two. There is also a regional dimension to the Romanian situation (for more detail see Turlea and Mereuta 2002). Conclusions are offered in the final section.

Domestic market context

The enterprises

In the early years of the transition, a complex and extensive process of administrative breakdown of communist production units took place, whereby the business services separated themselves from the producing units in the first round, followed by the separation of the production lines that could operate independently. This was especially the case in wood processing, textiles and clothing, some metal construction and foodstuff activities. As in the case of Hungary (see Whitley and Czaban 1999), the companies continued to be highly specialized in production inherited from communist times, further accentuating the effects of dissolution upon previous linkages without significantly improving efficiency.

The emerging structure of Romanian firms also raised concerns. Between 1992 and 1995, the number of new companies doubled, while between 1995 and 2000, the number of new enterprises slowed but still grew on average by 15 per cent annually. While the overall figures suggest that some convergence in the size structure of Romanian industrial enterprises towards that in the EU has taken place (Table 14.1), since 1997 the growth in the net number of new enterprises has stagnated at a level well below the EU. Currently, in Romania, there are less than fifteen active enterprises per 1,000 inhabitants, as compared to 45–50 in the EU countries. Decrease in the average size of the companies and their high rate of creation before 1996 is consistent with a disorganization process in the sense of Blanchard and Kremer (1997). However, the stagnating number of net entries, which is accompanied by an intensification of exit/entry rates, signals a different type of evolution, which is driven by *intensive market selection* and *significant barriers to firm growth*.[1]

Romanian private industry has almost the same structure of turnover in relation to size of enterprises as the EU (Table 14.2). This suggests that the distortions come from the state sector, which is inefficient and heavily concentrated in the energy and raw materials producing branches. Large state-owned companies (over

Table 14.1 Average employment per company in industry

	1989 (1990 for EU)	1999 (1996 for EU)
Romania	1756	52.9
EU	17.9	15.3

Source: Based on Marin *et al.* (2001) and EUROSTAT SME database.

Table 14.2 Breakdown of number of industrial enterprises and turnover by firm size

	No. of companies			Turnover		
Employees	0–49	50–249	250+	0–49	50–249	250+
Romania (1999)	88.9%	7.4%	3.6%	11.5%	12.4%	76.1%
Private sector only	NA	NA	NA	21.7%	21.9%	56.3%
EU (1996)	96.1%	3.1%	0.8%	20.2%	20.3	59.4%

Source: Based on Romanian Statistical Yearbook (2000) and EUROSTAT SME database.

500 employees) appear to be particularly inefficient. Their profitability rate in 1999 was −7 per cent, while the same segment of the private sector experienced a profitability rate of 1.6 per cent. The big loss-making enterprises, in both the state-owned and private-owned sectors, are concentrated mainly in raw materials, energy and infrastructure (transport and telecommunications) employing 15 per cent of the wage earners and generating 20 per cent of Romanian exports (Marin et al. 2001). They are also subject to considerable state interference and political pressure (Table 14.3).

Industrial networks are shaped largely by the behaviour of the big firms, which, in turn, are driven by their objective functions and corporate governance. Theoretically, the transition should shift the motivation of agents from compliance with plan requirements to profit maximization. However, instead, the state-owned firms that have been taken over by insiders maximize insiders' utility[2] and succumb to political pressures[3] (Daianu 1999; Dobrescu 1999; Marin et al. 2001; Turlea and De Sousa 2001). In such a situation, managers lack incentives for restructuring. As a result, corporate governance in Romania is short-term oriented and the decisions of the agents are most often reactive and very seldom aimed towards long-term investments. The state-owned enterprises (SOEs) survive on direct and indirect subsidies, but are often caught in relationships of adverse integration such as the so-called 'tick firms'.[4] By supporting state enterprises through such mechanisms, the state effectively redistributes the losses arising from private appropriation of state-owned firms' resources to private sector segments. At the same time, private loss-making firms rely on the practice of arrears, as non-interest bearing credit, to finance their operations.[5] They have neither the financial resources nor the willingness to be actively involved in network formation. Instead, as we show below, the big foreign direct investors play this role, although on a still limited scale.

State ownership

In countries in transition, state ownership of sensitive sectors could alleviate the social cost of disinflation (Roland 1994). However, in Romania, the asymmetric position of the state has favoured the emergence of a strong dichotomy between state and private sectors regarding pricing and wage setting, access to credits, speed of restructuring, compliance with economic legislation, etc. (Turlea and De Sousa 2001).

The state retained the property of the big enterprises, which are concentrated in the first stages of the production chain, *and* accommodated their monopolistic

Table 14.3 The top ten loss-making companies, 2000[a] (bn. ROL)

NACE	Company	Ownership	Region	Loss	% of GDP
Metallurgy	Sidex Steel mill	State	South-east	7,774.15	0.98
Extraction	National Pitcoal Company	State	South-west	5,941.31	0.75
Transportation	Daewoo Romania	Privatized	South-west	3,629.88	0.46
Energy production and distribution	National Company of Electric Energy Production	State	Bucharest	3,551.65	0.45
Extraction	National Lignite Company 'Oltenia'	State	South-west	2,222.31	0.28
Energy production and distribution	Energy Distribution Company – Bucharest	State	Bucharest	1,467.12	0.18
Foodstuff and tobacco	National Tobacco Company	State	Bucharest	1,197.97	0.15
Petroleum processing, coking	RAFO	Privatized	North-east	1,151.34	0.14
Petroleum processing, coking	Petromidia	Privatized	South-east	864.55	0.11
Transportation	Dacia SA	Privatized	South-west	847.83	0.10
Total	Ten companies	Four regions		28,648.1	3.60

Source: Authors' computations based on CEMATT database.

Notes

a The presence of automobile producers among the big losers is conjectural for year 2000.
€1 = ROL19922.

behaviour. This, in our view, is the main factor that prevented growth from resuming sooner and has implications for network formation and integration. We add to the Blanchard and Kremer (1997) framework of organizing production chains two specific hypotheses: (1) at each stage of the production chain, more than one use of the intermediate good is possible; and (2) the private firms can operate mainly at upper levels in the production chain.[6] In this system, the rent extracted by the energy and raw materials producing sectors will not be the lowest but the highest, while the competition for clients and suppliers will be tougher in more processed goods. In this case, the imposition of monopolistic/oligopolistic prices from the bottom of the chain will diminish profit margins and ultimately result in the exit of companies in more competitive downstream markets.

During the communist era, the central planner determined both relative wages and relative prices, which had weak (if any) correspondence to each other or to competitiveness criteria. Through various redistribution channels of the central administration this led to a permanent transfer of value-added from the more profitable sectors to others (Kornaï 1980, 1986). During transition, the liberalization of prices and economic structures has had a favourable net effect, especially on utilities and some raw materials (Pujol 1996). Therefore, even if these sectors were to experience tightening budget constraints, which is not particularly the case in Romania, the strong increase in their relative prices enables them to preserve their position in the market and lowers their incentive to restructure, despite a strong decrease in demand and production.

At the same time, the state presides over a number of harmful market distortions. By sheltering the inefficient state sector[7] and preventing the enforcement of hard budget constraints, Romanian economic policy decisions crowded out the chances for growth of a healthy private sector. Moreover, monopoly positions of the energy-intensive and extraction sectors have slowed down structural change.

Maintaining or even increasing the participation of the worst performing agents in economic life comes at the expense of diminishing the contribution of the best performing.[8]

The pre-conditions for network formation and alignment

The distribution channels that were administratively imposed during communism were disrupted, while a modern structure of mediators has started to emerge only recently. The wholesale trade seems comparatively well developed. The share of turnover in the wholesale trade compared to industry is 0.3 in both the EU15[9] and Romania.[10] The retail trade, characterized by pronounced atomization, by its nature cannot play an intermediary role in inter-firm interactions.

A variety of professional associations have been established and are active. The Chambers of Commerce and Industry support dissemination of information on economic activity in Romania and periodically organize specialist fairs and exhibitions in order to assist in matching supply and demand. However, these efforts are insufficient to enhance ties between firms, suppliers and customers.

In addition, financial intermediation is weak and inefficient, as reflected in very high interest rates for loans.[11] The insurance sector is facing low demand as a direct consequence of poverty and lack of market-oriented behaviour. Venture capital, which could provide funding for entrepreneurs in new economic areas like information technology (IT) and more especially software, does not exist. The stock exchange market is underdeveloped and few companies are actually traded. Therefore, the emergence of credible, market-type alternatives did not follow the collapse of past investment incentives and channels.

Indeed the characteristics of the Romanian economic system work against the development of networks:

- Highly volatile market share and economic performance of companies.
- Fragile links between suppliers and customers, lacking trust and fair business conduct, with contracts not being respected and long and costly legal procedures.

- Contracts between domestic agents typically short-term and cash-based, while firms are often faced with dramatic and unexpected changes in their portfolios of clients and suppliers and are exposed to moral hazard.
- Corruption, subsidies, preferential credits, arrears and value-added transfers from the new private and profitable sector to the inefficient or rent-extracting parts of the economy.
- Prices are not the main mechanism of resource reallocation due to pervasive subsidies coupled with other forms of protection of state enterprises.
- Economic agents face pronounced asymmetric information and the burden of an immature, evolving and unstable institutional framework.
- Government legislation in areas such as competition policy and bankruptcy is not implemented.
- Inherited structural bias and resistance to adjustment, partially motivated by the factors described above.
- An under-capitalized economy – most of the companies are operating on zero financial reserves, which increases their risk aversion and the probability that firms will build arrears as 'emergency buffers'.
- A segmented labour market, with strong unions, concentrated in the big, state-owned inefficient companies, with strong insider–outsider interests.
- Short-term *cost efficiency seeking* as the basic strategy of an important part of the foreign and the domestic capital.[12]

As a result, domestic industrial networks in Romania typically are temporary, fragile links between independent, opportunistic agents acting in unstable markets. We call this set of behavioural characteristics 'systemic unrest'. The difference between *systemic unrest* and the Blanchard and Kremer (1997) concept of *disorganization* is twofold. First, our concept of systemic unrest refers not to the reasons that the existing networks broke up, but to reasons that prevent new, stable networks from being formed. Second, the disorganization that precedes the formation of the new networks has some specific features. Underpinned by a system of subsidies, by barriers to entry and by protection from external competition, two types of sectors emerge, depending on whether monopolies or almost perfect competition arise at the upstream ends of the value chain. The value of the surplus is not distributed uniformly as in Blanchard and Kremer (1997), given that private agents do not have equal access along the production chain.

The emerging regional development pattern

These characteristics of markets and network formation are reflected in the pattern of regional development as well.[13] A preliminary analysis based on specialization indices and regional variance of revenues seems to show that urbanization effects are present in the Bucharest and Centre areas, concentrated primarily on manufactured final consumption. Zones with narrower specialization in extraction and heavy industry (south-west, south-east) do not show significant agglomeration effects.

Areas displaying urbanization effects are those with the most intensive market selection. Jacobs (1969) suggests that diversification of activities in a given area promotes innovation and knowledge diffusion from suppliers to their clients. Porter (1990), who claims that local competition is more growth conducive than a monopoly, supports this view. Such effects are to be seen in areas like Bucharest. It is not just that the location of the headquarters of most foreign investors[14] helped the development of services, trade, foodstuffs and clothing producing units, but the physical proximity of potential suppliers for these big investors also plays a role.

The more specialized areas are also those with the lowest revenue. Industries that dominate the poorer regions are state-owned, inefficient and face shrinking demand. Little innovation and accumulation of knowledge is actually taking place as the firms have both few incentives and few means to stimulate them.

With the concentration of some regions on lower value-added industries, interregional complementarities are not achieved. Instead, the self-sufficiency of the more developed, less specialized areas, brings growing regional disparity.

The world market dimension

The products and the exporters

Within the ex-Council for Mutual Economic Assistance (CMEA) network, the position of Romania was favourable, as the external trade was substantially more western oriented than for some other CEE countries. A pronounced reorientation of trade towards other markets was completed in Romania rather quickly. The export regime was liberalized in the early stages with simultaneous control of deficits through various import restrictions. The manufacturing industry provides 67.4 per cent of total Romanian exports,[15] of which two industrial branches, clothing and metallurgy, represent one-third. Six branches (out of thirty-two) cover 60 per cent of industrial exports, namely clothing, metallurgy, chemicals, furniture and other activities, machinery and equipment, and transport means other than road.

Exports are focused on two extremes of Romanian manufacturing. On the one hand, there are those companies that have received most of the FDI and have restructured with low labour costs. They are, to an important degree, integrated into the western networks, not only through commercial relations, but also through vertical production linkages. Sometimes Romanian firms are integrated horizontally, especially if they are part of a transnational corporation (TNC). On the other hand, there are those companies that are facing falling demand to which they react by lowering prices below costs and accumulating losses. Dobrescu (1999, 2002) suggests that the lack of correlation between Romanian exports and the appreciation of the exchange rate could be explained by the perceived cost of uncertainty in the domestic market, which is still higher than the disincentive of real appreciation.

A highly important vehicle for the trade integration of Romania is the outward processing trade (OPT). Table 14.4 shows that some of the sectors operating in the OPT regime are also those that have registered some growth in 1999. Clothing,

Table 14.4 Production growth and OPT production

	Production growth, 1999 (1998 = 100)	OPT production index[a] 1999 %
Manufacturing – total	98.84	12.1
Foodstuff and tobacco	115.87	2.3
Textile and clothing, of which	92.47	68.3
Textile industry	75.10	20.2
Clothing industry	105.51	86.3
Leather and footwear	101.70	76.3
Wood processing	98.41	2.9
Paper and cardboard, printing and recording	95.52	0.0
Petroleum processing, coal coking and treatment of nuclear fuels	74.40	17.0
Chemical industry, synthetic and artificial fibres	102.12	1.2
Rubber and plastic	78.20	1.7
Other non-metallic products	88.42	0.0
Metallurgy	63.28	3.2
Metallic constructions and products	116.86	1.6
Machinery and equipment	85.01	0.1
Electric and optical machinery and equipment	104.69	13.9
Transport means	98.35	0.0
Furniture and other industrial activities	105.73	2.8

Source: Authors' computations based on CEMATT database and Romanian Statistical Yearbook (2000).

Note

a The index of OPT production is the share of expenditures made by the foreign client in total production costs.

leather and footwear especially, but also electrical and optical equipment, seem to be positively affected by integration into the world economy. They are also top Romanian exporters. Foodstuff production grew, fuelled by the growth in demand and FDI, since Romanian agriculture is a good supplier to the food industry and is mainly domestic market oriented. The textile industry saw a pronounced decline after 1995. One of the reasons was the change in consumer preferences away from synthetic fibre production, since foreign capital is oriented towards natural fibre production and only specific enterprises or production lines, with a low value-added part of total production. Nevertheless, all major products saw a decline. The apparent growth in metallic construction is cyclical: it follows a few years of major decline (up to 50 per cent) beginning in 1997. A special case is the transport industry, which we discuss below.

The state and trade policy

Romanian trade policy was biased towards stronger protection against international competition of sectors producing raw materials and intermediate goods through higher import taxes.[16] As a developing country, Romania was allowed within the Uruguay Round to have a more protectionist trade system (see Table 14.5).

Table 14.5 Weighted average of import
custom taxes for all industrial
products of Romania

Before Uruguay Round	11.7%
After Uruguay Round	33.9%

Source: Based on Negrescu *et al.* (2001).

Table 14.6 Mean import duties by country and type of good (in %)

	Raw materials	*Semi-processed goods*	*Manufactured goods*
India	41.3	52.4	65.1
Turkey	20.9	40.4	46.9
Tunisia	29.1	32.5	35.5
Mexico	33.8	34.8	34.9
Romania	31.2	31.9	30.1
Thailand	17.9	26.9	29.3
Philippines	19.0	23.4	29.1
South Korea	8.7	8.0	14.3
Poland	6.2	9.3	11.6
Hungary	5.3	5.4	8.9
Czech Republic	0.9	4.2	4.9

Source: Based on Market Access; Unfinished Business, the Post-Uruguay Round Inventory and Issues, WTO Special Studies 6, 2001; pp. 14–16 (from Negrescu *et al.* 2001). Ranked in descending order for manufactured goods.

An important feature of the Romanian customs system is the excessive differentiation of import taxes[17] (Negrescu *et al.* 2001). In addition, Romania has slightly higher import taxes for the raw materials and semi-processed goods than for manufactured goods (see Table 14.6). Negrescu *et al.* (2001) point out that this is an example of negative protection and is part of the asymmetric attitude of the state towards different sectors.

Exchange rate policy also influences exports and the integration of Romanian industry. From 1993 to 2000, the exchange rate appreciated by 5 per cent if deflated by the price index of textiles and ready-made clothes, or by 22 per cent if deflated by the price of extraction industry products. The external competitiveness of manufactured products has improved through a lower appreciation of the exchange rate when deflated by production prices, while the internal producers of raw materials have been protected through import barriers.

Therefore, the external competitiveness of Romanian products is ensured by low prices, coexisting, in certain parts of manufacturing industry, with improved quality and management, especially in labour-intensive industries. Co-operation with western partners (through direct investment, OPT production or direct privatization) is essential.

FDI – agent of alignment

The vicious cycle could be broken by investment in new technologies that would reduce consumption of energy and raw materials. As market volatility makes investment in long-term restructuring risky and expensive, the role of FDI becomes critical. As envisaged in chaos theory, FDI can create *attractors*, around which the economic system could form stable structures. Such a process started in several branches, of which we will detail some examples, but according to Marin *et al.* (2001) their scale has not yet reached the critical level to generate effects on the national economy as a whole.

Greenfield foreign investment amounts to 80 per cent, while brownfield (privatizations) constitutes another 17 per cent of FDI.[18] The role of local stock markets is marginal (Dochia 1999b). The foreign investment is also very concentrated, as the top 100 investors made up 1 per cent of the total number of investing companies, but controlled 71 per cent of the total foreign capital by the end of 2000. Of these major investments, 50.25 per cent were made in industry (see Table 14.7).

Eighty per cent of FDI is of EU origin. From a regional perspective, the areas preferred by the foreign investors are Bucharest, western Romania and the free trade zones (Arad-Curtici, Giurgiu and Timisoara). The sectoral structure of FDI is rather close to the other CEE countries (see Table 14.8).

The top investors in industry range from US$252 mn invested by Renault France in car manufacturing at the end of 2000, down to US$7.9 mn invested by Ganahl,

Table 14.7 Share of top foreign investments (US$ million, 2000)

Total capital subscribed in hard currency	Capital subscribed by the top 100 foreign direct investments	Capital subscribed by the top 100 foreign direct investments in industry
5001.9	3574.46	1796.4

Source: Chamber of Commerce and Industry, *Foreign Investments in Romania*, Bulletin no. 35 and *Business Review*, 4(45).

Table 14.8 Sectoral foreign investments (% of total)

	Romania	Central and eastern Europe
Heavy industry	23.3	17
Light industry	10.2	14
Foodstuff industry	11.8	11
Agriculture	3.5	3
Construction	5.2	NA
Trade	18.2	12
Tourism	2.8	NA
Transport	7.8	9
Services	17.3	14

Source: Based on Marin *et al.* (2001).

Austria, in the manufacture of paper and cardboard.[19] With the exception of food-stuffs and the transportation industry, which are primarily oriented to the domestic market, the composition of the top investors has helped the Romanian producers to penetrate foreign markets as exporters (metallurgy, chemicals, petroleum processing, electrical equipment). In sectors where FDI is not common (leather and footwear, textiles and clothing), OPT production was the main mechanism for industrial integration. FDI has the potential to link national to international networks. For the time being, however, much of the FDI is oriented towards the Romanian market.

Strategic FDI: the car industry

The car industry has attracted the biggest foreign investments so far. The French car giant, Renault, purchased a majority stake (51 per cent) of the top local car builder Dacia Pitesti, followed by additional purchases up to 92 per cent. The investment has been considered as one of the most successful so far in Romania. Dacia currently holds 62 per cent of the Romanian market. The level of investment in the period 1999–2004 is planned to be €515 mn, of which €270 mn has been already invested, with the intention of turning Dacia into a major exporter. An additional €350–450 mn will be invested in the new X90 model, to be launched in 2004. The other investor in the car industry is South Korea's Daewoo Motors which invested more than US$850 mn between 1994 and June 2001 and has plans to invest a further US$20 mn. Since 1990, the US Trinity group has invested in the railway industry.

FDI in the transportation industry was one of the three industrial branches that recorded a growth of 74 per cent (1994–99) compared to −18 per cent for overall manufacturing. Daewoo and Dacia Renault dominate the local market by producing both average and good quality cars at affordable prices. The automotive industry typically has a strong influence on several other branches. In Romania, foreign investment in the car industry has attracted other investors, which see opportunities to supply car assemblers.

Other investors have also been attracted to the domestic market by the lure of import taxes. For example, the international tyre producers Continental (Germany)[20] and Michelin entered Romania in 1998 and 2001 respectively. Other investors provide spare parts, rubber and plastic products, etc. Given the inherited high level of vertical integration in the Romanian car industry, an increasing number of components are being produced within Romania. Daewoo chose to integrate some of the first-tier suppliers, instead of developing relationships with independent firms. Renault's local content is currently about 30 per cent. Although still modest, we can see the emergence of industrial networks focused around two large investors in the automotive industry.

Market seeking FDI – the food industry

The Romanian beer market has developed significantly since the entry of FDI in 1997. Domestic production grew from 7.5 million hl. to 12.1 million in 2000.

This sector is considered to be one of the most competitive in Romania, with around 40 beer producers, and many small regional breweries. However, 60 per cent of the total market is controlled by international beer producers. This is not surprising given that the domestic market is sheltered by very high import taxes of 248 per cent (55 per cent for imports from the EU).

Brau Union Romania, founded in 1998 as a subsidiary of the Austrian Group BBAG, is currently the leader in the Romanian beer market with a market share of 36 per cent. The leadership position came about through acquisitions of breweries in Arad, Constanta, Craiova, Reghin, Bucharest, Miercurea Ciuc and Hateg. Since its entry into the Romanian market, Brau Union has invested over US$100 mn and occupies the 12th position among the 100 top investments in Romania. Brau Union invested in product quality and technological transfer – it now produces Kraiser beer, a representative brand of the group, in Romania under licence.

Cost based subcontracting and FDI – textiles and clothing

Textiles and clothing have not attracted a single 'top' investment, but have attracted numerous smaller ones. The investments, both internal and foreign, have been quite extensive in this sector, which has led to significant technological transfer and restructuring. In the 1992–99 period, the clothing industry had one of the highest shares of investments: 5.7 per cent in 1995 and 9.8 per cent in 1999.

Since 1996, Romania has been the second biggest supplier for clothing subcontracting in the EU, after Poland, with a contribution of approximately €440 mn. The key feature of this sector is OPT production, which amounted in 2000 to 74.6 per cent of total local production: 26.1 per cent in textile products and 89.8 per cent in clothing.

Textiles and clothing are also the main single exports of the Romanian manufacturing industry. Their share in total Romanian exports grew from 15.9 per cent in 1994 to 24.2 per cent in 2000. In terms of exports to the EU, this sector contributes one-third (see Table 14.9). Essentially, the entire Romanian production from the textile and clothing sector is now exported to the EU.

The state and FDI

The Romanian government encourages FDI mainly through fiscal incentives, but throughout the last decade the policy for attracting FDI proved to be ineffective,

Table 14.9 The share of the textile and clothing (T&C) sector in total exports (%)

Indicator	1994	1995	1996	1997	1998	1999	2000
Share of T&C in total exports	15.9	19.8	21.4	23.0	26.0	25.9	24.2
Share of T&C exports to the EU in total EU exports	33.1	31.2	33.4	36.0	36.4	36.1	34.3

Source: Authors' calculations based on CEMATT database.

especially given its instability. A new Investment Law in Romania for the promotion of direct investment was promulgated in June 2001 and provides fixed incentives on investments exceeding US$1 mn. The investor is granted accelerated redemption of 50 per cent of the value of fixed assets, exemption from customs duty and delayed payment of value-added tax (VAT) on local procurement. The government also offers professional advice to foreign investors in the initial set-up phase of their business to facilitate interaction with Romanian government bodies. In addition, there are 'overlapping' facilities for disadvantaged areas, industrial parks and free trade zones. Companies with 100 per cent foreign ownership established in the free trade zones receive incentives regarding the payment of VAT, excise duty, income tax, customs duty, and the right to repatriate profits throughout the period of their activity. Yet, even these measures (in addition to special discretionary incentives associated with particular privatizations) have not succeeded in attracting foreign investment on a scale comparable to the central European countries. Nor are there policies which are able to foster linkages between FDI and local firms. In the past, there was a fiscal incentive conditional on 60 per cent of local content, but this was removed as part of the EU negotiations.

More generally, however, it has proved hard for Romania to adapt policies to help towards EU membership. In a number of respects the country has lagged behind other CEE states in aligning its economic policies and institutional frameworks with the EU acquis: as of late 2002 the country had closed only thirteen of the thirty negotiating chapters. Indeed the problems were such that the country was not included in the first wave of new membership, and future membership will depend upon reinforcing administrative and judicial capacity and the pursuit of economic reforms (most notably in the areas of tackling subsidies and arrears).

Conclusions

In this chapter, we have reviewed the emerging evidence on network formation and the relation of this process to the formation of markets, using the local-national-global dimension of the network alignment approach of Kim and von Tunzelmann (1998). As we lack direct evidence on network formation we have had to rely on indirect data to investigate the emerging structures of firms and their networks. Our conclusion is that the basic preconditions for vertical and horizontal integration and formation of industrial networks, like lack of entry–exit barriers, coherent competition enhancing government policies, a modern system of commercial mediators and other elements of the institutional framework including managerial culture, are underdeveloped and not fully functional. On the other hand, the early liberalization of external trade and the incentives for FDI enabled the best performing firms to integrate into EU markets. At the national and regional level, with the exception of the emergent industrial districts in western and north-western Romania, there is a lack of developed industrial networks. The only pervasive networks are 'meta' or 'relational' networks based on the personal contacts of the managers. The emergence of industrial networks is driven by FDI, which act as business catalysts and stabilizers. Our conclusion is that it is in these areas that the formation and alignment of the networks has started. However, a deepening of industrial networks would require a certain and stable environment, a more even attitude of the state, an enforcement of fair competition policy and an acceleration of institution building to continue and succeed.

Acknowledgement

We would like to thank Ms Gabriela Baciu (Arthur Andersen) for contribution of useful insights to the preparation of this text.

Notes

1 Between 1997 and 1999, the newly created enterprises represented approximately 6.5 per cent of the total number.
2 For sectors like metallurgy, electricity etc. labour costs amount to as much as 80–90 per cent of total value-added.
3 Policies such as insurance against managerial risk (malpractice) are not sold in Romania, which lowers even further the incentives of state-owned managers to restructure their companies and to make long-term investments.
4 'The most significant effect of the white-collar, managerial origins of the Romanian private entrepreneur comes from its special relation with the state and state companies. Many private ventures were from the start conceived to gravitate around a state company. Although some of them are legitimate and respectable businesses, in a very large number of cases they are simply devices aimed at siphoning profits and assets from state companies into private hands. The simplest and best known mechanism is the "tick firm": Two SRL (limited liability companies), usually having deep roots in the political environment, are placed on the "inputs" and the "outputs" circuits of a state enterprise. The first is selling the raw materials at higher prices; the second is buying the production cheaply. The tick firms are prospering, and the guest company becomes, in a few years, a true "black hole"' (quoted from Cercelescu 1999, extracted from Dochia 1999a).
5 According to OECD (2002) the volume of arrears amounted to an equivalent of 40 per cent of GDP in 2001.
6 In addition, in an unstable environment, private capital will tend naturally to locate into areas where entry costs to the market are low and business is adaptable to demand shocks, allowing a quick and efficient response to the rapid structural changes.
7 Blanchard and Kremer (1997) suggest that a gradual liberalization could help the state sector to follow a smooth decline.
8 Although the situation seems to reverse somewhat in 2000, further analysis for the following years is needed to confirm if there is a break in the negative trend.
9 EUROSTAT; data for 1996.
10 NIS (2000); data for 1999.
11 In the early years of the transition the interest rates were sometimes negative, but the banking system was state-owned, and access to credit was rationed.
12 Landesmann (2000) shows that in the CEECs the evolution of productivity drives the gap in unit labour costs at sectoral levels. However, in the case of Romania this does not lead to a gain in high and medium tech industries comparable to the central European economies. One of the particularities of Romania is that the bulk of the most profitable industries are included among the low-tech groups of Landesmann (2000) – food and tobacco, textiles and textile products, leather and leather products – and one from the resource-intensive group, that is, other non-metallic mineral products.
13 According to the EU model, Romania is organized into eight development regions: North-East, South-East, South, South-West, West, North-West, Centre and Bucharest.

14 Fifty-seven per cent of the companies receiving investments from the top 100 investors are located or have their headquarters in Bucharest.
15 Data for 1999.
16 Many import duties were lifted as of 1 January 2002.
17 At the end of 1999, Romania had eighty-one different groups of import taxes of which only thirty-one were applied, compared to the majority of countries where there are not more than ten different rates applied (Negrescu *et al.* 2001).
18 The contribution of privatization in attracting foreign investment became significant only after 1997, when the real privatization of bigger SOEs started.
19 The biggest investment will be reversed by the biggest privatization in south-eastern Europe, the sale of the Sidex steel mill for almost US$500 mn to the LNM Holding Company. The company produces 4 per cent of Romanian GDP and it is estimated to account for 80 per cent of the losses by state-owned enterprises in Romania.
20 The entry of Michelin seems to be clearly motivated by its link with Renault. However, there is little evidence that the entry of Continental is motivated by any opportunity to become a supplier of Daewoo.

References

Blanchard, O. and Kremer, M. (1997) 'Disorganization', *Quarterly Journal of Economics*, 112(4): 1091–126.
Business Review (2001), 4(45).
Cercelescu, Gh. (1999) 'Riscurile asanarii economiei', Adevarul, Bucharest.
Daianu, D. (1999) *Tranformarea ca process real*, Bucharest: IRLI.
Dobrescu, E. (1999) *Macromodels of the Romanian Economy in Transition*, Bucharest: Ed. Expert.
Dobrescu, E. (2002) 'Macromodel estimations for the Romanian "Pre-Accession Economic Programme"', mimeo, Bucharest.
Dochia, A. (1999a) 'New private firm contributions to structural change in the Romanian economy', in C. Ruhl and D. Daianu (eds), *Romania 2000 Conference Proceedings*, Washington, DC: World Bank.
Dochia, A. (1999b) *Corporate Governance in Romania*, Paris: OECD.
EUROSTAT (2001) *Enterprises in Europe*, Brussels: EUROSTAT.
Foreign Investments in Romania vol. 35, (2002), Bucharest: Chamber of Commerce and Industry.
Glaeser, E.L., Kallal, H.D., Scheinkman, J.A. and Schleifer, A. (1992) 'Growth in cities', *Journal of Political Economy*, 100: 1126–52.
Jacobs, J. (1969) *The Economics of Cities*, New York: Vintage.
Kornaï, J. (1980) *Economics of Shortage*, Amsterdam: Elsevier North-Holland.
Kornaï, J. (1986) 'The soft budget constraint', *Kyklos*, 39(1): 3–30.
Kim, S.R. and von Tunzelmann, N. (1998) 'The dynamics and alignment of "networks of networks": explaining Taiwan's successful IT specialization', SEWPS no. 17, SPRU, University of Sussex, Brighton. Available HTTP: <http://www.sussex.ac.uk/spru/publications/imprint/sewps/sewp17/sewp17.pdf> (accessed 14.9.03).
Landesmann, M. (2000) 'Narrowing the structural gap: structural change in the transition economies 1989 to 1999', in S. Arndt, H. Heindler and D. Salvatore (eds), *Eastern Enlargement, the Sooner the Better*, Vienna: Austrian Federal Ministry for Economic Affairs and Labour, Economic Policy Section.
Marin, D., Mereuta, C., Ciupagea, C. and Turlea, G. (eds) (2001) *Economia Romaniei. Sistemul de companii. Diagnostic structural*, Bucharest: Ed. Economica.
National Institute for Statistics (2000) *Romanian Statistical Yearbook*, Bucharest: National Institute for Statistics.

Negrescu, D., Ciupagea, C. and Goanta, L. (2001) 'Politica comercială a României în Perioada de Tranzitie. Lectii din Experientă și Perspective' CEROPE, mimeo.

Organisation for Economic Cooperation and Development (2002) *OECD Economic Assessment for Romania*, Paris: OECD.

Porter, M.E. (1990) *The Competitive Advantage of Nations*, New York: Free Press.

Pujol, T. (1996) 'The role of labour market rigidity during transition: lessons for Poland', IMF, mimeo.

Roland, G. (1994) 'On the speed and sequencing of privatisation and restructuring', *Economic Journal*, 104(426): 1158–68.

Turlea, G. and De Sousa, J. (2001) 'Institutional dimension of wage determination in Romanian industry', in W.W. Charemza and K. Strzala (eds), *East European Transition and EU Enlargement. A Quantitative Approach*, Heidelberg; New York: Physica-Verlag.

Turlea, G. and Mereuta, C. (2002) 'Markets and networks in Romania – life after disorganization', Project Working Paper No. 14, March. Available HTTP: <http://www.ssees.ac.uk/publications/working_papers/wp15.pdf> (accessed 14.9.03).

Whitley, R. and Czaban, L. (1999) 'Continuity amidst change: Hungarian enterprises in the mid-1990s', in A. Lorentzen, B. Widmaier and M. Laki (eds), *Institutional Change and Industrial Development in Central and Eastern Europe*, Aldershot: Ashgate.

15 The integration of Poland into EU and global industrial networks

Evidence and the main challenges

Stefan Dunin-Wasowicz, Michal Gorzynski and Richard Woodward

Introduction

Economic integration is much more than the reduction and removal of trade barriers. It involves links of producers crossing borders that span a range of relationships from the equity-based (foreign direct investment (FDI)) to the contractual (subcontracting, leasing of production equipment, etc.). The nature and extent of such relationships are key factors determining a given country's place in the international division of labour. In this chapter, we attempt a presentation of the achievements of one decade of transformation of the Polish economy in effecting the integration of its producers with those of the broader European and global economy.

The following section of the chapter presents a broad picture of the current situation in Poland with respect to the integration of the country's economy into European industrial networks. The section on Factors underlying Poland's emerging position in international networks examines the chief actors in the integration process (foreign and domestic firms and national and local governments), assessing the role they have played in that process over the last decade. The final section summarizes and discusses some hypotheses that we think worth investigating in further research.

Trends in foreign trade, foreign investment and specialization

We begin our discussion with a few key numbers that characterize the degree of integration between Poland and the European Union (EU). World Trade Organization (WTO) data indicate that in 2000, exports from Poland to the EU were worth 22 bn US\$, representing 70 per cent of all Polish exports. On the other hand, imports amounted to 29.9 bn US\$, which represented 61 per cent of total imports and 19 per cent of Polish GDP. These trade share figures are illustrated in Figure 15.1. The last five years have not brought fundamental changes in terms of the balance of trade or geographical orientation. During that period, Poland has fairly consistently sent 70 per cent of its exports to the EU and received 61–66 per cent of its imports from the EU.

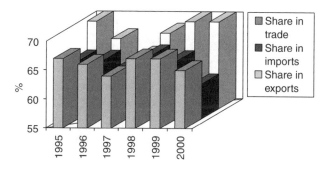

Figure 15.1 Trade shares, Poland–EU (1995–2000).
Source: Based on Central Statistical Office (2001).

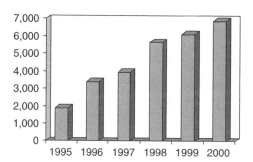

Figure 15.2 Total FDI in Poland, 1992–2000.
Source: PAIZ data.

According to data published by PAIZ (the Polish Agency for Foreign
Investment), the flow of FDI into Poland since 1994 has been impressive. Of the
total stock of FDI in Poland accumulated since 1992 and estimated at 49 bn US$,
about 59 per cent is held by companies headquartered in EU member countries.
As of the beginning of 2000, the total number of companies under foreign ownership was 13,369 (most of them small companies with fewer than nine employees).
Out of that total number, 10,369 companies were reported as having capital originating from EU countries, which would be equivalent to 77 per cent of the total
(with companies of German origin equal to 40.7 per cent of the total). Total FDI
for 1992–2000 is presented in Figure 15.2, while the breakdown with respect to
individual countries for 1998–2000 is presented in Figure 15.3. Germany initially
was the leading source of FDI to Poland, but an increase of FDI from France
starting in 1995 has resulted in even higher FDI growth in Poland, but also sectoral
diversification (which we will return to in a moment).

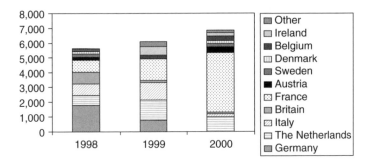

Figure 15.3 FDI in Poland originating from EU countries, by country of origin, 1998–2000 (US$ mn).

Source: PAIZ data.

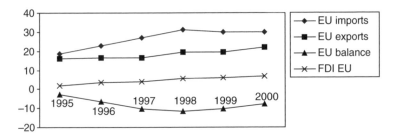

Figure 15.4 Foreign trade and FDI, Poland–EU (1995–2000; US$ mn).

Source: Based on Central Statistical Office (2001).

Table 15.1 EU–Poland trade and FDI year-to-year growth (%; in current prices)

	1996	*1997*	*1998*	*1999*	*2000*
Imports	21.8	17.5	15.2	−3.9	0.3
Exports	1.9	1.2	17.0	0.0	14.5
Balance	135.7	57.6	12.5	−10.3	−25.7
FDI	88.9	14.7	43.6	8.9	11.5

Sources: Central Statistical Office, *Yearbook of Foreign Trade* 2001, for trade data; PAIZ web site (http://www.paiz.gov.pl) for FDI data.

Putting FDI and foreign trade together we arrive at the picture presented in Figure 15.4 and Table 15.1. We see that while FDI from the EU has grown fairly steadily, Poland's balance of trade with the EU has been consistently negative, and dipped in the mid-1990s to recover somewhat more recently.

Table 15.1 summarizes annual percentage changes for trade and FDI between Poland and the EU (in current prices). The balance of trade with the EU started to improve in 1998 and, over the same time, the flow of FDI from the EU to Poland demonstrated steady growth of approximately 10 per cent per year.

Data reported by Poland's Central Statistical Office as of the end of 1999 present the following picture of the profits of the foreign-owned sector compared to all enterprises reporting profit and loss figures (see Table 15.2).

There are several important observations to be made based on the above comparison. First, foreign firms typically are larger than domestic firms in terms of revenues and employment (on average three times bigger in terms of revenues). Second, they are more profitable (also approximately three times more). Third, they are net importers, in contrast to domestic firms, whose foreign trade is more or less balanced. What this negative balance of trade means for the development of the Polish economy and its integration into European and global production networks is unclear. Are imports dominated by raw materials and supplies, or do they represent capital investment? Certainly there are elements of both and the respective shares are changing over time, but we are unable to say anything definitive about the magnitudes and directions and their effects without further research. At any rate, the fact that Poland's large domestic market generally leads investors to focus on production for domestic rather than export markets makes Poland's per capita export performance much less impressive than that of several of its smaller neighbours. This is presented in Table 15.3.

According to PAIZ, only about 41 per cent of FDI was directed towards manufacturing (with food and consumer products and the automotive sector each representing approximately 10 per cent). Investments in services accounted for 59 per cent, with 20 per cent of total FDI flowing into financial services, 11 per cent into infrastructure (transportation and telecommunication) and 8 per cent going to distribution and sales activities. Given the very diverse sectoral allocation of investments, mostly motivated by the search for local consumer market share (see section on MNC strategies), scepticism as to whether FDI is a significant force driving Poland's integration into EU networks seems justified. It is, however, true that the spillover effects in terms of generating local supplier bases have not been sufficiently studied to offer a conclusive analysis of FDI-induced growth of various Polish industries and their participation in European production networks. This is clearly one of the key research challenges for the future.

Another angle in the analysis of integration of Poland's economy into European industrial networks and the European division of labour comes from using specialization and integration indices. Simplifying somewhat, we can say that the specialization index corresponds to the balance of trade in the products of a given industry. Thus, an index with a positive value means that exports represent a large portion of total production in a given industry. Conversely, de-specialization (indicated by an index with a negative value) indicates that a large portion of domestic demand is satisfied by imports.[1] Integration indices are calculated as the simple average of specialization indices. (Similarly, industry network integration could be expressed as the average spread between specialization and de-specialization on the

Table 15.2 Activity of firms with foreign ownership, end 1999

Type of firms	No. of firms	Employment	In millions of PLN[a]				In millions of US$	
			Revenues	Gross profits	Exports	Imports	Exports	Imports
All	48,057	4,943,917	1,077,210	14,830	115,080	192,780	27,400	45,900
Domestic ownership	42,152	4,042,082	736,306	6,815	64,339.8	65,805.6	15,319	15,668
%	87.7	81.8	68.4	46.0	55.9	34.1	55.9	34.1
Foreign ownership	5,905	901,835	340,904	8,015	50,740.2	126,974.4	12,081	30,232
%	12.3	18.2	31.6	54.0	44.1	65.9	44.1	65.9

Source: Based on Central Statistical Office (2000).

Note
a Calculated at an exchange rate of 4.2 PLN to 1 US$.

Table 15.3 Exports per capita, 1999 (US$)

Poland	710
Hungary	1,800
Slovenia	4,200
Czech Republic	2,200

Source: Ministerstwo Gospodarki.

Table 15.4 Specialization indices for trade of various Central European economies with the EU

SITC classification	Poland	Czech Rep.	Slovakia	Hungary	Romania	Bulgaria	Slovenia
Rather labour intensive							
Rubber products	1	4	0	1	1	0	3
Wood and cork	5	3	1	1	2	2	7
Fabrics	−6	−2	−10	−12	−31	−19	−8
Iron and steel	1	1	11	−3	5	18	−2
Non-ferrous metals	4	−3	5	2	6	20	7
Furniture	11	9	3	2	10	2	21
Clothing	13	6	18	16	55	42	15
Footwear	1	2	7	4	15	6	1
Rather capital intensive							
Power generation machinery	0	0	−9	43	1	1	−1
Machinery specialized	−6	−3	−7	−9	−11	−9	−7
Gen. industry machinery	−7	−4	−11	−15	−5	−5	−4
Office machines	−4	−7	−2	17	−3	−5	−6
Telecommunication	−1	−9	−7	11	−7	−9	−7
Electrical machinery	1	−3	−3	−1	−6	−7	15
Road vehicles	−2	26	40	−26	−7	−16	11
Other transport equipment	2	2	4	1	3	−2	−2

Source: Based on Allen (2001).

subsectoral level – material, intermediary products and finished goods trade.) These indices are presented for various Central European economies in Tables 15.4 and 15.5.

As can be seen from Table 15.5, and as would be expected, smaller economies demonstrate overall higher integration levels. With respect to the specializations of the various countries, we can see from Table 15.4 that with the exception of Hungary, which achieved significant positive specialization in technology-intensive industries, all countries of the region demonstrate dominance of specialization in low-technology industries.

Table 15.5 Integration indices for trade of various Central European economies with the EU

	Poland	Czech Rep.	Slovakia	Hungary	Romania	Bulgaria	Slovenia
Integration index	0.81	1.38	2.50	2.00	1.75	1.19	2.69

Source: Based on Allen (2001).

Our conclusions are not very favourable for Poland. With the exception of furniture and clothing, there is no strong evidence of inter-industry specialization in trade between Poland and EU. The wood and textile industries' links with the international economy are historically strong and existed prior to transformation. These industries are relatively labour intensive and to a large extent domestically owned. By way of contrast, in the rather capital-intensive sectors we cannot find clear evidence of increased or decreased specialization of Poland *vis-à-vis* the EU. A slightly more optimistic picture is provided by Kaminski and Smarzynska (2001), who perform a similar analysis but divide products into four categories: natural resource based, unskilled labour intensive, skilled labour intensive and capital intensive. They find that in the period 1993–98 there was a shift in the factor content of Polish exports to the EU towards skilled labour-intensive goods, with a decrease in specialization in natural resource-based goods. Overall, however, the country remains most strongly characterized by a specialization in unskilled labour-extensive exports.[2]

Factors underlying Poland's emerging position in international networks

The position of Poland in international networks that has been emerging over the last decade or so can be considered from the viewpoint of three types of players: multinational corporations (MNCs), domestic firms and public authorities (both national and local). We will seek to provide a broad picture of the context within which this process has been taking place.

An underlying assumption of the 'alignment of networks' approach (Kim and von Tunzelmann 1998; Radosevic 2000) to the analysis of international networks is that for a full understanding of how international business networks are formed, it is necessary to look at three different types of forces – markets, policies and enterprise strategies – and how they interact. Consideration of any of these factors in isolation will provide an incomplete or even distorted picture. With this in mind, we now look at how the three aforementioned types of actors in Poland have worked over the last decade to integrate the Polish economy into the world economy by means of direct equity investments, trade and other contractual relationships.

The role of the EU as one of the actors in the process of network alignment deserves a few words. As we noted above, the radical reorientation of Poland's trade in the early 1990s led to the EU's becoming Poland's main trading partner several years ago. Accession will bring additional costs associated with more stringent regulations in such areas as environmental protection and workplace health and safety. It is, however, likely that positive effects due, for example, to the developmental and infrastructural investments supported by the Structural and Cohesion Funds and the elimination of political and currency risk will be achieved. However, we are not able to estimate the magnitude of these effects or determine whether (and in what time frame) they will outweigh the negative effects mentioned earlier.

MNC strategies

Generally, three types of MNC direct investment strategies can be observed in Poland:

1   *Market-seeking*, motivated by the attractiveness of a share in the fairly large local market.
2   *Efficiency-seeking*, exploiting low unit costs to manufacture low-end products for the world market.
3   Another form of *efficiency-seeking* investment, exploiting low costs and proximity to perform assembly and then re-import finished products into EU markets.

It is particularly important to note that a *knowledge-seeking* strategy, taking advantage of (or even developing) local technologies and innovation capacities, is conspicuously absent from this list. The sorts of strategies adopted tend to make facilities in Poland 'extended workbenches' for MNCs investing there and, therefore, offer little promise that they will bring about Poland's integration into international innovation networks. Some observers have noted a tendency for foreign investors not only failing to develop local research and development (R&D) capacity, but actually *reducing* it by eliminating local R&D facilities and concentrating R&D activities in their home countries (see, e.g. Gorzelak *et al.* 1995; Kurz and Wittke 1998). As we discuss in the next section, the private sector in Poland has a generally very poor performance in the area of R&D investments, and the inflow of FDI appears to have done little or nothing to improve this state of affairs.

Domestic firm strategies

With respect to FDI, the role of local firms in attracting investment has been limited in comparison to the role of the state (specifically, the privatization ministry). As a consequence, the role of foreign capital in the Polish privatization process has been determined largely by the state and foreign investors rather than the domestic enterprises themselves.

Lack of innovation makes many Polish small and medium-sized enterprises (SMEs) dependent on Original Equipment Manufacturing (OEM) arrangements in their contractually based relations with western European (particularly German) final contractors. Such arrangements are typically associated with small profit margins and low opportunity for investment and technological upgrading, generally limited to upgrading the capital stock by, for example, purchasing or leasing equipment (often second hand) from foreign partners (most frequently German and Italian), who are often helpful in making financing arrangements for the purchase transactions or lease agreements. Nevertheless, it is clear that for the most part these methods of modernizing production equipment are far from sufficient to bring Polish businesses to the forefront of technology; at best they allow them to be reasonable imitators, but never innovators (Dornisch *et al.* 2000).

Trade relations are, of course, another very important aspect of integration, even if of a 'shallower' kind. It has often been noted that the trade reorientation from the collapsing CMEA markets to markets in the most developed countries (primarily those of Western Europe) at the beginning of transformation was remarkable in Poland as well as in several of its neighbours in Central Europe (especially the Czech Republic, Hungary and the Baltic states). This was accomplished largely without the aid of foreign capital, and we have already shown that domestic companies' exports exceed those of foreign-owned firms in Poland. We therefore believe that, while the country's overall export performance may leave much to be desired, domestic firms have contributed more to the country's successes in this area than foreign-owned firms in spite of their relative disadvantages in doing so.

Finally, in evaluating Polish firms' capacity to steer the process of 'deeper' integration into European innovation networks, it is crucial to look at their role in what might be called the national system of innovation (NSI) in Poland. Here the key fact to note is the extremely low rate of expenditure in private industry on R&D activity. Table 15.6 illustrates the scale of Poland's problem with R&D investment in comparison with a number of other OECD countries.

As Table 15.6 shows, the largest portion of the distance between Poland and the other OECD countries is not due primarily to low government R&D expenditures, but rather the low level of private R&D spending by industry. Polish industry spending on R&D amounts to a mere 0.3 per cent of GDP, as opposed to the OECD average of 1.51 per cent (Pietraszewski 1997). This has not changed in more recent years, as data from the Central Statistical Office demonstrate. The share of R&D expenditures in GDP rose somewhat in 1999, and the private sector's share rose with it; however, in 2000, the share of expenditures in GDP, and the private sector share in those expenditures, fell back to the levels of 1995 (Central Statistical Office 2001).

The roles and strategies of public authorities

The role of Polish public authorities in the process of integrating the Polish economy with that of the EU can be summed up as unimaginative and defensive, based

Table 15.6 R&D expenditures (% of GDP)

	1965	1970	1975	1980	1984	1994 or 1995	Central government expenditures
Japan	1.27	1.59	1.73	1.91	2.37	2.69	0.63 (1994)
USA	2.91	2.65	2.27	2.38	2.62	2.45	0.99 (1994)
France	2.03	1.93	1.80	1.84	—	2.38 (1995)	1.05 (1993)
United Kingdom	2.35	2.10	2.02	2.19	—	2.19	0.71 (1994)
Germany (Federal Republic)	1.73	2.18	2.38	2.63	—	2.27 (1995)	0.84 (1995)
Poland	—	—	—	—	—	c.0.8 (1995)	0.5

Sources: Based on Pietraszewski (1997) and Parteka (1997).

on reaction to forces brought to bear on those authorities (interest groups) rather than active realization of coherent strategies. Most actions have consisted of attempts to defend existing employment in largely decrepit enterprises whose competitiveness has been severely threatened by the opening of the Polish econ-omy; there has been little or no concentrated effort to create favourable conditions for the development of new, internationally competitive industry. One of the most significant exceptions has been the extensive investment in infrastructure carried out by Polish local governments throughout the past decade.

The national government

The statement of the minister of industry in the first non-Communist government of postwar Poland that the best industrial policy is the lack of an industrial policy is very well known in Poland. This highly ideological approach to the issue of policy led to what one might describe as the formation of policy by default. By this we mean that the industrial policy that (inevitably) emerged in Poland was shaped primarily by the pressures of various interest groups bringing their influence to bear on successive governments rather than any conscious strategy choices of those governments.

One of the leading motives in the creation of this 'policy by default' has been the perceived need to protect jobs in industries and regions, threatened with obsoles-cence since the opening of Poland's economy over a decade ago. Classic examples include the coal and steel industries, the Warsaw tractor factory URSUS, and the Gdansk shipyard. These enterprises have been protected from the forces of competition by various methods, both implicitly (e.g. by allowing them to run enormous arrears in the payments of taxes and social security contributions) and explicitly (by means of import tariffs, etc.). Similarly, the nearly two dozen Special Economic Zones created by the government since the passage of appropriate legislation in 1994, in which investors have been favoured by extraordinary tax exemptions as well as exemptions from tariffs on imported components, have arisen in localities threatened by extremely high unemployment as a result of the crisis of local industrial monocultures.

Poland lacks anything that could be described as a coherent export promotion policy. In the early years of Polish transformation, the only policy instrument used for export promotion of any sort was exchange rate policy. It fairly quickly became clear, however, that the export promotion potential of this policy had been exhausted due to the lack of export credit and export credit insurance (World Economy Research Institute 1994).

However, many of the instruments subsequently introduced for export promotion have little more than symbolic significance (abstracting from the question of whether they are well designed in the first place). One of them is the export credit subsidy introduced in 1995: in 1999 only PLN 6.7 mn were allocated for such subsidies (see Pintera n.d.).

The Export Credit Insurance Corporation (known by its Polish acronym KUKE), founded in 1991, provides guarantees on export credits provided by banks. However, KUKE's role is limited due to the fact that its requirements concerning the minimum size of transactions insured effectively eliminate small businesses from its potential clientele. It is no surprise that while 25 per cent of German exports and 50 per cent of UK exports are credit based, only 4 per cent of Polish exports are financed by sources other than those of the exporters themselves (2.5 per cent by KUKE; see Ministerstwo Gospodarki).

Finally, we should consider the role of the public sector in the NSI. Alongside the low level of spending on R&D in private industry, it is very important to note the existence of 260 state-owned R&D institutes of which Polish firms without their own R&D facilities could potentially take advantage. Such institutes (as well as research facilities at universities and polytechnic institutes) could constitute ideal partners for small businesses, which often cannot afford their own laboratories. Nothing, however, could be further from the reality in Poland, where cooperation between these institutes and small businesses is practically unknown. Industrial R&D institutes prefer to concentrate on cooperation with their traditional clients, large industrial producers in the state-owned or formerly state-owned sector and, moreover, are heavily dependent on government grants. Polish universities suffer equally from many of the problems often observed in the West; resulting, for example, from the fact that universities are seldom well prepared for cooperation with business and lack the necessary administrative flexibility, professionalism in drawing up contracts and general awareness concerning business practices (Quevit 1997). Moreover, small business owners themselves usually lack both awareness of what the institutes could possibly offer them, as well as the financial resources to pay for R&D services. Possibilities for small businesses utilizing similar technologies to pool their financial resources in developing cooperation with these institutes remain unexplored, and the R&D institutes generally fail to engage in marketing or promotional activity on any significant scale.[3]

Local governments

Many local governments in Poland have been very active in developing policies to support investment in their localities. The types of policies they have implemented have been quite varied. Probably the most common, and arguably the least imaginative, is analogous to the creation of Special Economic Zones by the national government and consists of tax incentives. While it is questionable whether tax breaks offered by local authorities have more than a marginal effect on investors' decisions about where to locate new plants, they are undoubtedly an indicator of the priority that local authorities have placed on attracting investment as a means of stimulating local economic development.

It is also worth noting the activities of local governments (and, to some extent, regional authorities) in establishing business support organizations. The services offered by these organizations are targeted primarily at local SMEs and include, for example, training and various kinds of courses, as well as consulting, advisory and information services. Some disseminate information about trade fairs and various national and international business opportunities; some also participate in the organization of such fairs. A number offer assistance in preparation of documents, such as contracts, business plans and credit applications. Additionally, they sometimes assist in establishing contacts between local business and potential foreign investors.[4] There can be no doubt that only a minority of Polish municipalities have adopted such an active and creative approach to local economic development; nevertheless, their leadership can be expected to yield multiplier effects as well as (in the longer term) providing examples that can yield learning effects for other localities.

Some specific examples (drawn from Gorzelak *et al.* 1999) illustrate how other policies can be more effective in achieving the same goals.

The eastern town of Bilgoraj is very generous with its tax breaks, which it has used to stimulate investment by both local entrepreneurs and foreign firms. However, it is clear that these tax breaks were of little significance for the investment decisions; more important factors included provision, by the city, of land equipped with the necessary infrastructure and the existence of major clients in the area. The northern town of Ilawa, by contrast, gives almost no tax breaks to firms in the locality and is in fact zealous about collecting as much as it can in tax revenues from them (and seems to be doing a good job of it); nevertheless, it has a slightly higher ratio of existing firms to local residents. Ilawa has, however, implemented a policy of public infrastructure investments, which have improved its attractiveness to tourists and stimulated the general business climate of the town.

The case of the western rural borough of Tarnowo Podgorne deserves particular attention. By 1998, this borough, bordering on the major city of Poznan, had attracted 300 mn US$ in foreign investments. The mayor of Tarnowo Podgorne emphasizes that although one investor was granted a five-year exemption from payment of the local real estate tax, the revenue lost was more than compensated by the investor's construction of a sewage pipeline for its factory, which also serves the needs of the local population.

The literature, on the experience of Polish local governments in the 1990s, emphasizes their extensive activity in the area of infrastructure investment. Polish local governments typically spent more than 20 per cent of their budgets on investment in the 1990s, thereby accounting for 50 per cent of all public investment spending.[5] As the examples cited above illustrate, this appears to be a much more effective tool for stimulating foreign investment than tax breaks. Another tool whose effectiveness is demonstrated by Tarnowo Podgorne is spatial planning. The borough authorities in Tarnowo Podgorne were quick to gather full information about the area and its development opportunities, and prepared a new land-use plan in 1992. Thanks to the availability of this information, investors can obtain detailed information about available plots of land, their price, the infrastructure with which they are equipped, etc. (Gorzelak *et al.* 1999).

Conclusions and future possibilities

There were significant inflows of FDI to Poland from the EU in the 1990s. However, this burst of investment may be slowing down, as investment opportunities afforded by the privatization process are running out. Moreover, given the very diverse sectoral allocation of investments and their largely market-seeking motivation, scepticism as to whether FDI is integrating Poland into EU networks in a manner most conducive to upgrading and likely to yield significant positive spillover effects seems justified. It is true that the export intensity (exports per sales) of foreign-owned firms is higher than that of domestic firms. It is, however, important to bear in mind the disadvantages of domestic firms *vis-à-vis* foreign firms in access to capital and foreign markets, as well as the fact that foreign-owned firms in Poland are net importers while the international trade of domestic firms is, in aggregate, nearly balanced. Given these considerations, it is clear that, relative to their capacities, Polish domestic firms are making greater export efforts than foreign firms.

The fact that assembly units are being closed as trade barriers are reduced shows that many Polish production facilities – in spite of their much lower labour costs – are not competitive. This gives valuable insight into the nature of the structural weaknesses of the Polish economy and, consequently, into the nature of the main challenges that it will face over the next decade.

Probably the most important insight emerging from this analysis is that cost advantages are not enough. Our preliminary observations indicate that technology transfer and innovation processes are more important for the integration of Polish manufacturing into European production and innovation networks and, in this arena, Poland is particularly weak. Existing capacities for innovation and R&D have generally been neglected by all of the relevant actors – both the national government and the private sector (including both domestic and foreign-owned companies).

When we consider the interplay of three types of forces (markets, enterprises and politics) and three types of players (foreign corporations, local firms and the public sector) in the process of Poland's integration into the European economy, the general picture that emerges is one of weak developments in the direction of full integration (especially into cross-national innovation networks).

Ironically, one of Poland's main strengths turns out to be one of its great weaknesses: its relatively large domestic market, which relieves pressure on both local and foreign actors to look for export opportunities. Another key weakness affecting all three types of players is the low level of investment in R&D activity, which is aggressively pursued and stimulated neither by the public sector, nor by domestic firms, nor by foreign investors.

The public sector has generally played a rather passive and defensive role, with little active, strategic policy-making and much catering to special interests. The instruments used to promote foreign investment consist primarily of tax privileges and similar concessions. However, other instruments, which we believe to be more effective, have also been utilized by local and regional authorities in efforts to stimulate economic development and raise the living standards of their residents. The most important area of activity supporting (albeit indirectly) integration is found in the extensive infrastructure investments carried out by local governments over the past decade. Other activities, which are much rarer but potentially offer significant multiplier and learning effects, include involvement in the creation of business support organizations.

One might sum up our results with the statement that, in relation to their capacities, the most powerful actors – the MNCs and national government – have been the least active in trying to push Poland's integration in the direction of high value added and high innovation, whereas the least powerful actors (i.e. local governments and Polish small businesses) have made greater efforts in this direction.

As discussed in the section on Trends in foreign trade, foreign investment and specialization, it seems that on the whole foreign-owned companies tend to be net importers (of both supplies and investment goods), while it is domestic companies that provide most of the impetus behind Polish exports. We believe that this trend results from the strategic emphasis placed by foreign investors on domestic market share.

The relationships between market orientation and the resulting specialization on one hand, and the relative size of markets and relative average costs on the other, are fairly straightforward. A country will specialize in a given industry (i.e. will have a positive index of specialization and export large proportions of its production) if its local market is relatively large and the cost differential is neutral or relatively small such that it does not offset the market effect. The impact of asset and technology ownership is less easy to apprehend. In fact, the structure of asset ownership represents both the result of a historical process of accumulation of capital and – equally importantly – the source and the degree of technological autonomy. The domestically owned sector will tend to use locally developed or localized technologies, while the foreign-owned sector will tend to transfer in the technology and import components from the sources it taps in the home countries of the investors. Consequently, even when the relative size of the market and positive cost differential would justify the emergence of positively specialized industry, these effects can be overwhelmed by the effect of the technology and asset ownership structure if, as we hypothesize, this works in the opposite direction in the case of dominant foreign ownership.

Taking into account market, cost and ownership effects, we would argue that, market sizes and costs being equal, an industry's market specialization, characterized by the ratio of the trade balance to output, is dependent on asset and technology ownership. In other words, with market sizes in two countries being the same and no cost differentials, the flow of goods will be defined by who owns the assets and the technology embodied in those assets. Consequently, in looking forward to EU enlargement, the key will be to understand how fast the market effects will disappear and how fast the cost structures will converge. Then, as suggested, the ownership of assets and origin of technologies may become the decisive factors in successful integration into EU and global production networks.

Some countries and some industries are in a better position than others. With falling trade barriers and logistics costs arising from enlargement of the EU, in domestically owned industries we can expect to see potential amplification of positive specialization and gains in market share for suppliers from Central Europe (with increased competition between them). For industries dominated by foreign ownership our prognosis is more complex. On the one hand, we may see a decline in foreign manufacturing in Central Europe, where the benefits of fragmentation do not justify multiplication of sites and some companies with smaller local market shares will eliminate their manufacturing activities in the region. On the other hand, we may expect to see foreign suppliers refocusing on established brands and finished products manufacture, and accelerating the de-localization of their eastern manufacturing sites, with locally owned industry ramping up its technological and commercial capacities to move into the role of local and pan-European suppliers and contract manufacturers (Kierzkowski 2001). The latter scenario could even lead to a total reorientation of entire industries, depending on the strength and innovativeness of local supplier networks. In this context, the funding and effectiveness of the innovation systems in each country will become critical.

Notes

1 This index, known as the Lafay index or the 'contribution to trade balance index', is defined as the actual trade balance for a given good, minus a theoretical trade balance for that good if there were no comparative advantage or disadvantage, divided by GDP and multiplied by 1,000 (so that the index represents thousandths of GDP). The theoretical trade balance is calculated as the percentage share of total trade of the product multiplied by the nation's total trade balance (Allen 2001).
2 Similarly, Hotopp *et al.* (2002) find a shift from commodity-type exports to exports that are higher up the value chain in three Central and Eastern European countries. The strongest such shift is observed in Hungary, the next strongest in the Czech Republic and the weakest in Poland.
3 This discussion of R&D institutes and universities draws on Woodward (2001).
4 For more on local and regional business support organizations in Poland, see Woodward (1999, 2001).
5 See, for example, Gilowska (1994) and Levitas (1999).

References

Allen, T. (2001) 'Specialization of candidate countries in relation to EU', *Statistics in Focus*, Brussels: Eurostat, 5 July.

Central Statistical Office (1998, 1999, 2000, 2001) *Yearbook of Foreign Trade*, Warsaw, CSO.

Central Statistical Office (2001) *Statistical Yearbook 2001*, Warsaw: CSO.

Dornisch, D., Gorzynski, M. and Woodward, R. (2000) 'Networking for innovation: pre-feasibility study for transfer of foreign technology to Polish small and medium-sized enterprises'. Warsaw: CASE. Available HTTP: <http://www.case.com.pl/pdf/forum/ddmgrw_en.pdf> (accessed 29.09.03).

Gilowska, Z. (1994) *Gminy Gospodarujace* (Municipal financial management). Poznan: Krajowy Instytut Badan Samorzadowych.

Gorzelak, G., Jalowiecki, B., Kuklinski, A. and Zienkowski, L. (1995) *Eastern and Central Europe 2000: Final Report*, Brussels: European Commission.

Gorzelak, G., Jalowiecki, B., Woodward, R., Dziemianowicz, W., Herbst, M., Roszkowski, W. and Zarycki, T. (1999) *Dynamics and Factors of Local Success in Poland*, Warsaw: European Institute for Regional and Local Development, CASE.

Hotopp, U., Radosevic, S. and Bishop, K. (2002) 'Trade and industrial upgrading in countries of Central and Eastern Europe: patterns of scale- and scope-based learning', paper prepared under the project entitled 'The Emerging Industrial Architecture of the Wider Europe: The Co-evolution of Industrial and Political Structures', financed by the UK Economic and Social Research Council's programme 'One Europe or Several?' Available HTTP: <http://www.ssees.ac.uk/esrcwork.htm> (accessed 29.09.03).

Kaminski, B. and Smarzynska, B.K. (2001) *Foreign Direct Investment and Integration into Global production and Distribution Networks: The Case of Poland*, Washington, DC: The World Bank. July.

Kierzkowski, H. (2001) 'Joining the global economy: experience and prospects of the transition economies', in S. Arndt and H. Kierzkowski (eds) *Fragmentation*, Oxford: Oxford University Press.

Kim, S.R. and von Tunzelmann, N. (1998) 'Aligning internal and external networks: Taiwan's specialization in IT', Brighton: SPRU, University of Sussex.

Kurz, C. and Wittke, V. (1998) *Using Industrial Capacities as a Way of Integrating Central-East European Economies*. BRIE Working Paper No. 123.

Levitas, T. (1999) *The Political Economy of Fiscal Decentralization and Local Government Finance Reform in Poland, 1989–99*. Research Triangle Park, NC: Research Triangle Institute.

Ministerstwo Gospodarki (Ministry of Economy) 'Raport z konferencji "Polski system wspierania eksportu" (Report on the conference on the Polish system of export promotion)'. Available HTTP: <http://www.exporter.pl/forum/agencje_plus/2_sytuacja.html> (accessed 29.09.03).

PAIZ web site: http://www.paiz.pl

Parteka, T. (1997) 'Japońskie doświadczenia transferu technologii i pobudzania innowacji – lata sześćdziesiąte i osiemdziesiąte (Japanese experience in technology transfer and stimulation of innovation)', in T. Markowski, E. Stawasz and R. Zembaczyński (eds) *Instrumenty Transferu Technologii i Pobudzania Innowacji: Wybór Ekspertyz* (Instruments of technology transfer and stimulation of innovation: Selected papers), Warsaw: Zespol Zadaniowy ds. Polityki Strukturalnej w Polsce.

Pietraszewski, M. (1997) 'Innowacyjność gospodarki polskiej: Charakterystyka zjawiska (Innovativeness of the Polish economy: A description)', in T. Markowski, E. Stawasz and R. Zembaczyński (eds) *Instrumenty Transferu Technologii i Pobudzania Innowacji: Wybór Ekspertyz* (Instruments of technology transfer and stimulation of innovation: Selected papers), Warsaw: Zespol Zadaniowy ds. Polityki Strukturalnej w Polsce.

Pintera, M. (n.d.) 'Polska polityka eksportowa i pokonywanie barier (Polish pro-export policy and how to overcome barriers to export)'. Available HTTP: <http://www.exporter.pl/forum/agencje_plus/1_promocja.html> (accessed 29.09.03).

Quevit, M. (1997) 'Główne instrumenty wspierania innowacji technologicznych w kontekście restrukturyzacji polskiej gospodarki. Priorytety i testy ewaluacyjne istniejących instrumentów (Chief instruments for supporting technological innovations in the context of the restructuring of the Polish economy: Priorities and tests for evaluating existing instruments)', in T. Markowski, E. Stawasz and R. Zembaczyński (eds) *Instrumenty Transferu Technologii i Pobudzania Innowacji: Wybór Ekspertyz* (Instruments of technology transfer and stimulation of innovation: Selected papers), Warsaw: Zespol Zadaniowy ds. Polityki Strukturalnej w Polsce.

Radosevic, S. (2000) 'The emerging industrial architecture of the wider Europe: Conceptual and empirical issues for research'. School of Slavonic and East European Studies, University College London.

Woodward, R. (ed.) (1999) *Otoczenie instytucjonalne małych i średnich Przedsiębiorstw* (The institutional environment of small and medium enterprises). CASE Report No. 25, Warsaw: CASE.

Woodward, R. (2001) 'SME Support in post-Communist countries: moving from individual to cooperative approaches (Reflections on the Polish case)', in *MOCT-MOST: Economic Policy in Transitional Economies*, 113: 275–94.

World Economy Research Institute (1994) *Poland International Economic Report 1993/94*, Warsaw: Warsaw School of Economics.

16 Network alignment and pan-European industry networks

Conclusions, contributions and policy implications

Francis McGowan, Slavo Radosevic and Nick von Tunzelmann

This book has sought to explain the changing microeconomic architecture of the wider Europe in terms of the alignment of networks within countries of the east and also between east and west. Our analysis (and the findings of the contributors) has demonstrated the applicability of such an approach and at the same time the limits of such alignments in actual practice. In Chapter 3, the various network types that overlaid one another were described as functional (related to production, technology, finance and demand), resource (related to varieties of labour and capital requirements) and geographical (global, national and local). A first attempt to bring these together, for countries in transition, was depicted in Figures 3.3 and 3.4. Here we link these types in strategic ways, for instance, looking at foreign direct investment (FDI) in its global dimension (geographical), as a resource (tangible and intangible investment), to carry out functions of production, technology and of course finance. In this conclusion we synthesize the linked findings from our sectoral and country case studies and draw out broader conclusions and policy recommendations.

Comparative overview of country study results

Industry networks are to a great extent firm- and industry-specific. Nevertheless, their extent and nature differ significantly across countries. Although in the project our focus was on firm and industry levels, as at these levels the morphology and the processes of network alignment can be discerned more easily than at national level, our research objective was to link industry networks with the issues of industry upgrading and growth. In this respect, the national level is an essential complement to our understanding of how the broader context can affect industry integration.

Ireland and Spain as reference cases

In this section, we confine ourselves to issues of relevance for the central and east European countries (CEECs) from studies of industrial networks in Ireland and

Spain. We consider the role of European Union (EU) accession (from Figure 3.3) and of FDI and government (from Figure 3.4).

Common structural reasons for EU accession

Comparing the Irish and Spanish experience of integration into the EU economy with that of the CEECs reveals a common structural root: the exhaustion of one development model and the need to replace it with another model.

Until the end of the 1950s, Ireland followed an import substitution industrialization (ISI) strategy, which failed. This was followed by an outward-oriented and export-oriented strategy as the only remaining option. After thirty years of protectionism and economic difficulties, FDI entered in the 1960s to be followed by EU accession in 1973.

Spain followed an ISI strategy until the early 1970s, but did not exclude FDI (the beginnings of economic liberalization can be traced to policies devised in the 1950s). However, this FDI was oriented towards the local market, to fill investment gaps. During the 1970s, Spain experienced a structural crisis, which was resolved by liberalization and, subsequently, EU accession in 1986. EU accession came as a result of failures of previous development strategies as well as political choice.

CEECs have opened up after a prolonged crisis, which started in the 1970s, and was followed by the transition crisis during the 1990s, but which varied in duration and intensity across countries. As in the Spanish crisis of 1974–85, central and east European opening led to an increase in the share of services and a rise in industry productivity. As was the case for Spain and Ireland, EU accession for the CEECs is likely to follow after the crisis of their growth model, hence EU accession has deeper roots than is usually perceived through political debate. But, while both Spain and Ireland appear to have benefited from accession – aided by considerable structural assistance – it remains to be seen whether the CEECs will be as fortunate.

FDI vs indigenous industry

The opening of the Irish and Spanish economies led to FDI becoming dominant in exports and sales, raising the issue of the relationship between foreign and domestically controlled sectors, which is also a fundamental policy concern for CEECs. In Ireland, domestically controlled employment decreased in 1975–95 by 19 per cent and only thereafter became a net employment generator. Indigenous industry remained weak until the end of the 1990s when its revival became visible through its own overseas operations. Market opening and FDI also made it difficult for traditional Spanish firms to face up to the new competition. Indeed Spain seems to display elements of a dual economy: high-tech sectors are much more foreign controlled than traditional sectors.

In a similar fashion, in several central European countries there is a dichotomy between modern, foreign-dominated industries and traditional industries with many domestic firms. Only in Hungary, the biggest inward investor, has domestic industry become a net employment generator (Radosevic *et al.* 2003). The relative productivity gap between domestic and foreign firms has increased (Hunya 2000), though as shown in Chapter 12, domestic firms are beginning to catch up. If the Irish and Spanish experiences are any guide, then the next ten–twenty years of policy-making in CEECs will be concerned with the gap between domestic and foreign sectors.

Government role in network alignment

Spain and Ireland offer contrasting experiences with respect to the role of government in fostering industry integration. In Ireland, after twenty years of experience and many mistakes, the government has developed the capability of 'network supporter'. There has been considerable continuity in the role of government towards FDI, a policy being maintained of general attraction of FDI through the Irish Development Agency. Government has sought to cultivate closer ties between local and foreign firms through the National Linkage Programme, which has become selective to the point that the policy priority is to attract the key business functions and support subsidiary-based development. FDI policy is accompanied by programmes for vocational training and for advanced technologies, which are geared towards FDI and are designed in cooperation with them. By contrast, Spanish policy is much less sophisticated. There have been no conscious efforts to upgrade the position of subsidiaries within multinational corporations (MNCs) as in Ireland or explicitly to address the issue of linkages. In addition, there have been no vocational and technology programmes that are designed and geared towards the needs of foreign investors. Some selectivity exists at a regional level but the overall policy is aimed at attracting FDI in general.

Policies towards FDI in CEECs have been relatively undeveloped. Only recently has the Hungarian government, followed by the Czech government, started to address the issue of linkages between domestic and foreign firms (as in the Hungarian 'Integrator' programme). The government role in relation to FDI is not yet articulated except through privatization, which has become the FDI policy by default. Selectivity in FDI incentives has emerged in the Czech Republic with respect to electronics and high-tech sectors, and the results seem to be positive (Radosevic 2002a). Vocational training to meet the needs of FDI is the weakest aspect of FDI policy. Nor does there seem to be any consistency towards FDI. For example, in Hungary tax incentives for FDI were withdrawn in 1994–96 and then reintroduced together with the introduction of Free Trade Zones. In Slovenia, only after 1999 can a shift towards support for FDI be seen. In Poland and Romania incentives remain weak.

Comparison of country studies

Here we compare the results of the four studies of industrial networks in Hungary, Slovenia, Romania and Poland. These country studies show that the extent, nature and modes of integration into the global economy via industrial networks cannot be understood independently of the national political economy context of each country. This does not mean that other factors like EU demand and regulations, or strategies of MNCs, do not play important roles, for we conclude that these are key factors in structuring network alignment. Yet, if we want to understand the extent, nature and modes of integration of CEECs into the global economy at the micro level then the national context seems to be of paramount importance. This in no way contradicts our conclusion about the relatively limited importance of governments in sectors where network alignment is market-driven. In fact, the weak role of government here is part of the broader national political economy context, as emphasized in Chapter 4.

Country differences in integration into international industrial networks

There are great differences among these four countries in their degrees of penetration of FDI and their policies towards FDI and other forms of industry integration. Figure 16.1 shows the differences in terms of several indices concerning the manufacturing sector. The difference in the presence of FDI between Hungary and Slovenia is especially strong (we do not have data for Romania, which would show a much smaller presence of FDI compared to central European economies). These differences emerged as the result of several factors, of which the most important are: (i) differences in their levels of development and socialist legacy, (ii) the strategies of MNCs (which have anticipated EU enlargement), and (iii) the changing dynamics of government–business relationships in each of the CEECs (speed and pace of transition).

The legacy of socialist rule, especially in terms of previous levels of development, openness and degree to which the economies were reformed during the 1980s, was important in the initial stages of transition (e.g. Hungary vs Romania). These differences have been compounded by differences in modes of privatization as the most important policy towards FDI: contrasts between Hungarian direct sale privatization; Polish delayed direct sale privatization; Romanian protracted privatization; and Slovenian privatization to managers and employees, help explain the extent and modes of industry integration. The outcome of these processes has been very high penetration of FDI in Hungary, medium but rising penetration in Poland, limited penetration in Romania and low penetration in Slovenia.

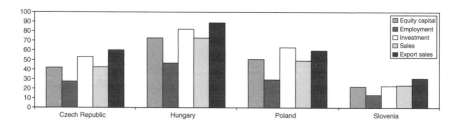

Figure 16.1 Percentage shares of foreign investment enterprises, manufacturing 1999.
Source: Hunya (2002), based on WIIW database on foreign investment enterprises.

These factors combined with the strategies of MNCs have generated diverse national patterns of modernization. For example, due to FDI the Hungarian export and industry structure has been radically restructured and technologically improved. In Bulgaria and Romania, changes were significant but towards technological deterioration of the export structure, while Poland represents an intermediate case (see Hotopp *et al.* 2002). Slovenia is the only central European country that has not increased its market share in the EU market (Chapter 13).

In Hungary, modernization is very much foreign-led while in Slovenia it is domestic-led. On the other hand, surveys suggest that Hungarian firms occupy low positions in international networks and are confined to production-only subsidiaries, while Slovenian firms are occupying higher positions in international networks with exporting firms having broader sets of functions in these networks (Dyker and von Tunzelmann 2003).

Integration of Romania into industrial networks via outward processing traffic (OPT subcontracting) (as in clothing) and, more limitedly, FDI is the result of the specific Romanian political economy described in Chapter 14 as 'systemic unrest', meaning that domestic industrial networks in Romania are 'temporary and fragile vertical and horizontal links between independent, opportunistic agents acting in unstable markets'.

The Polish political economy of government–business relationships is characterized by defensive 'policy by default' in response to interest group pressures (Chapter 15). The government focus is on budget revenues in conditions of fiscal crisis, which has led to the neglect of growth aspects of industry integration.

These national specificities do not necessarily apply across all sectors; for example, in all countries, despite different orientations of the state towards foreign capital, telecom operators have been privatized to foreign strategic investors. In this case, technology and finance gaps were too large for modernization to be carried out under domestic control. Yet, without understanding the political economy of government–business relations in individual CEECs we cannot understand delays in privatization of telecoms, shifts in attitudes or (in)consistencies towards foreign capital.

Overall, it seems that the Hungarian political economy was the most conducive to integration via industrial networks, though exactly why is not so obvious. While withdrawal of the Hungarian state was obvious in many respects, it did not exclude its active role in privatization and today in trying to enhance linkages between domestic and foreign sectors. The country's commitment to FDI dates from the socialist period of the 1980s. This is in stark contrast to Slovenia where FDI did not rank as a prominent policy objective until recently; since 1999 there has been a policy shift towards FDI as a means of industrial upgrading, but its implementation requires the consensus of various stakeholders and cannot be achieved only by fiscal incentives and promotion programmes. The Czech Republic is another case of a shift in policy from domestic-led modernization based on voucher privatization and (at least nominally) a 'minimalist government', towards a more activist role of the state in innovation and upgrading via FDI. This shift started with the new government of 1998. The Czech case, especially in electronics, suggests that implementation capability, rather than normative policy, matters much more for the effects of integration via industry networks (Radosevic 2002a).

Country similarities in MNC strategies

Strategies of MNCs, in particular market seeking, have led to a very high degree of integration of CEECs as markets into the global economy, notably the EU. Country differences in the political economy of government–business relations have not influenced the extent of market-seeking FDI. The main differences in the scale of international industrial networks across CEECs arise instead from differences in the presence of export-oriented FDI.

MNCs have managed to find their way through country differences in privatization modes and establish themselves as the major market players. Indeed, irrespective of country differences we find in all CEECs a dominance of foreign investments in breweries, tobacco and many other segments of the food industry, and in telecoms. This to a great extent reflects the resource superiority of MNCs, and their market-seeking motives.

In addition to the country case studies some additional data support this conclusion. For example, the absolute amount of foreign patenting is extremely similar across all CEECs, varying only between 35,000 and 38,000 thousand patents (1997). Given the big differences in population size (1.5mn in Slovenia to 38mn in Poland) this is striking and, again, indicates that country differences do not matter in this respect. MNCs seem to be primarily concerned with protection of their market position via intellectual property rights (IPR) protection, and differences in the technological capabilities of CEECs do not seem to concern them. Figures for non-resident patents in EU economies also show striking homogeneity in this respect, though at three times as high a level (Radosevic and Mickiewicz 2003).

The deeper the penetration of FDI the more it is expected to be accompanied by a higher share of exporters than distributors and local suppliers (Radosevic *et al.* 2003). However, this does not mean that export-oriented FDI is determined by a clear set of fixed variables. The motivations and strategies of MNCs are not fixed but are multiple, overlapping and change through self-discovery and learning by investors. For example, MNCs in the food industry have learnt that they will have to embark on restructuring of upstream sectors if they want to continue to serve local markets on competitive terms (Chapter 6). Companies like the contract manufacturer Flextronics discovered the central and eastern Europe as a location for electronics production, despite underdeveloped electronics competencies, leading to a wave of other MNCs that have established their operations in CEECs (Chapter 8). In the car industry, initial market-seeking investment has been transformed into efficiency-seeking operations after the abolition of tariffs with the EU (Chapter 15). In power engineering, we find examples of initially efficiency-seeking FDI being transformed into technology-seeking FDI as local technology capabilities have been recognized and plugged into global networks (Radosevic 2001).

These processes of learning and entrepreneurial discovery by MNCs are not country-specific. Country differences in political economy have influenced the pace and to some extent the modes but certainly not the scale of market-seeking FDI, or at least not in the long term. In all CEECs, we find significant presence of local personal computer (PC) assemblers; particularly in Poland, which has been the only country where they have the dominant share. However, international PC manufacturers are gradually starting to hurt established local manufacturers, because the former have developed strategies to cater to the price-sensitive central and eastern European PC market (Radosevic 2002a).

However, country differences remain important if we want to understand differences in export-oriented FDI. In this case, the future dynamics of industry integration can be understood through the interplay of national differences and strategies of MNCs compounded with a variety of other factors like EU accession and local governments.

Domestic vs foreign firms

A common feature of industry integration of the CEECs is the big gap in performance between domestic and foreign firms. Table 16.1 shows that labour productivity, capital productivity, export intensity and profitability are much higher in foreign investments than domestic enterprises.

This feature is common across CEECs countries and differences are due to sectoral differences in FDI presence rather than to country-specific variables. For example, in Poland foreign firms are oriented towards the domestic market, which reduces the scope for possible spillovers that are usually higher in export-oriented activities (Chapter 15). The sample constructed in Chapter 12 of foreign firms in Hungary found very few backward linkages, domestic subsidiaries very strongly dependent on MNC headquarters and local small and medium-sized enterprises (SMEs) involved only occasionally in supply chains. The sample of automotive suppliers in Slovenia in Chapter 13 indicated that ownership cannot explain technical complexity, sourcing patterns or differences in strength between suppliers and buyers, thus indirectly confirming the absence of spillovers. Foreign investors are motivated by low labour costs as long as they are able to realize similar or higher levels of productivity to those in their home country.

Table 16.1 Foreign investment enterprises relative to domestic enterprises, 1998 (%)

	Labour productivity	Capital productivity	Exports per sales	Profits per sales
Czech Republic	189	133	188	3,200
Estonia	150	62	138	300
Hungary	287	150	260	333
Poland	194	110	162	277
Slovenia	197	129	152	103

Source: Based on Hamar (2001); Hunya (2000); Mickiewicz *et al.* (2001).

The restructuring of domestic firms

The overall dominance of foreign investment across CEECs does not mean that domestic firms do not play a role in industrial integration. We find across all CEECs examples of domestically controlled firms that have managed not only to survive but also to restructure and grow. While many domestic 'blue chip' companies have been taken over, in these cases the management has usually succeeded in retaining control. In some cases, the state has considered it inappropriate to sell all the 'family silver' and been keen to support entrepreneurial management. In our project we analysed some of these cases (Elektrim, Vistula, Videoton, Dobrogea). In many cases, resource deficiencies, rent seeking as well as oligopolistic competition from foreign investors, or simply a bad coincidence of several events led to failure. In successful cases, these companies have managed to attract foreign passive investors and continue to retain autonomy.

However, these favourable examples seem to be more the exception than the rule. From our industrial networks' perspective the most significant are those domestic firms that have managed to become network organizers. Based on country studies we would assume that the frequency of successful domestically controlled firms should negatively correlate with the degree of presence of FDI, as might be expected in Slovenia where the relative presence of foreign firms is small and the domestic economy is healthy. The research on the relatively high Slovenian outward investments in Chapter 13, however, shows that these are still market seeking, greenfield, trade-oriented affiliates with specific products that are accepted in these markets. This suggests that they are still far from being agents of deepening industry (production and technology) integration but mainly operate as a mechanism of market integration. Romania has an even lower presence of FDI but, given the 'systemic unrest', it is unlikely that many domestically controlled companies could operate as network organizers.

In this respect, national studies have confirmed the general picture from firm and sectoral studies, which suggests that domestic firms (large and small) and related national networks (R&D institutes, infrastructure institutions) are the weakest links in network alignment.

Regional authorities and network alignment

The unexpected conclusion from firm and sectoral studies, which has been confirmed by country studies, is the importance of regions or local authorities for network alignment. This is surprising given the generally poor state of local governance in CEECs.

Until 1989, the system of local government was relatively unimportant across CEECs. In centrally planned economies proximity was not an asset and potential local linkages were not used as sources of efficiency improvements or innovation (Radosevic 1999, 2002b). The dominant linkages were inter-regional and were organized within individual sectors or within large combinates. This created a dependence of regions on the centre and reduced regional policy to sectoral policies for the industrialization of rural peripheries (Gorzelak 1996).

From the onset of the transition period we immediately saw a trend towards decentralization and fragmentation of local government into municipalities and communes. These lowest levels of governance were given broad autonomy, including finance. Given this new freedom, local governments have tried to strengthen their position by, as Peteri (1993) describes it, 'enterprising local government', or transferring the rule of the private sector into areas of public services. They established production and service companies along with an increase in institutional and council rents and revenues. However, given their small tax base and small size, this trend towards fragmentation of regional governance into municipalities and communes was followed by a re-concentration of power into national government. The meso or regional level was either abolished (Czech Republic, Slovakia), became an appendage of central government (Poland, Bulgaria, Romania) or had only marginal powers (Hungary) (Horvath 1996; Hughes *et al.* 2001).

During the 1990s, there were no comprehensive regional policies formulated in any of the CEECs. Even after ten years of transition, no coherent regional policy agenda had been set. The impression is that most CEECs are still in the process of learning and defining regional policy within a policy discourse that has been dominated by transition issues and recently by the accession agenda. However, there are regional aspects to the FDI policies in some CEECs (Hungary, Poland, Czech Republic) in terms of greater incentives for investors in backward regions.

In Poland, typically over 20 per cent of municipal budgets in the 1990s went into infrastructure investments closely related to the needs of FDI. Some localities have explicitly designed policies (e.g. spatial planning) for attracting investments, like industrial parks and new capacities for electronics in Hungary. It is no coincidence that the role of local governments has been most notable in Poland and Hungary as the only two CEECs where the system of local governance is comparatively developed, though only in Hungary can the system of public finance be called relatively decentralized (Gorzelak 2000: 144–5). In contrast, in Romania the role of regions in relation to FDI is almost non-existent (Chapter 14): regional effects are confined to urbanization effects or growth of urban centres but not with agglomeration effects.

Foreign-supported programmes in central and eastern Europe have involved piecemeal attempts to construct an entrepreneurial local state in the sphere of regional development (Smith 1998: 281). This involved the formation of Regional Development Agencies as the mechanism to bring into partnership the range of local and external agents, by acting as a 'broker' or catalyst for the formation of a wider network of relations both at central and at local level. While being important agents of change in the long term, the weaknesses of the enterprises and other organizations in the region have undermined the role and potential of agencies for inter-regional networking. These new organizations must re-establish themselves as political as well as administrative agents and create linkages with county, municipality and national levels.

Role of the EU

One of the important points of departure of this project was that there is an important inter-relationship between EU policy integration and the depth of industrial networks. Our firm case studies have shown two things. First, the impact of the EU on demand is essential in understanding strategies of MNCs as the main actors in structuring network alignment. Second, EU accession and related policy alignment have only a modest impact. However, our industry studies have shown that this latter is true only in sectors where network alignment is market-driven (electronics, food, clothing). In electricity, where network alignment is based on strategies of MNCs, which, in turn, are based on and strongly conditioned by the regulatory regime, the impact of EU enlargement is significant. In this respect, our conclusions are identical to the recent McKinsey (2002) study of the business effects of enlargement.

However, the important point is that the major effect of EU enlargement on industrial networks does not operate via direct EU regulations but via nation states, in particular, their orientation and capacity to comply with EU regulations while at the same time pursuing their own growth or restructuring objectives. Chapter 4 concluded that overall the impact of the EU upon member states' economic orientations appears to be strongest in the regulatory mode. The expected shift towards the regulatory mode of the candidate countries will depend on:

(i)   the degree of compliance with EU regulations. Implementation gaps (different degrees of compliance) may increase significantly with enlargement, and thus may enable the pursuit of sectoral policies inconsistent with EU policies, like competition policy. Such gaps may emerge because of individual group pressures and/or weak administrative capacities;

(ii) exploiting ambiguities in the orientation of EU policy. These might allow adoption of more developmental strategies while conforming to the regulatory policy mode of the EU. For example, Ireland is often quoted as an example of a 'developmental' state operating within the EU regulatory model and in this respect is seen as a model by many CEECs.

For further research at the country level, we believe that the above framework is a powerful guide to exploring the interaction between EU regulations and CEECs on the impact of policy integration on industrial integration.

Sectors in a network alignment perspective

The technological and organizational homogeneity of individual industries makes comparisons within a network alignment perspective easier than across countries. In Table 16.2 we summarize the results of the four industry studies from the alignment of networks perspective.

The food industry has attracted a considerable number of EU MNCs primarily in search of market share. The early entrants were companies operating in downstream segments like confectionery, soft drinks, tobacco, sugar, dairy and brewing. The entry of MNCs has a strong impact on industry and market structure and on competition in the sector as they have bought up key local players. Being oriented

Table 16.2 Network alignment factors in four CEEC industries

	Clothing	Food	Electronics	Electricity
MNCs	Efficiency-seeking investments; buyer-driven supply chains	Market-seeking investors	Efficiency/market-seeking investors	Market-seeking investors
CEECs firm(s)	Subcontracting trap; long-term aim to develop OBM-based exports	Competing with MNCs	Mainly 'dependent subsidaries'	In competition with new entrants
CEECs national networks	Weak	Limited and weak	Limited	No clear pattern across countries
CEECs local networks (SMEs)	Linked to large firms (Poland); very weak in Romania	Limited	Limited	Non-existent
CEECs government	No impact on industrial networks	No impact; weak support in upstream agriculture	No strong impact, except in Czech and Hungary; stronger impact of local governments	Key source of regulatory change; strong direct impact
EU as regulator	No impact	Impact via food standards	No impact (limit on investment incentives?)	'Regulator of last resort'
EU demand	Strong attractor	Potential attractor	Strong attractor	Potential attractor
Overall network alignment	Integration via subcontracting networks, export-oriented	Integration into MNC production and technology network, local market oriented	Hungary, Czech and partly Poland strongly integrated into MNC-led production chains	Network alignment strongly shaped by state orientations

Source: Authors.

towards local markets and wishing to retain market positions, but faced with the low quality of domestic agricultural produce, investors were forced to do something about the poor state of upstream sectors. Case studies (Soufflet, EBS, Sokolow) show that MNCs have started to restructure those segments of upstream value chains on which they directly depend. Foreign retailers have also made a strong impact on the food sector by starting to source locally (Tesco).

The size of the local market has restricted the degree of commitment of MNCs, though prospects of export to EU markets may change this. However, for the time being food standards, strong competition in the EU market and an un-restructured upstream sector reduce the potential attractiveness of EU markets to foreign investors. Those local firms that have not been taken over are competing with MNCs and have managed to improve considerably their quality, marketing and distribution (Dobrogea, Sokolow).

The biggest obstacle to further industrial integration and upgrading are the weak national networks, in particular links with local R&D organizations. Foreign companies are not linked to national R&D institutes in the food industry primarily because of their lower technological and R&D level. Such 'network failure' partly has to do with the lack of commitment of governments to improving agricultural technology. Local networks in Poland are developing through cooperation with large firms, foreign and domestic. By contrast, in Romania, local networks are undeveloped. Overall, MNCs dominate the scope and scale of network alignment, though we also observe growth of domestic firms in the food industry.

In the clothing industry, foreign buyers are the main drivers of integration and network alignment. They seek low-cost efficiency with relatively limited commitments in terms of equity. Local firms are unable to export on their own and are highly dependent on buyer-driven supply chains. They are oriented towards meeting the quality, delivery time and flexibility requirements of buyers. Industry dynamics are driven by exports, in particular to EU markets. In Poland, domestic firms are trying to reduce dependence on subcontracting and strengthen their presence in the domestic market. The most successful clothing firms in Poland have started to operate as network organizers by subcontracting SMEs. Government impact is absent, and operations are very much market-driven.

Network alignment in electronics is strongly driven by MNCs, by first movers like Philips and Samsung and then by contract manufacturers like Flextronics. They are targeting central and eastern Europe in order to achieve flexibility and low costs. Relatively flat hierarchical structures limit the extent of local subcontracting. Networking is mainly confined to subsidiaries and parent firms, or subsidiaries in other countries. There is patchy evidence that local sourcing is confined to low-cost components like plastic and mechanical parts. Local sourcing beyond local subsidiaries is limited because the quality of local SMEs has not yet reached the required level, but it has started.

Local enterprises are not strong actors in the strategies of MNCs or meeting opportunities which arise from integration into EU markets. This is the most serious handicap of central and eastern Europe for deeper industry integration and largely reflects differences in historical heritage across CEECs. Large ex-socialist electronics conglomerates lagged behind in many respects in technology, finance and market access. The few cases of successful restructuring, like the turnaround of Videoton in Hungary, are difficult to generalize. Since their specific network alignment approach is difficult to replicate, domestic firms are likely, with few exceptions, to play a dependent role in global production networks. Possibly, driven by contract manufacturers (turnkey suppliers), we might see some clustering of different-sized local firms.

In the Czech Republic and Hungary, which are leading locations in electronics, government policies have been important in understanding the patterns and timing of investments. Local governments in CEECs, jointly with MNCs, have become the most active agent for integrating FDI into the local economy. The example of the Videoton industrial park shows that local authorities played one of the key roles in its success. Case-study evidence suggests that the EU accession process plays a sec-ondary role as the effective obstacles to trade and FDI have already been eliminated.

Network alignment in the electricity industry is determined by the interplay between strategies of large EU energy operators and the behaviour of the CEECs governments in privatization and then in regulation. The EU is important but sec-ondary in this process too, though governments and MNCs make their decisions on the basis that regulatory regimes and market structures will converge. Local firms have played a limited role in this process and local networks play a negligible role in this sector. The key role of governments and the tensions between them, foreign investors and the EU/Organisation for Economic Cooperation and Development (OECD) regulatory rules are strongly shaping the depth and scope of industry integration.

An overview of the four sectors shows several general features of the alignment of industrial networks in CEECs.

1   Network alignment is driven by the strategies (motives) of MNCs, which strongly influence its orientation, depth and scope. This is especially strong in sectors where alignment is market-driven (clothing, electronics, food) but less so in sectors where it is driven by strategic decisions of national governments (electricity).

2   Domestic firms are dependent on foreign firms for market access (clothing), competencies (electronics) or capabilities to compete and to restructure upstream suppliers (food). This does not mean that domestic firms are not important players but they are faced with significant constraints in terms of access to technology (electronics), markets (clothing) and finance (food). Those domestic firms that have managed to operate successfully have done so again in cooperation with foreign partners, irrespective of the sector.

3   A common feature of all sectors is the weakness of national and very often local networks. Cooperation with other domestic firms or local infrastructural insti-tutions is limited. This is partly the result of weak governments, pursuing a vari-ety of conflicting objectives (liberalization vs protection of national champions, budget revenue vs privatization, support for industry R&D vs market-oriented government policy). However, in cases where governments have pursued sec-tor-specific policies, like electronics and electricity, their impact is more visible.

4   EU demand operates variously as a strong attractor (electronics, clothing) or as a potential but still unrealized attractor (food, electricity), while the EU as regulator has a strong influence in food exports and in electricity as the 'regulator of last resort'.

5   In all sectors the role of foreign capital in network alignment is critical. This underscores the weaknesses of domestic networks and local firms, and governments' difficulties to moderate industry integration. The network alignment framework shows how simply opening themselves to foreign markets and MNCs, and conforming institutionally to EU, World Trade Organization (WTO) or OECD requirements, will not correct the weaknesses that have been building up in CEECs.

Policy implications

We have shown the importance of complementarities that mutually reinforce the effects of factors like firm strategies, national R&D policies, FDI policies and EU regulations that operate over quite different time scales. In that context policy-makers have to aim to maximize these complementarities while taking into account that many variables for the alignment of industrial networks are not under their control. From this perspective, policy should have a long-term focus and try to maximize opportunities for alignment to take place. Based on our findings, several key ideas have emerged which policy-makers in CEEC and the EU should consider.

Support the weakest link!

Our project has concluded that domestic large and small firms are the weakest links in industrial network alignment. Hence, there is a strong need to enhance national systems of innovation in the CEECs within an EU-wide system of innovation. In particular, this relates to support for local and international networking and diffusion activities. The past focus of policy on transition-related issues and, more recently, on EU-accession requirements, created a situation where the only industrial policy was FDI policy. We have seen in the last few years the emergence of innovation policy, but mainly normative and without effective mechanisms (EC 2001). Further weakening of national innovation systems will inevitably undermine prospects for industrial upgrading by any other means apart from being FDI-driven.

Two steps forward, one step back

EU accession will further remove prerogatives for decision-making from the candidate countries in areas like Free Economic Zones (FEZs) and tax incentives. It is not yet clear what will be the effects of abolishing export processing or FEZs for the CEECs, like Hungary and Poland, that have used them with differing success as an instrument for attracting and supporting FDI. Unless EU accession, through further momentum for institutional change and/or improved attraction for FDI, can compensate for some of these factors, the net effect may even be negative. FEZs can be considered as second-best institutional solutions, at most; if abolished, the EU actions should compensate for reduced policy freedom by enhancing first-best institutional solutions. Interim outcomes in this process may not always be positive.

Window of opportunity: strategic FDI policies and supply chain policies

Vertical industrial policies are today a thing of the past. We may expect that the CEECs will increasingly shift their state aid towards horizontal types of assistance, which comply with EU rules. The drawback to horizontal policies like R&D and innovation is that they have broad objectives, broad target groups and long gestation periods. The example of countries such as Ireland suggests that there is scope for policies that are market-friendly, but which target specific areas of FDI and thus can have quicker effects. Two such policy directions are strategic FDI policy, and targeting and supporting supply chains.

Most of the CEECs apply so-called first-generation policies like liberalization of FDI flows. Some CEECs have embarked on second-generation policies like marketing countries as locations and setting up national investment agencies. The most advanced CEECs have started to entertain, implicitly or explicitly, third-generation policies like targeting foreign investors at the levels of industries and clusters. In order to catch up, CEECs must learn fast how to implement second- and third-generation policies.

In order to assist industrial upgrading the CEECs should take into account the increasingly networked character of local and global companies, implying that particular nations or companies matter less (Sharp 2003). This has already been recognized (implicitly or explicitly) through National Subcontracting programmes (Czech Republic) and the Integrator programme (Hungary), which aim to integrate domestic firms with foreign firms through supply linkages.

EU-wide FDI contests

Even after the EU accession, CEECs will remain heavily dependent on FDI for industry upgrading. In some ways, the competition to attract FDI may even increase. Instead of trying to limit competition for FDI between the EU regions, the EU could entertain using contests for FDI between regions as a mechanism to improve the business environment in the weakest regions. As Kuznetsov (2002) points out, the existing pattern is limited to large MNCs and national governments. Instead of implicitly accepting this state, the EC should make these contests public 'as an incentive device for private and public actors to come together to develop innovative solutions to improve the investment climate on a sub-national level' (p. 12), with matching grants from the EU level. In this way, contests could serve as an incentive device for local government and domestic firms to engage in meaningful joint action and reform, as a coordination device to link activities at national and EU level under the umbrella of private–public competitiveness projects and as a mechanism to share policy knowledge.

Enhancing coordinative capabilities of national governments

A shift in policy focus towards value chains complicates policy-making, as value chains can only be fully supported from the national level. They require a multi-level approach with support from national, regional and EU levels. In addition, our network alignment perspective indicates that a focus on commodity chains is not enough, as upgrading based on value chains may be related to technology, skills and national innovation systems rather than to direct production chains. The main challenge at a national level is to coordinate diverse policies with very different life cycles and constituencies (Sharp 2003). Government capability to integrate policy objectives and actions from the different tiers of government (EU, national, regional) is essential for promoting industrial upgrading through industrial networks.

References

Dyker, D.A. and von Tunzelmann, N. (2003) 'Networks and network alignment in transition: the experience of Hungary and Slovenia', *Progress in Economics Research*, 6: 69–88.

EC (2001) 'Innovation policy issues in six Candidate Countries: the challenges', Luxembourg. Available HTTP: <http://www.cordis.lu/innovation-policy/studies/geo_study1.htm> (accessed January 2004).

Gorzelak, G. (1996) *The Regional Dimension of Transformation in Central Europe*, London: Jessica Kingsley Publishers and Regional Studies Association.

Gorzelak, G. (2000) 'The dilemmas of regional policy in the transition countries and the territorial organisation of the state', in G. Petrakos, G. Maier and G. Gorzelak (eds) *Integration and Transition in Europe. The economic geography of interaction*, London and New York: Routledge.

Hamar, J. (2001) Multinacionalis vállalatok Magyarországon, Európai Tükör, No 80. és 'A külföldi és a hazai tokével muködo vállalatok szerepe a magyar ipraban, Külgazdaság 2001, No. 65, pp. 4–34.

Hotopp, U., Radosevic, S. and Bishop, K. (2002) 'Trade and industrial upgrading in countries of central and eastern Europe: patterns of scale and scope based learning', Project Working Paper No. 26, June, www.ssees.ac.uk/esrcwork.htm.

Horvath, G. (1996) 'Transition and Regionalism in East-Central Europe', Occasional Papers No. 7 (Tubingen: Europaisches Zentrum fur Foderalismus – Forschung).

Hughes, J., Sasse, G. and Gordon, C. (2001) 'The regional deficit in eastward enlargement of the EU: top down policies and bottom up reactions', ESRC Programme 'One Europe or several?', Working Paper 29/01.

Hunya, G. (2000) 'International competitiveness impacts of FDI in CEECs', paper presented at the 6th EACES Conference, Barcelona, 7–9 September. Available HTTP: <http://eu-enlargement.org/> (accessed 12.09.03).

Kuznetsov, Y. (2002) 'Waking up, catching up and forging ahead, institutional agenda for knowledge-based growth in Russia', Washington: World Bank, mimeo.

McKinsey & Co. (2002) 'Business consequences of EU enlargement. Major change or non-event?', London: McKinsey & Co.

Mickiewicz, T. and Radosevic, S. (2001) 'Innovation capabilities of the six EU candidate countries: comparative data based analysis', Background paper for the study on 'Innovation Policy in Issues in Six Applicant Countries: the Challenges', EC DG Enterprise. Available HTTP: <http://www.cordis.lu/innovation-smes/src/studies3.htm#studies_candidate_countries> (accessed 17.09.03).

Mickiewicz, T., Radosevic, S. and Varblane, U. (2001) 'The value of diversity: Foreign direct investment and employment in Central Europe during economic recovery', April 2000,

Working Paper 5, ESRC Programme 'One Europe or Several?'. Available HTTP: <http://www.one-europe.ac.uk/pdf/WP5.PDF> (accessed 27.09.03).

Peteri, G. (1993) 'From the "enterprising" local government towards local economic development', in *Public Policy Institute Foundation Private Sector Development and Local Government in Hungary*, Papers and Proceedings of the Conference Organized by the Centre for International Private Enterprise and the Public Policy Institute Foundation, Eger (Hungary), 10–11 September, Budapest.

Radosevic, S. (1999) 'Prospects for building regional technology policy in central and eastern Europe', in K. Morgan and C. Nauewealers (eds) *Regional Technology Strategies*, London: Stationery Office Press.

Radosevic, S. (2001) 'European integration and complementarities driven network alignment: the case of ABB in central and eastern Europe', *Electronic Working Paper in Economics and Business*, 4 (June). Available HTTP: <http://www.ssees.ac.uk/economic.htm> (accessed 18.09.03).

Radosevic, S. (2002a) 'Electronics industry in CEE: the emerging production location in alignment of networks perspective', Working Paper No. 21, March. Available HTTP: <www.ssees.ac.uk/esrc.htm> (accessed 17.09.03).

Radosevic, S. (2002b) 'Regional innovation systems in central and eastern Europe: determinants, organizers and alignments', *Journal of Technology Transfer*, 27: 87–96.

Radosevic, S. and Mickiewicz, T. (2003) *Innovation Capabilities of the Seven EU Candidate Countries*, Study prepared for EU DG Enterprise Study on Innovation Policy in Seven Candidate Countries, Luxembourg. Available HTTP: <ftp://ftp.cordis.lu/pub/innovation-policy/studies/slavo_final_report_march_2003.pdf (accessed 27.9.03).

Radosevic, S. Mickiewicz, T. and Varblane, U. (2003) 'The patterns of foreign direct investment and employment in central Europe during economic recovery', *Transational Corporations*, 12(1): 53–90.

Sharp, M. (2003) 'Industrial policy and European integration: lessons from experience in Western Europe over the last 25 years', Project Working Paper No. 30, March, UCL – SSEES, London.

Smith, A. (1998) *Reconstructing the Regional Economy. Industrial Transformation and Regional Development in Slovakia*, Cheltenham: Edward Elgar.

Index